Practical Technology Business Management

Reviews and recommendations

With this book, Jon brings forward helpful, actionable advice for leaders and practitioners looking to apply TBM and get some wins of their own. I learned early on to listen and learn from Jon's advice, throughout our respective journeys building and applying TBM. Jon came into the TBM scene very early in its inception, where he applied it while managing a global, multi-billion dollar TBM implementation for five years – managing costs, service catalogs, and unit prices. I saw how he drove annual improvements in IT efficiency by identifying opportunities, measuring progress, and incentivizing stakeholders in meaningful fashion. Jon takes what is often misunderstood as a mechanical modeling exercise and shows how to apply core principles effectively, how to change behavior and accelerate the IT roadmap, all in the name of business value and competitive advantage.

- Jesse Lee, Apptio Co-Founder, VP Customer Success, VP TBM Adoption

Thought provoking for someone considering implementing TBM ... a raft of examples around different approaches and considerations, which is very valuable

- TBM Consultant, London

The rich content means that even the more seasoned TBM experts will still be able to gain great insights and knowledge. I really enjoyed reading the book, great content throughout and not a single chapter out of place.

- TBM Director, Singapore

Practical Technology Business Management

Ideas And Approaches To
Drive Efficiency And Value
Through A TBM Implementation

Jon Sober

2020

Copyright © 2020 by Jon Sober

All rights reserved. This book or any portion thereof may not be reproduced or used in any manner whatsoever without the express written permission of the author except for the use of brief quotations in a book review or scholarly journal.

The TBM Taxonomy is ©2020 Technology Business Management Council, All rights reserved. Used with permission.

First Printing: 2020

This copy : 2020-10-30

ISBN 9798614538583

Chapters

1. Introduction 1
2. Technology and Business and Management 6
3. Where are you going? 12
4. Where can you go? 24
5. Be realistic about getting there 38
6. Some decisions are hard to undo 51
7. Don't do it 68
8. Gathering information 84
9. Modelling vs Reality 98
10. The mid-point(s) 117
11. Reaching the point of 'But …' 143
12. Who's making decisions? 156
13. Reporting 167
14. Changing Behaviour 182
15. Delivering Capability and Succeeding 199
16. The Bloopers reel 224
17. Glossary 232

Appendix : TBM Taxonomy 238

Contents

Chapter 1.   Introduction 1
Structure of the book 2
Outline of the chapters 2

Chapter 2.   Technology and Business and Management 6
The Cost Model at the core of Technology Business Management 8
The TBM Taxonomy provides a structure for Cost Modelling 10
How does TBM relate to ITIL and other Technology Management
   approaches? 10

Chapter 3.   Where are you going? 12
Who's asking? 12
Setting a destination 13
What's the purpose of Technology Business Management? 15
Technology cost within the business context 19
Beyond the objective and preparing for Cost Modelling 21
Benchmarking in a Technology Business Management context 23

Chapter 4.   Where can you go? 24
A Picture of TBM Utopia 24
The Business View 24
The Technology View 29
The Finance View 32

Chapter 5.   Be realistic about getting there 38
Modelling your organisation or using a standard model 38
How long will it take? 38
What level of accuracy is possible? 40
What level of detail should be managed? 42
Who needs to be involved? 45
Where should TBM sit in an organisation? 48
Getting it right first time 49

Chapter 6.   Some decisions are hard to undo 51
TBM and ITFM 51
Implementing a Budget or Actuals model first 55
Is your Technology function seen as a Cost Centre or a Profit Centre? . 60
How separate is the cost of Change and Investment from the cost of
   Running your business? 62
Who owns and manages Products and Services? 64

Chapter 7.	Don't do it	68
Using a TBM Cost Model as an Accounting system		68
Quarterly, Bi-Annual and Annual modelling		71
Reuse of common terms		71
Recursion		74
Managing Fixed and Variable Costs		77
Transparency		79
Replacing Finance functions		83

Chapter 8.	Gathering information	84
Collecting and managing data		84
The value of data		88
Filling in the gaps		90
Improving data quality		93
Data and time		95

Chapter 9.	Modelling vs Reality	98
Centralised and federated models		99
Different models for different purposes		99
A standard model has exceptions		101
Limitations of modelling		104
Technology challenges		111
Modelling the future		115

Chapter 10.	The mid-point(s)	117
What is a Product and what is a Service?		118
Product and Service Catalogues		119
What should be in a Catalogue?		124
How a Catalogue changes behaviour		129
Ownership and governance of Catalogues		132
Enabling Operation of a TBM Cost Model		140

Chapter 11.	Reaching the point of 'But …'	143
But … this information is wrong		143
But … this doesn't match with other numbers		147
The total's right, so we're talking about details		148
But … that isn't how it actually works		149
But … I'm different		154

Chapter 12.	Who's making decisions?	156
Good for me, good for the business		156
Who wants what?		158
Service, Strategy, Risk and Cost		163
Prioritisation		164

Chapter 13.	Reporting	166

Levels of overviews and details 166
Relevance and timing 168
Designing reports 172
Governance and maturation of reports 174
Use cases 179

Chapter 14.   Changing Behaviour 182
Service ownership 182
Customer expectations and behaviour 186
Financial Ownership 187
Overhead and Orphaned costs 191
What people want: Picture, Purpose, Plan, their Part 194
Managing change and driving specific change 196
Standardisation and Patterns 197

Chapter 15.   Delivering Capability and Succeeding 199
Moving from costing to pricing 200
Pricing of Products and Services 202
Value delivered 211
Identifying opportunities 214
Measuring impact 218
Governance 219
Documentation 222

Chapter 16.   The Bloopers reel 224
$100 trillion gap in the budget 224
Individual pay affecting behaviour 225
Measuring at a point in time or for average usage 226
Thousands and Thousandths 227
Unrealistic expectations 228
Changing the Unit of Measure 229
The difference between succeeding and going viral 230

Chapter 17.   Glossary 232

Appendix : TBM Taxonomy 238

Acknowledgements

Technology Business Management is not a discipline which suits everyone who gets involved with it. However there are many who make up the community that find it interesting and even fun. That community has grown and matured over the last decade but has consistently been made up of people who have openly discussed their own understanding of TBM and been willing to listen and talk with others about it.

Through several years of attending Technology Business Management events in Europe and the annual TBM Conference, I would like to particularly thank those whose friendliness and openness have made this a great community to work in. I'd particularly acknowledge those who presented Pecha Kucha presentations at the second TBM conference and who have always sought each other out at subsequent events, particularly Carl Stumpf, Suzanne Chartol and Lisa Stalter. Other specifically memorable and valuable conversations with Nate Bender and Kelly Morrison stand out from those events for helping me develop broader understanding.

I was fortunate to start working with what has now become Technology Business Management with Paul Sillett, a hugely foresighted individual who had implemented the billing and reporting system for an internal Technology Catalogue in banks that became JPMorgan Chase. Along with him I would particularly thank Martin O'Sullivan, Melvyn Jones, Ed McHugh, Valentina Ruiz and Richard Lupfer, who helped develop TBM Cost Modelling and implement other ideas in this book through multiple iterations.

Although not explicitly needing to be mentioned in the book, as the principles involved are not product specific, the staff and management at Apptio over the years have been hugely important to the development and success of TBM. Having worked with many of them over the last decade, I'd like to particularly thank the London team for their friendliness, knowledge and drive, including Nitin Patel, Pete Cunningham, Adrian Smoothie, Doug Silk, Aaron Russell and Paula Darvell. There are many others in the team who I have also relied on at different times and thank similarly. In the global team I've also gained huge insight and value from working with many people whose skill and resourcefulness have developed Technology Business Management. These include Todd Tucker, Chris Pick, Catherine Picknell, Matt Halls, Rob Booher and Ed Hayman.

Over multiple TBM implementations, I've learnt from the varied skills, knowledge, approaches to management, detail and experience of those around me. Thank you to Rob Grassie, Lisa Kelly, Mukhtar Ashrafi, Terry Howlett,

David Bull and Nasir Omar; Spencer Cunningham, Mark Steckel, David Taylor, Zenith Ahmed and Neil Clarke; Stefano Raggi, Frank Seifert, Massimo Fuser, Jürgen Maurer, Angela Mühlhölzer, Annette Dilger and Alina Marcu, and all the others in those teams, too numerous to mention.

Most recently and during the development and publication of this book I'd like to thank all those who have helped push me to the point of finishing the writing, and for their help in reviewing and editing, including some already mentioned, Amanda Deschenes, Vasily Sakharov, Ian Talbot, Michael Moulsdale and Colin Woodford.

Finally, I'm hugely grateful to my family; Rosalyn, Louisa and Gabriel (who insisted I thank our cats …) and everyone else who has helped the book reach this point.

Chapter 1.   Introduction

This book has been written to assist those people who are starting, and also those that are already involved, with the process of managing the cost of Information Technology, and looking for the appropriate way to manage that cost to deliver business value. A structured method to deliver this, Technology Business Management (TBM), will be introduced in terms of the ideas, approaches, challenges and responses that are involved.

TBM has developed and formalised as a consolidated set of disciplines since the late 'noughties,' previously having been activities carried out piecemeal and usually prioritised on an ad-hoc basis or to firefight specific organisational issues as they arose. In larger organisations, the activities which are now grouped together under a TBM banner were separate functions, with little or no recognition of the value to be gained by improving their cross-functional interaction. Without any formal structure to guide this, alongside the necessary level of professional expertise, and the training and focus needed to maintain core capabilities, the isolation of finance and technology functions was only broken down in a few companies.

This book takes the practical disciplines of TBM and builds on the central concepts related to value which were covered in the 2016 book by Todd Tucker, "Technology Business Management: The Four Value Conversations CIOs Must Have With Their Businesses[1]". The development of TBM is as much founded on in its practical delivery as in the recognition of its value, and this book brings together structured guidance on that, based on real-life implementations and conversations about the concepts.

The increasing capabilities of tools which help integrate information from multiple business functions paved the way for many innovative business improvements, and continue to do so. The recognition of the value to be gained in bringing this ability to the combination of management disciplines from technology, finance and business is where Technology Business Management derived its core propositions. Gradual development of the formality around this, with incremental value being able to be delivered over a sustained period, is why TBM has grown to its current state. A particular

---

[1] Published by Technology Business Management Council, Ltd., Bellevue, Washington. ISBN 978-0-9975127-4-5

backbone of this is the TBM Taxonomy, which is included in this book as an Appendix.

The other major factor in the development of Technology Business Management as a discipline has been the recognition of the value of a community of common interest, rather than the previous islands of competence. TBM is what has developed in the last decade from the starting point of those far-sighted individuals, companies and suppliers who saw a common interest in fixing problems that many organisations looked at as "too hard".

Continuing to build those communities of interest around TBM is a route to innovating and continuing to gain value, both within an organisation and within and across industries. There is still a gap between what it is possible to communicate and teach, as against what can be built through more direct relationships between those who are thoughtful, skilled, inquisitive or knowledgeable in a topic. A common understanding of the challenges and failures that are likely to affect those working in this space is, however, useful. That is what this book targets.

Structure of the book

One of the items learned from experience by those involved in multiple TBM implementations is that the breadth and depth of difference between organisations is only infrequently recognised by those working in them. The approach within this book is to roughly follow thought processes, planning, implementation, and challenges that can be associated with delivering TBM methodologies into an organisation, covering enough of the main areas of business difference to give guidance to all. It is highly likely that any business will already find that some elements of the mindset, tools and processes already exist, so some of the information covered here will already be well understood and, even more likely, maturely delivered.

Outline of the chapters

1. Introduction

The purpose of this book and its structure. You are here.

2. Technology and Business and Management

Background on Technology Business Management, including the Cost Model at its centre showing the value of technology expense, who TBM is useful for and how it fits into an organisation.

3. Where are you going?

Working out the potential and purpose of TBM, who the specific customers are and what they should gain from it, together with some ways to take action and show immediate value while preparing for the more complex tasks.

4. Where can you go?

Illustrating how some of the best practices available with a complete and mature TBM implementation can work, from the perspectives of the main groups involved; business, technology and finance.

5. Be realistic about getting there

Setting some expectations around the balance between complexity and achievement, this chapter looks at some approaches to implementing TBM, the organisational changes and impacts that may need to be planned, and the realistic effort and timelines for doing so.

6. Some decisions are hard to undo

Although there is a definition of the core TBM Taxonomy (see Appendix) and a structure associated with TBM, there are many routes to implementation. This degree of flexibility allows organisations to choose some options which may appear simple at the start, based on current knowledge or operations, but which need to be looked at more closely when they overlap into TBM. This chapter highlights several decisions which should be reviewed at an early stage of defining a TBM implementation strategy, and the implications.

7. Don't do it

The flexibility and extensibility of TBM can also suggest that options for implementation may be realistic which are better avoided. Extending from the previous chapter, some specific approaches are reviewed here that are advised against, along with the reasons why.

8. *Gathering information*

The basis of creating a TBM Cost Model is the collection and integration of a range of information sources, where the value is then identified and managed by building relationships between those sources. The initial and subsequent processes for identifying, collecting and managing that data are reviewed.

9. *Modelling vs Reality*

The temptation in building any model is to aim for perfection in every detail, but neither perfect accuracy nor perfect understanding are required. This chapter looks at understanding the relevance of using standard approaches instead of customisation, plus setting expectations about the key limitations of modelling.

10. *The mid-point(s)*

Returning to the broader process of implementing TBM, this chapter focuses on the importance of Product and Service Catalogues and their governance within an organisation. This can be a critical factor in creating linkages between business processes and the underlying technology and costs.

11. *Reaching the point of 'But ...'*

Providing output from a TBM implementation usually introduces people to information in a form, or with a scope, that is different from what they are used to. One of the natural reactions to this is to challenge the information, so this chapter looks at some general objections that are heard and approaches to mitigating the information being rejected.

12. *Who's making decisions?*

The value which TBM offers can be realised and recognised at both an individual level and at a business level. Understanding who is going to be able to gain in what way from TBM, and how a perceived negative impact in one area may be managed as part of a larger positive change, is reviewed.

13. *Reporting*

With a new range of information relationships available for review through TMB, this chapter provides an overview of how to understand and design reports that are relevant to the range of people who can benefit from TBM involvement.

14. Changing Behaviour

As all organisations change over time, the potential exists to use TBM to inform and drive change based on data rather than instinct. This section looks at a variety of changes and the impact they can have on behaviour through defining ownership, leaving gaps, and with both explicit and implicit goals.

15. Delivering capability and succeeding

It is possible to measure the maturity of TBM in multiple ways, so defining success can be incremental. This chapter looks at some of the measures used to identify progress on specific capabilities and how the level of maturity is not limited by reaching the point of implementation but continues into ongoing governance and continuous improvement.

16. The Bloopers reel

Despite everyone's best efforts, it is still possible for things to go wrong. This final chapter anonymously documents some of the more unusual ways this has been seen.

17. Glossary

A glossary of terms used in this book.

Appendix: TBM Taxonomy

The full TBM Taxonomy.

Chapter 2. Technology and Business and Management

… and risk and service.

A question that regularly underpins conversations about Information Technology (IT) is "Why does it cost so much?" although it comes in different varieties depending who is asking and the context in which it is being asked. In many large organisations it has been strikingly difficult to find an overall response, although if there is a very specific question being asked there is usually an answer … "What does this application cost?" or "How much are we spending on datacentres?"

If you think of the same question but about your personal expenditure for buying a car, you quickly move on to asking yourself about what you value in the purchase. You have examples readily to mind about the aspects of brand, model, aesthetics, fuel type, engine size, performance, comfort, reliability and colour that will give you value. You then start to put a price against each of these in your mind, even if not formalising it in the same way that a manufacturer would.

Technology Business Management, as a set of disciplines, offers a way to take the basic question and answer both what IT costs, but more valuably answering "why" and whether it is providing value to the organisation. It allows you to provide detailed understanding of costs and cost drivers of IT to the people who need to drive value and efficiency, whether they are specialists, users or managers in both IT and business roles.

One challenge in delivering on this direction is that of specialisation and the way that this drives the use of language. The perfect example of this is the acronym "TBM" for Technology Business Management, which takes three generic words to create a specialised acronym. In the early 1990s, when Microsoft first started to use the Windows name for software, its application to register the name with the United States Patent and Trademark Office was rejected several times. Although "Windows" is now generically understood in the computing sphere without needing additional context, it is useful to use the phrase Technology Business Management (or the acronym TBM) with enough context to establish its position and value.

One of the practical issues with delivering value from TBM is that you need to be aware of your position and strategy in many more areas than just technology, business, or management. TBM is a useful acronym, but as well as the individual knowledge associated with each letter, you also need to think about the combinations of technology as a business, management of technology, and general business management as part of the process. Depending on your business environment, you may also need to review the alignment of risk measurement and management, service quality and delivery, and organisational design and management, across your TBM evolution.

Management perspectives for each of technology, finance and business will be analysed throughout this book. This is necessarily quite loose however, as an organisational structure can join or split these in multiple ways, although in a large organisation it is likely that the roles have only limited overlaps. It is worth reviewing your own discipline within these sections, to evaluate your own and your organisation's maturity, and ensure that you have taken precursor steps to enable progress.

It is also worth reviewing the other disciplines and identifying who in your organisation has that responsibility and their level of engagement and process maturity.

It will appear possible in many places to summarise the responsibilities and maturity levels, but you will notice that the chapter summaries do not do this. The range of organisational, functional and management disciplines and specialisations involved in running any business are huge. It would neither be realistic nor reasonable to try to suggest a 'one size fits all' checklist, or to assume that a single organisation's successful implementation of TBM could be lifted and dropped into another.

> *The use of generic words in Products can lead to some interesting comparisons, such as the software named 'Best/1' and 'Good'.*
>
> *Would you buy software named 'Adequate' or 'Poor'?*

Stepping back to what you need to do to deliver TBM, a view that has been independently developed in many TBM implementations is that the function delivering TBM (sometimes called a "TBM Office") needs to engage with Technology, Finance and Business management.

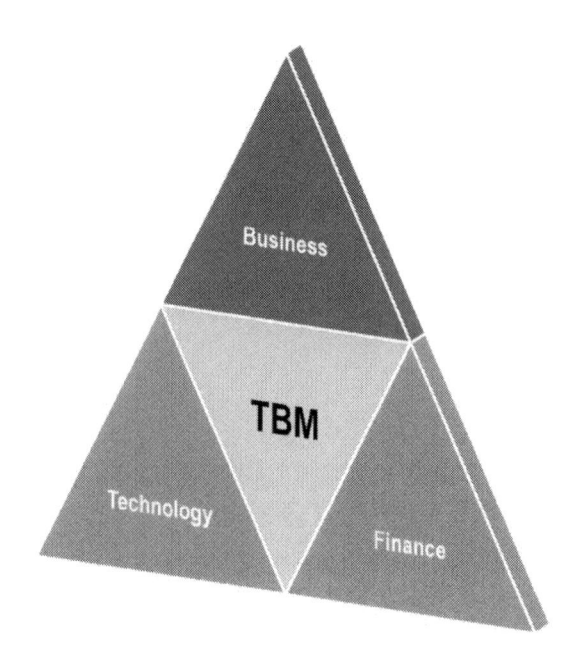

Can you succeed without one of these three areas? It is possible to run a TBM effort within a finance organisation without technology's full engagement, and vice-versa. It is harder to succeed without business engagement at senior levels, but still possible. Overall, the objectives for TBM implementation and the measures of success need to be set realistically at the start of the effort, considering the level of involvement of each of the main groups.

A TBM programme without full engagement from any one of technology, finance and business management can be successful, up to a point, with limited engagement from a second of the functions. The quality of the outcome will however be hugely compromised in that situation, since both the confirmation of the strategy and the evaluation of the delivery may turn out to have been fundamentally wrong.

The Cost Model at the core of Technology Business Management

There are many actions which can individually deliver improvements to the cost-base or efficiency of IT spend. Traditionally these become the responsibility of individual managers and projects, as a single overall synthesis of them is seen as too difficult. Immediate tactical improvements to the management of project, labour, asset or external supplier (vendor) expense all provide cost reductions, but most business activity relies on combinations of these, and the efficiency to be gained by managing them holistically is harder to achieve.

TBM provides the approach to delivering this by showing the business that the money spent on technology is delivering value and ways to control it. The tool to show this is a Cost Model; a logical flow that demonstrates how the costs of technology relate to the business usage and demands. It is unlikely, particularly in a large organisation, that any one person will ever know or be able to accurately model all aspects of finance, technology, and the business. If such a person exists in any organisation, they potentially have more value to add in running the business than in modelling it for others.

Cost Modelling can be a formal discipline and is part of an accountant's training under the name of "Activity Based Costing" (ABC). As the name suggests, the general concept is that costs can be related to activities, and activities related to business purposes. The most complete implementations of this are usually related to the calculation of the cost of physical products in a manufacturing environment, where the cost of each component can be identified along with the quantities used. The same concepts are brought to Cost Modelling for Technology Business Management, adjusted for the needs of the situation. This includes variability in component cost and, often, that the final technology 'product' is for the internal use of the organisation rather than for sale to customers.

How well will the business, technology and finance functions understand a Cost Model?

Each of the functions involved in TBM, if they compare the Cost Model to the level of complexity at which they normally function, will say that parts of the Cost Model are inaccurate and could be improved. Those do not stop the model from providing value. This lack of perfect accuracy does not negate or even significantly reduce the potential value of modelling, since the model will have built in the key elements for each function, on top of which they can each deliver additional value through operational efficiency.

As an example, a Cost Model running across multiple countries and currencies can be built using a single currency and fixed exchange rates. This is clearly inaccurate from a financial perspective, but the finance function can add further value through currency hedging and planning. Do the business or technology functions need to know or understand this? If the answer to either of these is yes, it is likely that the relevant currency fluctuations are large enough to impact business decision making and they should be fully modelled, but in many cases this might be best left to the experts rather than modelled centrally. The understanding, by the experts in their functions, that the TBM Cost Model should hold all key information but not every detail, is a core part of making TBM work in an organisation.

The TBM Taxonomy provides a structure for Cost Modelling

When building a Cost Model, there is always a choice between building a bespoke view of an organisation and following a pre-existing template. Both have benefits and detractors in terms of aspects such as the ease with which they will be understood, the need for up-front understanding of the target end state, flexibility and accuracy.

The TBM Taxonomy (see Appendix), provides one view of the detail for modelling relationships between finance, technology, and business. This is a basis under which many organisations have built Cost Models and specifically provides sufficient detail and structure to enable that goal.

As a taxonomy is fundamentally an ordered, detailed hierarchy or list, making changes that are relevant to a particular business situation is possible, but this particular version has been successfully used across multiple business segments.

A logical understanding of the structure of the Taxonomy and its main points is an important level of understanding to bring into a TBM implementation. As will be repeated at several points later, perfect adherence to the detail of the TBM Taxonomy is not a requirement for success. It is, however, valuable to understand the TBM Taxonomy to the level where it is possible to assess the benefits and challenges which come from alternative choices, large or small.

How does TBM relate to ITIL and other Technology Management approaches?

With technology companies constantly developing new products and new approaches, whether it is hardware, software, digitalisation, cloud or service-based, the management discipline for these has also been subject to a degree of standardisation. As examples;

- The IT Infrastructure Library (ITIL) provides a source of good practice and discipline across functional and operational management of technology.

- CoBIT (Control of Business IT) takes a structured view of how to integrate process, risk and security management into the management of IT.

Neither provides significant depth to questions of overall management of finances for IT, although there are specific functional approaches around vendor and project expense. This is the area where TBM provides an additional management capability and value, integrating with the other management approaches and standards where needed.

Technology Business Management, particularly a TBM Cost Model, should not therefore be the discipline which owns information about the functional and operational delivery of technology or its cost. It is more correctly identified as the way in which this information is consolidated, analysed and delivered throughout an organisation, to understand the value of technology and the business choices for its use.

Chapter 3. Where are you going?

This chapter will discuss the preparation for a TBM implementation, setting scope and expectations. Although a technology Cost Model can range upwards from creating a simple spreadsheet for one technology function, the larger value is gained when the scope is broad enough that most technology costs in a business are included. As such, the chapter will start to review organisational sponsorship, objectives and scope. While not defining a single route to success, the intent is to show the decisions that should be made at the start of an implementation, to help set realistic expectations and to show suggested approaches.

Who's asking?

The requirement for some form of Technology Business Management implementation can come from business, technology or financial functions. The potential exists for an implementation to exist largely in either technology or finance with specific input from the other, but this will have limited value compared to a jointly agreed and sponsored effort.

Each of the business, technology and finance functions can gain benefit from TBM but will have different specific requirements and expectations, which should be collected and synthesised into a common objective and deliverables.

While it is possible to only take direction and sponsorship from a single part of the organisation, the destination and outcomes will differ. This is also noticeable when one area of sponsorship or leadership is more actively involved in the implementation processes and decision-making for TBM than another. A simple example is in the balance between technology and finance management and the outcomes that they are looking to achieve.

As will be returned to in Chapter 6, 'Some decisions are hard to undo', a strong focus on financial discipline may lead to reduced engagement and accuracy on the technology side of TBM and later challenges to the accuracy of the overall outcome. The reverse of this, with leadership and focus only from technology without all relevant involvement from finance, can result in outcomes that have limited acceptance throughout the organisation due to inconsistencies between TBM and related financial outputs.

The best balance to look for in defining objectives for TBM comes with sponsorship from both technology and finance functions; understanding what they can jointly achieve which would not be feasible separately. Starting from there also supports continuing engagement and involvement throughout the detailed decision-making of a TBM implementation.

Setting a destination

When taking a trip by road you'll often start by choosing your destination, setting the location in your sat-nav (which already knows where you are starting from), allowing it to specify the route before starting driving. The parallels to Project Management disciplines are clear and can be carried through the actual act of driving to your destination, with waypoints and re-routing as needed.

Implementation of some aspects of Technology Business Management can be as straightforward as taking a trip with a single destination. The challenges come when you are not, or cannot be, specific about your destination.

The level of specificity that is needed in setting the scope for a full Cost Model implementation is significant. It is possible and realistic to make some early decisions about your destination that you will later find to be wrong enough to require an almost complete rebuild. This seems less likely when the TBM discipline is offering a common approach, the Cost Model, to deliver business value. Unusually, the choices that require a complete rebuild can even be correct at the time they are made, so you should plan for this situation from an early stage.

The first step in identifying the scope and target for TBM is to understand and document the expected scope and business requirements; your starting point and destination.

As a part of this definition, it is more than usually important to set the boundaries and exclusions to the scope of activity. The range of inputs, functionality and potential outputs that can be included in a TBM Cost Model implementation is very broad, with both complexity and expectation growing as they are identified. The implementation of a model does not require all items to be delivered at the first stage, although correct scheduling of core components and later requirements and data relationships are important to analyse.

One productive approach is to plan to implement a TBM Cost Model twice. While it is usual to plan projects to deliver correctly first time, this is made less practical for TBM by both the range of quality of information and data usually available, and the level of change being introduced to an organisation.

The initial implementation is used as a process to collect and qualify the value of all available inputs and educate each of the (usually newly formed) TBM team, finance and business stakeholders on the concepts of TBM. The target implementation provides a limited but defined set of reports showing the potential of the system.

The second implementation is expected to be faster and more functional than the first, with the ability to add or re-prioritise requirements from all stakeholders. The delivery time can be shortened as there will be a base of data, as well as common understanding of tools, processes and the people involved.

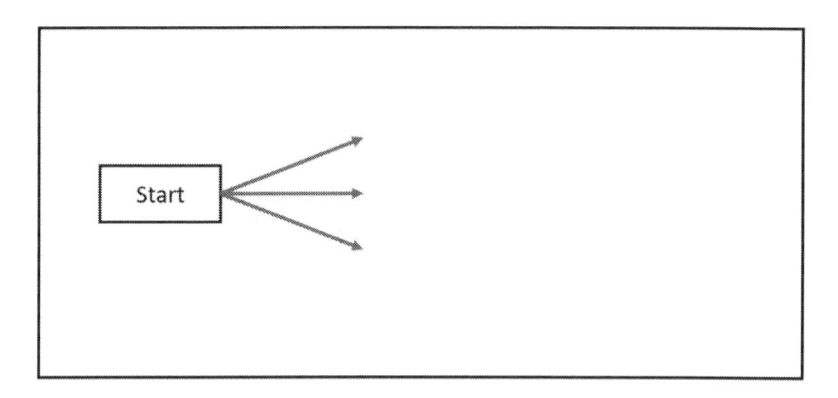

Returning to the road-trip analogy, if you only have a generic destination you may choose a generic start to your route. If you are travelling to 'the East' you may start on a Eastbound road, until you find out whether you are going due East, North East or South East. If these are the only three roads available, choosing the wrong one will result in you reaching the wrong destination first, or having to retrace your steps and start again. To further add to the complexity, you may not know or be told where you are starting from, resulting in the need to revisit a different start point having gone some way into your journey.

The potential complexity of business requirements for a TBM Cost Model may be similarly unstructured or incomplete. This leads to a need to set an expectation of 'waypoints' being reached with the deliverables and for rework, possibly from an early stage in the model. A waypoint becomes a recognised point that you reach, indicating that you are on at least a roughly correct path. It drives an approach to Cost Modelling that has specific points at which to control the process, such as the ensuring that all costs are accounted for at a particular waypoint in the model.

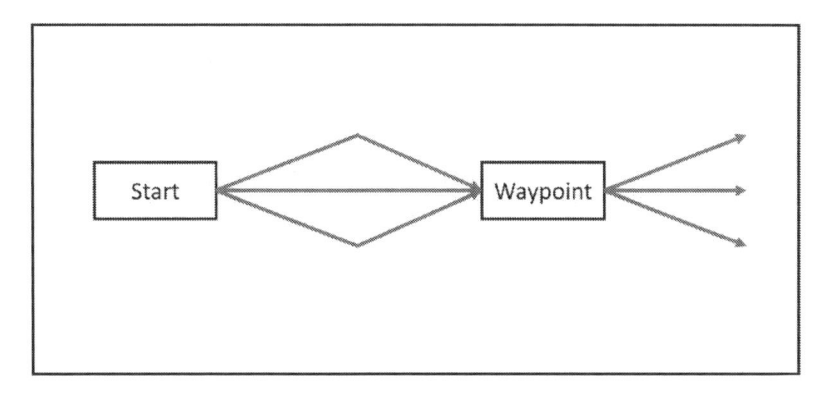

```
        Start  <====>  Waypoint  <===
```

Returning to the analogy, if you are building the road system, you are setting up at least one point that you will reach regardless of your starting point or destination. You will reach the waypoint, limit your requirement for retracing steps to the start, and have better likelihood of reaching your destination efficiently.

What's the purpose of Technology Business Management?

In defining a project, the initiation steps include sponsorship being defined and objectives being set. The breadth of business impact and coverage of a TBM Cost Model means that sponsorship is often from a board level position, potentially with multiple senior sponsors holding business, technology and finance accountabilities.

When looking for common understanding of objectives, the business focus will be primary, but not unique. Consolidating to a single statement, the best answer I have found is 'To manage IT efficiently, and equitably align the cost to its consumers.' A detailed breakdown of the statement is below, however the intention is to establish the targets for a number of activities and behaviours across Technology departments, finance and technology users.

This statement of objectives is generically for activities in TBM based on Cost Modelling, and inherent in the statement is the understanding that meeting the objectives delivers and shows the 'value' of IT.

To manage IT efficiently ...

As a statement of project objectives this is lacking some of the Specific, Measurable, Attainable, Relevant, Time-bound ('SMART') criteria which can be added as appropriate, but the first words can be interpreted by Business, Technology and Finance to show common understanding.

To the business, IT efficiency needs to be defined as more than cost, meaning that their understanding of what they are consuming needs to be developed in parallel. The business view will include service quality and risk management The measure of IT efficiency that a Cost Model will deliver should tie these together in a way that allows business users to link and manage their cost based on their business products and services.

This is about the cost of technology per "transaction" or "unit" that the business delivers. This is not about the "cost per server" or "cost per application" which, unless they are the business product, are not relevant business metrics.

To the IT functions, efficiency covers both internal cost efficiency and the business requirements in the delivery of technology. Technology management need to demonstrate to the business that they are managing the balance of delivering all aspects of their service, which with TBM will include its cost.

IT is also a shorthand term that can variously cover infrastructure, application development, technology support and operations. The move from a simple hierarchical view of technology to delivery of interrelated services complicates the measure of efficiency, which can be mitigated in Cost Modelling by using similar 'waypoints' to those already mentioned.

Implementing measures of cost efficiency will often be an addition to pre-existing service and risk metrics. The integration of these is possible, to provide modelled and calculated cost against service and risk levels, however this is not a primary objective or specific TBM deliverable and has the potential to be misleading.

Financial input to a Cost Model is the first requirement, but in most respects the hardest to measure efficiency for. This is the point at which the question of "Why does IT cost so much?" is expected to deliver answers but is unable to do so.

Having cost reduction as an objective for IT, without balance related to business requirements, service quality, or risk, can lead to reduced service levels and failure to meet business needs.

The implementation of cost management objectives, rather than cost reduction, alongside IT cost efficiency objectives, can be implemented in an organisation to reinforce both.

... and equitably align ...

Internally within many businesses, IT cost has become an increasing proportion of the overall expense base.

At a financial level, the implementation of IT cost alignment with the financial books and records of a business can take a wide variety of approaches, but in all events needs to be explainable and justifiable. This is the 'fair' or 'equitable' alignment that needs to take place since, both for day-to-day operations and in planning for change and investment. Inaccurate alignment and understanding of those costs can lead to incorrect decisions and unexpected impacts.

The implicit requirement behind 'equitable alignment' is the basis of cost modelling; that there is sufficient information to allow costs to be grouped functionally and then aligned to those functions' consumers. The output of this is that the business consumers of technology have costs aligned to them based on their usage, which they recognise and value.

It is an important aspect of this overall objective for TBM Cost Modelling that it does suggest 'equitably' rather than 'accurately'. The implication is that the output takes into account all major cost alignments to the business, to the best current extent possible, but is not perfect.

One of the expected limitations of TBM Cost Modelling derives from there being a large number of separately managed inputs to the system, often with multiple and complex relationships. This leads to a significantly complicated model, based on many decisions, which are 'most accurate' or 'best alternative' rather than absolute.

... the cost ...

In the absence of a central TBM Cost Model, many IT managers feel the need to understand how technology runs "as a business". The common answer to this is for them to build their own model of costs, usually based around their own scope of control, cost centre or technology. These models are usually highly detailed, can be fully supported and justified, but almost invariably are limited as they do not account for the full range of costs that should be included.

To gain the most value from TBM Cost Modelling, the scope of IT costs included should be both tightly defined and broad. This does not require that every IT function or cost be modelled, but the business leadership should be able to look at the Cost Model output and know, simply, what is and is not included.

A similar critique can be applied to investment planning and Business Cases. The role of a Project Manager in presenting a Business Case is effectively that of a salesman rather than an independent adviser; to prove that the cost of an investment is lower than the value it will earn. However true this is, the temptation is to minimise the cost and maximise the value predictions. A critical appraisal of a Business Case will often show this up and cause reassessment of the viability of the investment.

Definition of the financial scope of a TBM implementation requires multiple dimensions to be reviewed. These can include

- Organisational and business hierarchy to be covered, irrespective of technology structure.
- Financial scope in terms of timescale; historic, actual and forecast costs.
- IT organisational and functional structure; infrastructure only or inclusion of Application Development and management.
- Region and location coverage.
- Run the Business only or both Run and Change/Investment costs.

Decisions about some of these need to be made early in an implementation, as will be reviewed in Chapter 6 regarding financial scope. Others need not be immediate but can be phased, without negating the ability to derive value from a TBM Cost Model.

There is a risk that the more dimensions you look to manage through a Cost Model, the less likely you are to achieve your primary goals, as complexity overtakes the ability to deliver. It is practical to start with a clear and simple set of targets to build towards, explicitly limiting the opportunity and directly managing out scope changes.

Once the scope is defined, the expectation is set that the costs to be aligned to customers will be equal to the costs spent. This may seem like an obvious statement but needs to be reiterated. There will be situations where alignment of management, overhead and 'orphaned' costs need to take place, and 'the costs' provided to the business by Finance need to be able to be reconciled to those from the TBM Cost Model.

... to its consumers

The argument for Cost Modelling and TBM is at least partly to help consumers of IT ensure that their decision making is capable of including IT costs. The scope of TBM within an organisation may not immediately reach all the way to the ultimate business user, so the definition of the consumer is important.

For the consumer to accept both the calculation of cost and the fairness of their share of it, they must have a clear understanding of the details of these factors. This is where they can be expected, both implicitly and explicitly, to make decisions based on the value of IT to them. Conversations about how to manage the cost can then turn from the internal goals of efficiency, to business goals and business value delivered by technology.

It is quite possible to build an entire TBM Cost Model and implement TBM disciplines on a smaller scale than for all IT expense in a company. Major corporations regularly rotate between centralised and decentralised IT Infrastructure departments, business- or centrally-aligned Application Development and Operations, etc. and any of these can have a TBM Cost Model.

Whichever organisational model is in place, there will be a set of Services provided, which are utilised both inside and outside the Technology department, and the costs of those are the output of the model.

Technology cost within the business context

The business view of technology cost changes according to context and time, but the cost it is usually an enabler of business rather something that generates business revenue directly. From that position, the capability to align technology costs to business outcomes becomes an underlying requirement for business decision making. A TBM Cost Model provides the potential for this to be delivered on a historic and current (Actuals) basis and to enable planning based on trends and business direction.

With the number of ways in which Technology and Business Services outputs from a Cost Model can be used, the phases of presenting results from a TBM implementation to business users must be considered. A first step can be consideration of whether a business wants to just see the cost of technology from a Cost Model (sometimes known as 'Showback'), or to have a TBM Cost Model cause actual movement of costs in the financial records as an internal allocation. Between these choices there will be significant differences in the planning, implementation and communication needed. There is also a further considerable difference between an allocation, with 100% of costs going to business users, and a 'Chargeback' mechanism, where businesses are given more direct control over the management of their use of technology and its calculated cost to them.

From a business perspective, implementation of a new level of technology cost visibility through TBM Cost Modelling can be used to help drive positive behavioural changes. These can be supported by clearly identifying to the business how they can directly affect their own technology costs. In the context of both Chargeback and Showback this can include providing the business with metrics on the amount of technology used and how to request changes e.g. how to reduce IT cost by decommissioning applications, servers and storage.

There can also be less positive or limited change if the business identifies negative impacts to the approach being taken. An example of this is the use of the term Showback, which is relatively commonly used within a TBM context, but rarely otherwise.

In some business contexts, a Showback implementation for the business cost of technology may be seen by some as irrelevant if it is not backed up by reductions in the actual financial allocations.

Similarly, in a 'fully allocated' model, where all costs are mathematically calculated to align to businesses, an individual business unit may identify that the cost reduction from their decreased use of technology will actually be shared between all business units, rather than directly benefiting them.

In both these contexts the loss of value through inaction is to the overall business, which is being impacted by parochial concerns at the business unit level. The implementation of the TBM Cost Model can be used, in conjunction with both, to drive more positive behaviour. When it is understood by business units that their actions will be of direct benefit to them as well as to the overall business, as shown in their financial allocation of technology cost, they are provided with an incentive to show efficiency in their use of technology.

Beyond the objective and preparing for Cost Modelling

With the potential for complexity in a TBM Cost Model, it can take a significant amount of time to build a functional system. As a result it is useful to look at individual areas of TBM discipline and capabilities for quicker results, aligning those activities with the overall objectives and preparation for Cost Modelling.

At a financial level, apart from the relevant general ledger input, the key information that is needed for modelling is in terms of the relationships of the costs to specific technology functions. The main strands of this are labour, assets, vendors and projects. It is possible to align these costs to their IT functional use, but there are often more appropriate or accurate tools available that can provide further business value.

Time tracking and headcount management

For headcount management, aspects of general management that can be incrementally valuable to TBM Cost Modelling include measuring time spent on functional roles through a time-tracking system, projected increases and decreases through a headcount management system, and similar functions.

The level of detail required for some aspects of this are usually outside the scope of TBM, for example the specific cost of personnel in particular locations. Information on the alignment of personnel to technology activities, both for general activity and projects, is generally required but will only be used on a monthly basis and will not need perfect accuracy.

Similarly, information on planned directions for overall staffing levels are important to have available for TBM budget or forecasts, but not necessarily at a detailed level.

Fixed Assets

With assets, there is often a gap between the financial Fixed Asset Register and technical inventory. This can be the effect of many different circumstances such as single purchases covering multiple systems, lack of common inventory keys, tracking of financial incentives separately from the assets, system upgrades with a single serial number, and others. A review and alignment between the Fixed Asset Register and technical inventory, for the highest value assets, can help prepare for Cost Modelling and at the same time identify stranded assets for reuse or write-down.

Vendors and contracts

A review of vendors and contracts is likely to cover an increasing proportion of IT spend with current industry trends such as outsourcing and Cloud Services. The requirement to track a large number of these relationships and to actively manage them throughout their contractual lifecycles means there can be high value information available for use with TBM.

There is also the opportunity for additional information to be added to contracts for further analysis and management, with the possibility that each contract is treated as more of a legal than a technology relationship.

Technology inventory

Beyond the financial inputs to TBM, the most critical information that is required is of technology inventories and relationships; in ITIL terms this information is held in a Configuration Management Database (CMDB). Practically, few businesses have a fully functioning CMDB that shows correlations of technology with applications, or applications with business usage, so the definition of Cost Model scope should account for this limitation, and any improvements will be useful preparation for a TBM implementation.

Service Catalogues

Implementation of Service Catalogues can provide common understanding of the items available and being delivered to customers, which in turn provides benefits to a TBM Cost Model by specifying targets to align cost to.

As described earlier in this Chapter, the goal of a Technology Business Management implementation is enable a business to run efficiently and for business and technology management to be able to identify the opportunities for improving that. This means that there must be a view of cost that is understood by the business. A Service Catalogue, which may exist already in multiple sources or in a single place such as an Enterprise Architecture system, will become a key focal point, as described in Chapter 10 on 'The mid-point(s)'.

Early identification of the detail of the Service Catalogue (or Catalogues) helps define the later stages of creating a TBM Cost Model, beyond what is held in technology inventories.

Benchmarking in a Technology Business Management context

There are multiple views of the value that can be taken from comparing costs against industry benchmark measurements of the cost of technology. Historically this type of measurement and comparison has usually been mandated at senior levels of an organisation to target areas of perceived high expense. The benchmark comparisons show the cost of specific technology services, from which actions are developed to target improvements through cost-reduction by vendor negotiation or other efficiency targets.

This traditional approach to benchmarking is often a contentious process, requiring multiple cycles of financial and technical input to reach a common understanding of the cost-base and a realistic comparison between organisations.

As a precursor to a TBM implementation, benchmarking in this manner has limited value except in increasing focus of technology managers on the structure of their costs.

Benchmarking is significantly simplified through a TBM Cost Model implementation as the TBM Council's standard TBM Taxonomy provides a well-defined and common set of technology descriptions to which cost will be assigned. An outcome of this is that a TBM Cost Model implementation provides most of the information needed to enable initial benchmarking of individual IT Towers without rework. If the model is being run on a regular basis, it also makes it possible to see 'live' data on the same basis as the benchmarking and to set targets based on that.

An alternative management approach to the use of benchmark data, within the context of a Cost Model implementation and either at a standardised TBM Taxonomy level or in the context of a Product Catalogue, is to identify "best in class" costs and then target the technology function to deliver the services at that cost or better. This has also been used in some organisations to help set Service prices prior to using TBM.

Chapter 4.   Where can you go?

What does a successful Technology Business Management implementation look like and how will you know when you have achieved it? This Chapter will give some idea of what broad benefits, processes and behaviours you might achieve once you have a mature TBM environment. Many of these can also be seen in isolation within organisations without an integrated TBM capability, but the full benefits occur when they are integrated and have clear central governance.

The need for central governance does not mean that TBM functions require centralisation, but that business, finance and technology management need to identify and drive clear ownership of decisions, and those should be aligned to the interests of the business rather than individuals.

A Picture of TBM Utopia

This description will cover multiple views of a fully mature TBM implementation within an organisation, starting with a business view and then covering technology, finance and other functions. Some parts of the description overlap between the different views, which will generally be a case of multiple groups being involved in the same decision-making process or benefits being derived through cooperation.

The Business View

The business view of Technology Business Management is that it shouldn't have to care about how it works (or how IT works). This doesn't mean that a TBM implementation should be considered successful when the group managing TBM (the TBM Office) is disbanded, but when its deliverables are so closely integrated into business functions that they do not need to be separately marketed.

The heads of business functions will have two main requirements of the TBM capability; firstly that they should be able to run and manage their own business with clear, consistent and efficient technology inputs, and secondly that they should be able to plan for changes, whether they are tactical or strategic.

The Service Catalogue

The engagement of Technology Business Management into the business on a regular basis will be based around a Service Catalogue that is relevant to the business. The Service Catalogue will primarily give the business a description of what they are paying for in the way of service and how their actions will affect the cost of it. At the same time the Catalogue will be clearly understood by the Technology organisation through its relationship to the Technology Services that it is delivering.

The description of a Service in the Catalogue will not initially describe the underlying technology components, but will relate to the business value delivered and expected service levels. The relationship to the underlying technology components is an important part of providing transparency to the business on the cost components and drivers, but not primary to their understanding.

The second fundamental deliverable of the Service Catalogue to the business users is the information on how they can affect its cost to them. This may be shown as a price for a Service, but will not always be quite so simple. The key reason for this being included for each Service is to give the business a clear and consistent view of how their costs will change in a stable environment. If they increase their use of this Service their cost will increase, and vice versa. There is significant additional complexity to pricing, even for internal use, which will be explored in Chapter 15.

With a structured list of Services in place through the Catalogue, the Catalogue owner needs to put in place the processes to manage changes and a defined schedule for doing so. Business Services within the Catalogue should be at a level where only a small proportion of them change in each cycle. This implies that the Services should not be so consolidated that they appear to be independent of strategic changes to the organisation or management structure. It also implies that the Services should not be at so detailed a level that they need to be grouped before being understandable and relevant to the business.

The process for managing changes to the Catalogue needs to be led by the service provider, rather than consumer. It must involve collection of change requirements from the business, qualifying each request for relevance and value, and integration into the future version. The communication of the timing of the request cycle is vital, along with the results and impacts.

A business requirement in a stable environment is to be able to plan strategically, so part of their annual financial planning cycle will be reliant on the availability of the current, and potentially next, Service Catalogue.

What is the right number of Services in a Catalogue? From a purely capability-driven perspective, a dedicated business manager is not likely to be able to review and manage the usage of more than around 80 Services, so with a normal distribution of the cost of Services it is realistic to aim for between 80 and 120 in a Catalogue.

Both the business and its service providers need to understand the limits and limitations of the Service Catalogue. Although it will be relevant for normal business growth or reduction, major changes to the business or its environment should cause a review of whether the financial impact requires changes to be made to either the Service or the Catalogue.

Service Cost and Service Levels

The Service Catalogue becomes an assumed part of the processes of the business in a mature environment. Business and Technology management expect the Catalogue to show them relevant services and prices, so the only times that they focus on it is when there is a change or error.

On a more regular basis, the main management discipline where the Business relates to the Catalogue is in reviewing their costs and cost trends.

In this area, the delivery of a 'bill' to the customer for their use of Services is likely to be monthly. It is possible to run shorter cycles where the inventory for each Service is available, however this is of limited value to the business except in industries with fast-moving changes that directly impact IT cost.

The Business view of costs should, wherever possible, be at the level of a Price times Quantity (PxQ) for each Service. Monthly review of these values can then take place in the Business, or jointly between Technology and the Business. Where specific actions are being taken to affect change in the usage of a Service, it is a useful practice to hold separate finance and action review meetings for this purpose, keeping the actions being taken and their impacts separate from the review of the entire cost base.

The disciplines of Service Management, such as those within ITIL, have common goals and requirements to TBM for a Service Catalogue, business relationship development and other disciplines. Where a business already has a Service Catalogue, apart from cost management the main additional capability brought by integration of TBM is usually with the ability to define different Service Levels and price points in the Service Catalogue.

With a mature TBM capability the business can potentially be proactively shown the costs associated with Service Levels and exceptions, such as the costs of supporting out-of-date hardware and software, increases in cost due to technology or service failures, or the impact of slower helpdesk responses.

Similarly, an extension into Risk Management disciplines, such as the CoBIT framework, can enable consolidated reporting against the cost and value associated with risk measurements and classifications. The identification of high-risk Services and Applications with low investment, or opportunities for rationalization of Applications with similar functions identified by risk management taxonomies, can be delivered through TBM systems integration with Risk Management.

Financial Planning and Investment

With standard annual planning cycles, business leaders are asked to set targets for their expenses as well as their revenue. Several levels of capability can be achieved with a TBM implementation that ease this process.

With a Service Catalogue and regular reporting showing the cost and volume trends for a business, business leaders have an immediate capability to simply identify their baseline costs for the future.

The business should also have an expectation that prices for technology should be reducing over time. For Technology, this will be a calculated and defensible change rather than identical for every item in the Service Catalogue, but will be visible to the business as an overall trend.

To improve the accuracy of the price-setting process it is necessary that the business provides information on their expected demand trends for each Service. This identification of their projected Business as Usual requirements added to their planning of technology related Investments, should be based on the same Services in the Catalogue wherever possible.

In this process the Business is not asked to identify the demand for technology components directly, but it is expressed in terms of the Service volume. From this the Technology department will identify overall technology demand, and integrate underlying technology price changes and efficiencies, to return updated Service pricing.

Where an investment requirement cannot be met by Services already in the Catalogue, a new Service may eventually be required. Even in these cases, the cost of technology components to deliver the capability will usually be available to enable a calculated price to be defined.

A level of trust and discipline is required from both sides of this process, which is generally going to be one of the steps towards a fully mature TBM implementation. If business managers are given targets that include their Service cost, some may take actions to reduce it without actually reducing the Service cost base.

The same processes for demand planning and cost planning can be extended to provide multi-year forecasting capabilities. This is no more accurate than any other crystal ball, although there is an illusion of precision due to the level of detail involved.

Strategic planning

In line with most business development requirements, the core financial capabilities delivered by TBM are targeted at understanding and delivering historic, current, and short to medium term outlook reporting and analysis. The same information can be used for a number of strategic purposes, both for planning and for measurement of the impacts of strategic change.

Dependent on business priorities, the cost of some technology may be seen as non-core to the business and an opportunity for outsourcing or offshoring. By having a clear view of the Services provided by technology and the ability to transparently manage the costs and their drivers, a business has a clear position from which to challenge their suppliers on the value they provide. As this can include both internal and external providers, the data enables direct negotiation on Service and price as part of an outsourcing arrangement.

While TBM can also provide information on the sources and types of cost that are involved in providing specific technologies and business services, they do not provide the capability to inform all decisions. The location of staff is not always an input to a TBM Cost Model, and unless this has been envisaged and built as a specific requirement of the Model it is unlikely to be accurate enough to properly inform decision making.

Another area where business strategy can be informed by outputs from a TBM Cost Model is as a source of information on the costs of technology involved in larger activities such as mergers and divestments. A TBM Cost Model will be able to provide multiple views of how technology costs relate to business functions, including the total cost of technology for a business, how that is composed in terms of shared and business-specific technology, what the financial basis is in terms of regular and investment spend, etc. While these will be unlikely to be the primary deciding factor in defining a business strategy, the ability will exist to use this as a tool in decision making and action planning

The Technology View

While the business requirements and strategy are going to be tightly integrated with technology direction, technology strategy also needs to account for developments in its own marketplace, supplier relationships and products. This is a basic concept, and one which impacts into TBM in terms of readiness to show business consumers how you are delivering improved value of technology to them through those changes.

The Service Catalogue and Technology Services

Having established that your business customers relationship with TBM is through the Service Catalogue and Technology Services, their first expectation in a mature environment is that the 'price' of Technology Services will decrease over time. Regardless of your mechanism for aligning cost to business customers, the ability to demonstrate this reduction develops a level of trust and confidence that technology is being run efficiently.

A key to ensuring this visibility to customers is through a proper relationship between the volume of the Service that they see and its price. Establishing that each Service is defined with a Unit of Measure for its volume helps define and deliver the relevant level of granularity in a Service Catalogue. One effect of this is that it may not be relevant to put a price on individual Applications, either due to them being part of a larger Service, or because they lack a measure that relates their cost to their level of business usage. As a result, pricing the underlying Technology Services can become the critical business-relevant capability for TBM to deliver.

The technology market generally helps in delivering reductions in price over time, since natural competition and technology improvements are constantly delivering more capability for the same amount spent. There is still a gap between Moore's Law (i.e. how much the cost of computer processors reduces each year) and the cost of a computer, since the actual processor is only a fraction of the cost of a computer. Demonstrating that overall Technology Service prices are reducing, and the net impact of these to Business Services, is part of the annual planning and communication cycle for TBM.

Financial Planning and Investment

Although there are multiple characteristics of finance and technology disciplines which appeal to people of similar mindsets, both are highly detailed and it is unusual to find people who are trained and qualified in both. In general, technology managers come from a technology background and their engagement in financial planning and investment will be as part of a finance-driven process. This is not a barrier to success and the interaction of technology teams in financial planning can bring the benefits of each discipline to the other.

At its full maturity, the speed and regularly of the planning process can be reduced to the point where updates to cost forecasts and business demands are made on a monthly basis alongside the calculation of actual costs. If extended to cover all technology components, this can provide for (at least a first cycle of) annual planning for technology to be delivered without separate processes.

Technology Architecture

The level of detail at which Service costs are reviewed will vary between organisations. It would generally be expected that the detail of underlying technology costs for a Service would not be regularly provided to the business user for review, as this is a function of technology management to deliver efficiently.

Whilst this is true within a stable environment, changing capabilities and technologies require that it is independently reviewed at times. A business manager will not know when there is the need for underlying structural change to the technology components of their Service or what its value might be.

An interesting by-product of changing technology to both Business and Technology is the handling of market-impacting technology developments. There is a constant cycle of these, currently including Cloud, Artificial Intelligence, Robotic Process Automation, etc. The introduction of these into the Technology Catalogue should be treated as a longer-term activity, starting with a business and technology investment decision and finishing with the delivery of a Technology Service, or a decision not to invest further.

One component of the introduction of a new Technology Service is ensuring the smooth delivery of change. The Technology function is constantly managing component-level change. The technical aspects of Technology Service changes are similarly managed, generally by grouping the components of a Technology Service and managing their lifecycle. The main change to this, which TBM introduces, is in the financial relationship with customers and the additional incentives and behaviours which need to be managed. In delivering a new Technology Service, Technology Business Management needs to be used to ensure that the initial investment is not going to adversely affect the price and disadvantage the first mover. While pricing strategy will be further discussed in Chapter 15, setting a price for a new Technology Service needs to balance the expected ongoing cost (once the technology is established) with the cost of investment. Users should be given a realistic incentive to use a technology without causing the need for too much investment cost to be covered in other services.

Similar preparation for the termination of a Service needs to be applied through TBM, using a combination of project and financial planning to help ensure that costs are equitably aligned. A large-scale example, of exiting a Data Centre, shows the need to manage technology cost jointly between Business and Technology. While there will be significant cost of the Real Estate during the entire process, there will eventually be only one application (or a small number) left. In a mature environment, the cost of the application will be kept at its standard rate through the Data Centre Exit project, with a penal rate available to be applied only if the project is delayed through an application's failure to migrate.

Strategic Planning and Enterprise Architecture

The challenges to a technology organisation in delivering controlled changes to its Services should not be seen as a standalone activity, and the impact of changes in both technical and financial direction need to be integrated with other business factors. Some of the most effective ways to achieve this can be through the integration of TBM outputs with Enterprise Architecture, although the interface can be complex to achieve and manage.

Enterprise Architecture is a business discipline where a set of processes and tools enable an organisation to document its current business and technology estate and processes, describe a future state, and drive change to reach that future state.

There is an overlap between this and the goals and expected outcomes of Technology Business Management, although the TBM discipline is more specific in its focus. Chapter 2 starts with the words 'Technology and Business and Management, and risk and service' which starts to show possible areas of integration with disciplines such as Enterprise Architecture.

Although the Enterprise Architecture can be used to manage 'changes necessary to execute (business) strategies' that include cost, this is often not its primary target and may only be added to the outputs as a final step. Introducing a level of integration from TBM into Enterprise Architecture can enable detailed assessment of financial impact at multiple levels, which are not possible otherwise.

Enterprise Architecture is a significantly complex discipline, where the delivery of the core functionality is often already focused on business outcomes, so the integration with TBM may well be one that is only available to organisations which are reaching a significantly mature level of understanding of both disciplines.

The Finance View

Choices in how to implement Technology Business Management can affect how a Finance team interacts with its stakeholders in the business and technology organisations, and how its processes and interactions help to steer the financial aspects of decision-making.

As there will already be existing processes and relationships for this, TBM will bring change. This section, particularly, goes on to describe one specific implementation outcome for the integration of TBM into financial processes. This is not expected to be correct for all organisations. The benefits and risks of this and other approaches are not going to be fully explored, although some alternatives are explicitly cautioned against or supported in later chapters.

Business and technology integration

Where financial management has often been aligned to organisational structure, a fully implemented Technology Business Management approach gives more people responsibility for aspects of financial oversight, if not management.

The accountability for reporting and managing finances is not removed from the Finance organisation, who are still the ultimate 'source of truth' on all financial matters, reporting and regulation, but the responsibility for ensuring that costs are understood, appropriate and managed is matrixed between the organisational structure and the technology service structure.

The first notable impact of this for the Finance organisation is in the level of engagement of additional people and teams within the Technology function. In an organisation using TBM, many of the technologists, as well as their management, will be aware of how their customers identify their products. A technology specialist working on delivering a networking service to office users might initially only have considered the technical difference between a wired and wireless connection, and would now be more likely to be aware of the cost differential between them as that is how their users are being shown it.

Although that individual would be unlikely to interact with the Finance organisation, the development of the Business Case for such an investment, the calculation of the cost and the price to be charged to users, would all now be disciplines delivered by the owner of a Technology Service and the TBM organisation.

This wider engagement can in return bring additional demands on the Finance function. The level of scrutiny of TBM outputs is often more distributed and more detailed than with pure financial reports. Starting with the business expectation that TBM outputs are consistent, these are based on the quality of the Finance inputs into TBM, causing feedback to drive improvements and a rise in the level of data quality in the Finance organisation.

In any large and complex organisation, there is still a likelihood of costs being put in the General Ledger in an unexpected manner, such as late and unexpected financial inputs, resulting in the appearing in a different Cost Centre or different account to where they were due.

The visibility of this type of item is increased when the data is shown through TBM, for example as an inconsistency in a cost trend for a Service. The Finance organisation will usually be aware of these items before anyone else and know both the reason for them and whether they are due to be changed at a later date (e.g. journalled to a different account). These items can be brought proactively to the attention of the TBM Office and through them the relevant Service Owner, so that any impacts are approached as known exceptions rather than errors.

This can bring unexpected benefits to a Finance team, including a level of integration and understanding with both business and technology functions that is hard to achieve otherwise.

The simplest benefit is in the wider involvement of staff across an organisation in understanding and helping to manage the financial impact of their activities.

Finance as a continuous process

The initial and core integration of Finance with Technology Business Management is as a supplier of financial data, with periodic (usually monthly) updates providing the basis for the TBM Cost Model. This input of 'actual' information is backward looking and can be enhanced by the integration of 'future' views, such as budget and forecast data.

One target implementation for the integration of TBM and Finance is to build on the discipline of monthly TBM reviews of Actuals to provide regular feedback into the Forecast.

For non-investment costs in a business, the inputs that a Finance team require to build forecasts and budgets have the same structure as the outputs that are used in a TBM Cost Model. Changes that affect the Model, such as changes in the business demand and the volume of products or services that the Technology function is providing, are directly visible as trends in TBM reporting. From this information a useful view of the basic direction of business usage and cost of technology can be presented back to the Finance team.

This is not a complete process, however, as additional information on both Business and Technology direction and strategy need to be collected and their impacts integrated. The communication of technology cost to business users is a standard process within TBM, so this additional question about business direction impacting technology becomes a part of the regular communication between functions.

With this information flow in place and enabling TBM managers to aggregate business demand, technology direction and financial impact, the 'feedback loop' into financial systems can be completed. Where some businesses run an annual budget cycle and a mid-year re-forecast, this process can be run as frequently as the TBM cost review with the business occurs, which would be monthly at a detailed level and quarterly for a more structured overall review.

The accuracy of any forecast reduces the further ahead it looks but identifying a six-month view of business change in these reviews gives the ability to create a basic extrapolation for a year (or more). A mid-year forecast then becomes an exercise of extracting the pre-existing information from TBM systems, at least for non-investment costs, and can possibly be extrapolated to produce a full-year budget.

Investment planning

The integration of investment planning into budget and forecast development does require additional processes and effort, although the focus of Technology Business Management enables some of these to be more efficient than otherwise.

TBM helps to overcome one of the challenges of Investment Planning in that it provides a higher level of clarity around true technology cost than is often available otherwise. This applies both for larger projects and at the level of individual technologies, although it will not usually extend to the benefits analysis of a Business Case.

For a large project to deliver new business functionality by developing an application, the costs of the project will include application developers, infrastructure and operations. TBM will provide standard capabilities to calculate the costs of infrastructure and operations, based on current cost and internal prices. These are 'fully loaded' so that the cost of computing, whether in the Cloud or in-house, would not just be the price shown by a supplier but would include the other required costs of management infrastructure and support.

Within this context, where the function of a Business Case for a project is to prove that the investment will pay back its cost (or more), this helps ensure that costs are not accidentally ignored.

An example of an area where TBM may provide additional information on the benefit side of an investment decision is the requirement for additional capacity for technology infrastructure. While some organisations do not treat this as Investment cost, the purchase can be a significant outlay and needs to follow those processes.

The business requirement for additional capacity will have been identified through the regular reviews described in the previous section, in terms of volume of demand.

Outcomes of a fully mature TBM capability and Cost Model include a detailed understanding of the description of a Technology Service, its total cost and, from that, its cost per unit. Reductions in this Unit Cost, including the impact of both Investment cost and capacity increases, can then be used to demonstrate that the technology is being managed in a cost-efficient manner.

The business benefit of additional capacity is less of an issue than ensuring that a purchase is well-priced, since lack of capacity will limit business capability. The level of information available to the technology owner, who is putting forward the case for additional capacity, is such that both pieces of information will be directly available as part of the justification.

These examples do not remove or change the need for a business to look at investment planning as a whole or as part of a regular cycle, but do provide some additional flexibility in allowing some business cases to be more rapidly evaluated and accepted as business requirements, rather than business wishes.

An internal market in IT

The idea that services and products have a price is something that everyone understands and provides a common basis for communication within business and outside. This is one of the reasons why it is useful to enable Technology to sell its Services within an organisation, with the relevant financial processes in place to support that.

The basis for integrating this capability into the financial systems is to have a simple and straightforward relationship between a Technology Service Catalogue and a Financial Service Catalogue, so that customers of technology can see relevant and equivalent information for their cost of technology from the Finance organisation, and its details in the TBM system.

The Technology organisation will review the costs of their Services in their TBM Cost Model and use that as a basis for setting prices annually. Businesses will see their costs for technology each month on the basis of the price and quantity used, both as an allocation in the Financial system and with all necessary detail from the TBM system.

They understand that they can affect their technology cost by only 'purchasing' the amount of technology they need and they can also use this as a basis for budgeting and forecasting, since they only need to understand their changing demand for technology and multiply this by the price.

This is not an opportunity for the Technology department to make a profit at the expense of its users, as they have a target to break-even or take a small margin. It is relevant, however, that normal technology cost reduction and demand increases often lead to an over-recovery, which can be handed back to the business.

The extent to which a TBM system integrates with the business, and is implemented in financial systems, is only limited by choice. The potential to integrate non-technology costs and functions into a model exists, but is generally seen as outside the scope of the TBM discipline.

Choices to be made with this type of implementation include at which level within a TBM model it is relevant to identify services with a price. This can be for technology and infrastructure services, for applications, or for business services, or at more than one level.

The understanding of business users is that being shown a price for a measurable service implies that they have the ability to impact their cost by changing the amount they purchase. As such, there is a clear justification for setting prices at the level of Technology and Infrastructure Services, where the ability to measure the level of use is expected to exist.

Calculating the 'Total Cost of Ownership' (TCO) for Applications is then a matter of consolidating all of the charges for Technology and Infrastructure Services that make them up. The alignment of Applications to Business Services becomes more complex as there is often no 'Unit of Measure' which can be used to define the business demand and usage, although multiple mechanisms can be implemented within a TBM Cost Model to calculate and demonstrate these.

From a Finance organisation's perspective, this discussion is less relevant unless the business wishes to create a further integration of their technology and non-technology costs, or to charge customers on the basis of these Service TCO calculations.

Once the charge to a customer is being made on the basis of a proportion of the TCO, rather than on price and quantity, the relationship changes from being that of a market to that of a centrally managed economy based on business relationships and requirements.

This is a mechanism which may be acceptable to business users and gives them both a degree of control and visibility of the reasons for their costs. It removes some of the level of visibility of the underlying technology value, which must be considered within the context of TBM communications.

Chapter 5. Be realistic about getting there

In the same way as with any other business process, the development of a Technology Business Management capability in an organisation needs to start with the pre-existing capabilities and to organise these, fill in gaps, and develop maturity. The broadest TBM value will not be immediately available, or even within a short period, so it is best to look at how to deliver specific shorter-term changes that build towards the goal.

Modelling your organisation or using a standard model

The choice needs to be made at the start of a TBM implementation whether to buy into a standard approach or build a custom model to match current processes. While the latter approach would naturally appear to be more easily understood and faster, this is a false impression based on familiarity with a limited range of data. There is more likely to be a limit to the scope and success of this custom model than a gradual implementation of a larger goal. Organisations who follow this approach often find that once they have completed their first Cost Model and understand the concepts and data, they move to rebuild to the TBM standard.

When building a Cost Model, the TBM Taxonomy provides a standard which may not match the way an organisation is currently structured. The gaps at the financial structure layer are usually easily reconciled, as the TBM Cost Pools and Sub-Pools, and separate treatment of these cost groupings are generic concepts.

When it comes to the concept of consolidating costs in IT Towers and the later phases of a TBM Cost Model, this may be a larger step for an organisation to integrate.

How long will it take?

To deliver a TBM capability that enables decision-making aligned with business strategy based on a Cost Model, the minimum time required is likely to be six to nine months. You will identify areas that need improvement during that period, and take actions on that basis, which can also extend the overall time needed.

One step that can be planned for each phase of a TBM implementation is to take a baseline measurement i.e. where you are starting from, as soon as possible.

The time required to embed a full TBM implementation in an organisation and see the self-reinforcing maturity is likely to be in the range of three to five years but, as identified in Chapter 3, there are multiple practical components of TBM which can deliver short term value.

These can vary from implementations relating to Vendors and Contracts taking two to three months to identify and deliver value, through to larger changes that can help with technology inventories and financial integration.

While it may be organisationally difficult to accept that there is a requirement to build preliminary TBM Cost Models, this may prove to be the most effective way to introduce TBM discipline to an organisation. The inter-organisational requirements and multiple data sources that are needed are often not immediately available during an implementation. Starting with the intention to build a model as rapidly as possible, identifying and temporarily working around gaps, gives a shorter timeline for demonstrating the potential value.

Results from this approach are going to be useable but must be treated as 'a good fiction' rather than fact. The benefits of this approach include giving adequate notice to organisations of data gaps and quality issues that will need to be resolved, sometimes along with visibility of overlapping responsibilities and inconsistencies.

A Cost Model is going to have to change according to business requirements and priorities. Don't allow it to change too fast, but don't hold on to it when you know things have moved on. A complete review and rebuild of the model every two to three years is likely to be valuable.

A further phasing approach to Cost Modelling is to relate progress and delivery to the TBM Taxonomy. The adoption of this standard, its communication and the education of stakeholders, are pre-requisites for realising the full benefits of TBM, so this becomes an important component of TBM implementation.

There are specific points in the TBM Taxonomy at which it is possible to measure the completeness of modelling in financial terms. The first of these is validation that all relevant costs are in the input to the model and are aligned to the Cost Pools. Once these are being aligned to their IT Towers, it is possible to show the level of achievement as a percentage of the original cost which has been aligned at that level.

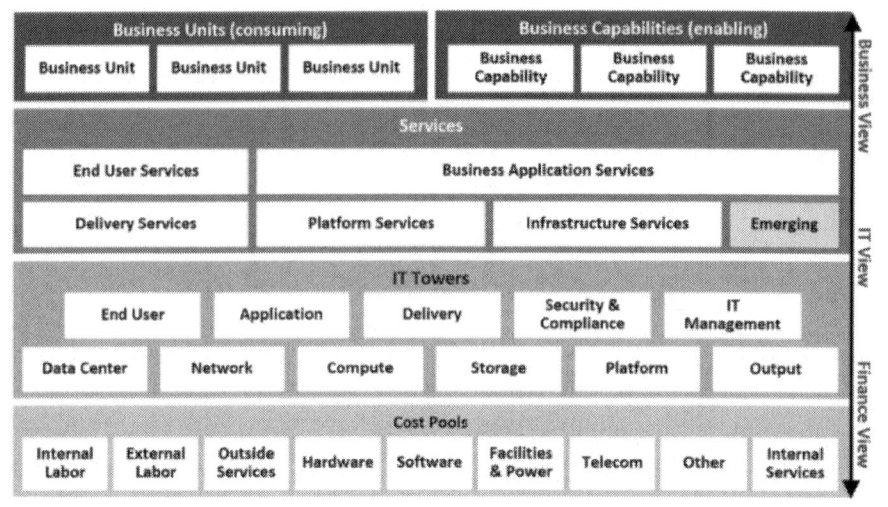

Figure1: The TBM Taxonomy (from the TBM Taxonomy v3.0. Appendix p1)

A similar measurement of implementation progress at Services and Business layers is possible, although measurement of individual components within the layers is not reliable.

What level of accuracy is possible?

If your requirement from a Cost Model is for perfect accuracy, it is unlikely you will succeed. Most organisations believe that they know and have good control of their data. When challenged on this, they are able to provide systems, files and tables which contain the relevant information to justify its correctness.

This often turns out to be true, but only when the review is limited to the context of each piece of information separately, and the level of quality is not maintained when information joining the data sets is reviewed. Those type of gaps are highlighted by a TBM Cost Model, since the relationships between data sets form the basis of creating the model.

One example of this which is found regularly during an early phase of implementation is in the different approaches to Fixed Assets by the Finance department and the equivalent equipment inventories held by Technology. From a financial perspective, the Fixed Asset Register should contain a list of all equipment which is being depreciated, its purchase and go-live dates, cost, depreciation period and similar details. For a server, there is likely to be an Asset Number assigned, and the serial number is likely to be an identifier included in the Fixed Asset Register, but it is unlikely to contain information on the hostname of the Server as that is not relevant to the Finance department and may be changed. The technology department will have a list of the servers that they manage including their hostname, operating system, software versions, network and storage connections. Within that list there are no common points that would enable accurate alignment of Fixed Asset Register and server inventory, although that would be fixed if the serial number of the Server were included in the inventory.

Similar issues can often be found when modelling how technology is associated to applications. While an Application Manager may keep track of which servers, storage and other technology they are using, this is not generally seen by the Technology department as a requirement for them to manage. When looking at the technology inventory to identify what applications are being delivered through what equipment, there will be gaps that imply that some equipment is not being used by any application, and that some applications appear to run without any technology.

In both of these cases, and other similar situations, there may be a need to create temporary mappings for costs to flow into and within the TBM model. This is not a failure, but relevant thought needs to be put to what interim model will be built, based on the expected replacement data.

A TBM Cost Model is open to challenge, as there will be multiple ways to treat cost components and also multiple alternatives for the relevant level of granularity of data. During the implementation of a Cost Model there will be groups which are already business-focused and have worked out their own equivalent model capability. A centrally controlled Cost Model is unlikely to be as detailed as this, or to have access to the same level of knowledge or data that is needed to build and maintain it. These groups are often willing to support a central model and migrate to using it, as they see both the wider value of their efforts being recognised and the time they can save from their manual administration.

What level of detail should be managed?

No amount of effort is likely to turn the complex reality of a business into a completely accurate model. One choice is whether a model should follow a standard approach such as the TBM Taxonomy, or alternatively if it is better to directly model the current business structure, methods and processes.

Implementation of either type of Cost Model provides the ability to understand the use and value of technology expenditure in ways that are not viable without a model, so the question moves on to what level of detail is important.

In practice, the choice of which details are managed in a model, which are excluded entirely, and which are used in summary form, can change over time. The challenge of modelling is that adding granularity to a data source may not just be about making data available but may change the model itself and cause unexpected inaccuracy.

How many inputs are needed to build a Cost Model? Organisations are known to have up to 200 per month. Don't be surprised at that but do plan for how you operationalise and manage it.

Aspects to look at when choosing what level of data to use are its granularity, its manageability, and its impact.

Granularity of data

It is useful to ensure that, when data is used for modelling, as much granularity is brought in as is available, with a choice then being made on how to summarise this to a useful level.

At the same time, it will always be good practice to ensure that the data used in a model comes directly from an 'authoritative' source and has not been subject to manual adjustment or manipulation.

These two goals overlap since authoritative but pre-summarised data provided for a model may be provided based on assumptions and filters which run counter to the requirements of the model.

The decisions on how to manage granularity and summarisation for any data source tend to be a balance between accuracy and manageability. Within detailed data you are more likely to find that there are exceptions, so understanding the data that is being used and how to integrate it into the model must account for both the usual cases and exceptions.

Exceptions will occur in almost any data set, from financials, through technology, to billing. Examples at each of these levels include the use of Journal entries in Ledgers to move costs from one Ledger or Cost Centre to another, the inclusion of Converged Infrastructure in a server inventory, or negative volumes being charged to a customer to generate a credit.

All of the above examples might be legitimate exceptions that are built into a model, or might be consolidated within the data source and treated as standard. The decision on which approach to take is about whether these exceptions affect the results of the model, so comes down to a combination of the impact of the exceptions and their management.

Applying this style of logic to each of the examples in turn,

- If small financial adjustments are a regular occurrence there is little value in treating each one separately as an exception. If there is a major misstatement being corrected, some exception handling in the model may be required.

- Converged Infrastructure is usually a high cost and low volume inventory compared to standard servers, requiring additional information which would not be included in a server inventory. This should be treated separately.

- When the charge to a customer is based on an inventory volume, the ability to give them a credit based on negative volumes must already exist and have an exception process for its input prior to the data being loaded to the Cost Model. In this case it is about understanding the data source before modelling.

Manageability and impact of data sources

A complete TBM Cost Model, running through from the initial financial inputs from the General Ledger to Business Services, will require tens of data sources even at its simplest implementation level. During the process of building a model, these will need to be discovered, understood, consolidated or summarised, and integrated into the model. The integration should be made on a standard basis and with exception management capabilities for all known and required exceptions.

These data management processes apply to each individual input so, in a regular monthly process, multiple steps must be taken to ensure correctness.

The overall manageability of a TBM Cost Model, and the acceptance of its accuracy, requires this level of commitment to the management of data. In any cycle of model calculation, the validation of results must include the ability to identify, trace and resolve exceptions.

In a complex organisation, the TBM Cost Model can use two to three hundred separate data sources, so the manageability of these becomes a significant operational overhead. Starting with this expectation, the management of data sources needs to becomes an early part of the process of building a Cost Model, rather than a retrospective clean-up.

The core outputs and value of a Cost Model will be developed from standard data and granularity. The number of exceptions to the standard data that occur is affected by both the granularity and volume of data in use, and your willingness to manage both. Exceptions will need to be managed through identifying the exceptional circumstances and data points.

The other time that you need to manage exceptions is when they are material to your model. These can be both positive and negative. Although most people tend to think more immediately of the negative, in either case if there is a material exception it is better to treat it as such directly.

When building a model, build the general case and make provision for exceptions. Be careful on how you manage the exceptions, particularly if they become a significant cost flow.

The management of exceptions in a Cost Model can usually be approached as a problem of data management rather than modelling; managing a class of exceptions so that they can be identified by the creation of an 'exception management' data source rather than through updated modelling.

Returning to the earlier examples

- Unusual material entries in the General Ledger will generally already be identified by the Finance department as part of the Finance processes. Ensuring that this information is available as an input to the team running the Cost Model enables them to identify whether there is a need to take exceptional action or not. A set of credits/debits which move significant cost between two technology Cost Centres may have no impact to the model (e.g. if they are both part of the same function) or may be business impacting (e.g. if the costs shift from one application to another).

- One method to give a credit to a customer is by charging them negative volumes of a product. Even if this is done, the original inventory should show the real volume with a separate entry for the credited volume. If these are hidden within a consolidated inventory the model may only show the net effect, but the negative volumes will have to be manually entered somewhere, so would always be better treated as an exception inventory rather than core.

Who needs to be involved?

The central players in both implementing and running TBM are the Technology and Finance departments, both for targeted implementations and for a fully integrated Cost Model. More detail on the specific roles or levels of engagement that you need to have in order to succeed are described below.

Organisational sponsorship

The value that is available to be achieved from TBM is something that can be recognised at the top of both Technology and Finance organisations, so it is always useful to have the 'Chief Officer' roles engaged as backers of an implementation. Without both types of support, it is harder to achieve full value as the results count not be accepted due to lack of engagement, disagreement about the principles and processes, or lack of correct understanding of input data.

This should not stop you from using TBM due to lack of cross-organisation sponsorship, but is a guide to what limits you might see without it.

An example from a Finance organisation perspective is where there is a lack of understanding of technology infrastructure and architecture. The initial stages of a TBM Cost Model can be built based on a financial view of the cost, with limited technology inputs. Taking these costs and aligning them correctly to Infrastructure, Applications and Services requires a significant amount of information from Technology departments and an understanding of how these relate to each other, and without these it will not be feasible.

To understand the cost of something as 'simple' as email may require knowledge of servers, storage, server software, user software, security and multiple other components, as well as an inventory of email users and their mailbox sizes or service levels.

These same questions about technology would also need to be managed within an implementation led by the Technology organisation. The benefit of a joint project becomes the ease with which the required underlying information is accessible and understood, regardless of its source.

The reverse of these issues, where Finance is not involved in the implementation of a TBM Cost Model, might be the situation where a single software license covers multiple cost components of the email cost-base along with other unrelated software. With limited input from the Finance organisation, the ability to identify and split this cost into its different IT Towers may be difficult for the Technology organisation. While a decision may be easy to make, the justification for that decision would need to be defensible against any query from Finance on the output and methodology used.

In both cases, sponsorship of TBM from both Technology and Finance organisations limits gaps of this nature.

Subject Matter Experts

Technology Business Management integrates skills from technology, finance and business which are not similarly required in many other jobs. The range, if not the depth, of each of the skills needed in each of these disciplines is very broad. As a result, the expertise to build a TBM Cost Model will either need to come from cross-functional teams learning and using each other's expertise, or from previous Cost Modelling experience.

Cost Modelling, specifically Activity Based Costing (ABC), has been an accounting discipline for a long time, with the implementation following various routes in different business domains. It has often been implemented in manufacturing environments, as the costs of both individual components and overall products can be usefully modelled and measured to show the total cost per item produced.

The expertise required that relates to technology is not that of depth of understanding of a single type of technology, but general breadth. This can be limited to knowledge of the technologies used in an organisation, but should also include interest and awareness of technology trends that may be applicable to the organisation in the future. The value of this expertise to a TBM implementation is also improved by pre-existing relationships with the relevant technology managers who will be involved in the process. This can help both technically and practically with closing knowledge and information gaps.

> *Describing TBM and Cost Modelling requires people to understand abstractions and technical or financial detail they are likely not to have seen before. Some of these will not fit their current understanding.*

Knowledge of business processes and drivers becomes most relevant as a TBM implementation reaches its later stages. This is often an area which is not well understood by technologists, whose achievements are built on technical excellence. As for technology expertise, the skills needed by a Business expert working with TBM are related to general knowledge of an organisation, its processes and priorities.

There are multiple approaches as to how to resolve these challenges, but the key is for financial subject-matter experts to be able to identify and enable these approaches. This type of change to financial systems can be significant to an organisation, again relying on the organisational sponsorship with the Finance department that has already been mentioned.

TBM, particularly with regard to developing a Cost Model, requires the combination of a wide range of skills and disciplines which are otherwise rarely consolidated. You are unlikely to easily find someone who understands all necessary aspects of finance and accounting, the full range of current and historic computing capabilities and trends, application development methodologies and processes, and business imperatives and direction. Even if you find that person, they also need to be able to engage with all the relevant groups to change your organisation's use of information and operational processes to deliver and bring maturity to your TBM implementation.

Where should TBM sit in an organisation?

With its reliance on input from multiple functions, Technology Business Management is usually subject to conflicting requirements. Large scale business cycles of growth and contraction, organisational cycles of centralisation and federation, global versus local management requirements and others, can all cause changes to how expense is managed. In a similar manner to other central functions, the TBM discipline needs to be capable of understanding and synthesizing these changes with a degree of independence.

The level of independence required for successful TBM generally means that wherever it sits organisationally, its role is to work with and reach into the other functions to help all to benefit. Acceptance and trust of TBM usually takes time to build and is often based on visible delivery of information and value. As with many approaches to teamwork, success is not individual but based on understanding what the goals of each group are, then working to communicate how you can help them deliver their goals using TBM tools and discipline.

The choice of where to control TBM within an organisation can end up being with either a single sponsoring organisation such as the Finance or Technology department or, when both are sponsoring TBM, whichever of them is seen as building the business relationship that will drive value from TBM. As the value can be delivered to any combination of stakeholders, rather than being specific to one specific group, this does not identify any particular answer.

Organisations have chosen both approaches successfully, so the choice is less important than other aspects of an implementation, such as the staffing of the TBM function and the connections between organisations and stakeholders. One choice which has had success in several businesses is to focus on the function and capabilities of the TBM team more than its ownership. Recognising the range of required skills and bringing them into a team which sits with 'one foot in each camp' between Technology and Finance organisations is one way to do this.

This can be related back to the first diagram in this book, of the position of TBM sitting between Technology, Finance and Business functions within an organisation. Any choice which is not balanced in this respect is likely to require change to meet the objectives of the under-represented function.

Getting it right first time

As with the choice of where Technology Business Management should be managed within an organisation, the range of knowledge and control required of stakeholders is rarely going to be found in one individual.

The result of this is that it is important to set realistic expectations for the achievement of TBM value. Those largely relate to identifying phased objectives rather than delivering everything at once. It is also likely that a degree of repetition and rework will be needed, or larger scale rebuilding to account for operational improvements or failures.

Across large organisations it is frequently possible to find inefficiencies due to 'islands' of information and processes, such as where a group has created their own inventory which does not relate to any central capability, or has even created their own 'cost model' for the service they deliver.

The alternative implementation approaches for these situations largely follow the choices available for Application Development methodologies, and can depend on the level of organisational knowledge that is available.

The challenge of a 'waterfall' development of a TBM Cost Model in a large organisation is that both the knowledge of the detailed target outcome, and the component inputs, are rarely sufficient for analysis in advance

> *Regular team meetings to establish a common understanding of the logic of a TBM Cost Model during its implementation give significant value to a TBM team. This carries into the process of maturing the use and understanding of TBM across an organisation.*

of implementation. The inclusion of 'islands' of information is likely to be based on individual knowledge and give undue weight to them. This results in the development being delayed in either, or both, the analysis phase and the implementation phase, while the 'islands' are built into the model and then removed or replaced.

The reverse of this situation applies to a Rapid Application Development approach to putting in TBM. The expectation is that information will be available much quicker from TBM with this implementation methodology. This can be met, but the amount of change that needs to be managed, even at a relatively fundamental level, is likely to be high. This can bring fast delivery of early results, but also cause increasing delays when early development stages need to be rebuilt.

As both the traditional and modern methodologies are not perfect, it is useful to understand how to take value from a TBM Cost Model during its implementation. An expectation that a Cost Model will be perfect in its first implementation is unlikely to be met. It is much more likely that a rebuild of a TBM Cost Model will be able to effectively deliver on expectations, based on lessons learnt during the first build. These can be lessons about the quality and source of data, the target outputs, or the scope of the model.

One of the tools which organisations implementing TBM can use to gain appropriate engagement and traction during an initial implementation is to provide an assessment of the accuracy of their model and be honest about the known challenges. This needs to be carefully managed so that the focus of the output is on where value can be derived rather than where the gaps are. Accuracy of the Cost Model is often a subjective measure rather than quantitative, so must not be perceived as negative to the organisations or groups whose information is of lower impact or quality.

The development of TBM skills, knowledge and maturity in an organisation will enable a significantly faster assessment of the quality of data, the shape of a Cost Model, and the approach to gaining value from the results.

In planning a TBM Cost Model implementation this effectively suggests scheduling a relatively fast initial implementation, while tracking errors and issues. This is followed by a reassessment and rebuilding exercise to reach a more mature outcome. Bringing these into a strategic implementation plan and timeline increases the likelihood of value being realised, both in the short and longer term.

Chapter 6. Some decisions are hard to undo

At the start of a Technology Business Management implementation, there are a number of decisions which need to be made that are hard to reverse or undo once action has been taken.

As mentioned in the previous chapter, this does not mean that you will be unable to make the change, but that you should understand that this will be a larger, more time-consuming and more involved activity than just taking the decision.

The reverse of this is that while you might be tempted to decide on targeting the most complete and capable TBM implementation as your first step, the path to a mature capability is more likely to be achieved successfully through multiple phases and the ability to learn from intermediate successes and failures.

This chapter identifies five key decisions which should be understood and made at the earliest stages of a TBM implementation:

- What are you implementing: Technology Business Management or IT Financial Management?
- Should you start by looking at your budget or your actual spend?
- Are you treating your technology function as a Cost Centre or a Profit Centre?
- Is the cost of Change and Investment separate from the cost of Running your business?
- Who owns and manages Products and Service?

TBM and ITFM

While the focus of this book is Technology Business Management, the related discipline of IT Financial Management (ITFM) is important to understand, particularly where your implementation approach for one may not match with the objectives of the other.

TBM has developed as a set of disciplines to help identify and deliver business value. The management of data in a TBM Cost Model and the flow of costs is not designed to follow formal accounting codes and practices, although this can be built in to a certain degree. ITFM has developed from a financial background and is more directly focused on ensuring correct accounting and alignment of IT costs for financial management and reporting, although it is increasingly including the approach to value recognised by TBM.

A TBM Cost Model can be developed to deliver data into an organisation's Finance systems in a number of ways, or may be treated as an offline capability for business management. The key to which capability is to be delivered is derived from a direct understanding of

- The inputs to the TBM Cost Model; the source, scope and the periodicity,
- The outputs of the TBM Cost Model; whether these are used as a direct input back into Finance processes and how,
- The controls on changes to data and model within a TBM Cost Model.

Taking each of these in turn, some detailed questions can help clarify what degree of ITFM capability it is expected or possible to deliver.

Inputs to the Cost Model

The inputs to a TBM Cost Model are finance, technology and reference data. For both TBM and ITFM there is an expectation that financial data (Ledgers) will be managed in a capable system, but this tool may be part of ITFM and only a data source for TBM. TBM tools are not required to deliver Ledger, Fixed Asset, Headcount or Contract management capabilities directly. In this respect, the most complex financial capability required from a TBM Cost Model is to function as a 'sub-ledger,' which takes inputs from the formal Finance system and delivers equivalent outputs back to it.

The scope of what is within a TBM Cost Model must be managed closely if it is going to be used for ITFM, starting with the inputs. The straightforward situation in which it is possible to deliver ITFM capability with TBM is when the scope of the input cost is the entire cost of an organisational unit, which implies that it will also reconcile with the 'sub-ledger' output that is expected. There are numerous situations where there is potential for the scope of data input to the Cost Model to change. These can include organisational change management, phased implementation of a Cost Model, changes to reference or technology data.

While it is possible to create a Cost Model for ITFM which allows for financial/organisational constructs and their cost to be included or removed over time, the entire construct becomes harder to reconcile if there are external organisational costs impacting the scope and cost-base of the model. An example might be for a variety of Real Estate costs;

- The exclusion of Data Centre costs from a model could be seen as reducing the overall completeness. Its subsequent introduction on an organisational (Cost Centre hierarchy) basis could be managed within a TBM/ITFM implementation
- The inclusion of office-space costs in a model based on external reference data, such as the percentage of Real Estate Office Space Cost by business, headcount and/or role, would be spread across the Cost Model's Services.

This can create a situation where the identification of the data coming from the General Ledger into the model and its reconciliation to the model outputs is not possible at the level of detail required for ITFM.

The outputs of the Cost Model

The clearest difference between TBM and ITFM use of a Cost Model is whether there is an interdependency between the General Ledger and the Cost Model.

A standalone TBM implementation will take the financial inputs from the Finance systems and will output a variety of information, reports and data for management use. The integration of this into standard technology management processes, targets and direction, are not reliant on understanding the detailed finances. From a Finance department perspective, this is seen as a Management Information System rather than a financial tool.

If there is a need for the Cost Model to be treated as an 'input' to the Finance systems, this becomes part of an ITFM capability. With this requirement come additional checks on how the Cost Model is built, explained and its definition of formal outputs. While this requirement can be described as a 'sub-ledger,' the Cost Model itself is not required to conform to accounting standards. The integration of the output back into the Finance system does need to be managed so that it meets financial standards, as that information is again auditable, which is the Finance department's responsibility.

There are multiple intermediate approaches between a standalone TBM implementation and a fully integrated TBM and ITFM implementation. However, these all tend to use a standalone TBM Cost Model output as an input to an intermediate process for Finance, so would not properly sit within the ITFM definition.

A common target example of an intermediate TBM/ITFM implementation is of a Price times Quantity (PxQ) Chargeback model. In this instance the Cost Model will be used to calculate the cost of each chargeable component and set a price for it. The price will be used as an input to the Finance systems, set for a year, although the quantity changes regularly. In this instance, the TBM capability is in providing information only on the cost component of Technology Services, while the ITFM capability is the actual charging mechanism in the financial books and records.

Controls and changes

The final area of difference between TBM and ITFM is in the level of required formality around change. Within a financial system, it is clearly not acceptable for the value recorded to change, except under specific and very tightly defined circumstances. While this capability can also be made a characteristic of a TBM Cost Model, it is not a basic requirement in delivering the business value of TBM.

The requirement for control and co-ordination is particularly vital when a TBM Cost Model is using monthly finance inputs, but dealing with changing reference and technology data at the same time. Once data has been taken from a TBM model for integration into ITFM, it becomes unacceptable to change the outcome for a prior period. If it is discovered that a technology inventory had 10% of its data filtered out in error, this cannot be fixed in an ITFM context by replacing the data and running the model again, although this may be acceptable in a TBM system.

Integrating TBM and ITFM, these control requirements extend to all non-financial data sources, not just technology. Change to the organisational construct, by moving a Cost Centre within the hierarchy, does not change the cost in that Cost Centre but may change the calculation of how much other cost is aligned to a target within a Cost Model. This particular type of change is even more complex if there is a requirement for historic restatement of the cost of a department based on a new organisational hierarchy, as the TBM

Cost Model will no longer match ITFM for any historic period without major rework.

The other basic requirement within an ITFM environment is for reconciliation between inputs and outputs or, in other words, the amount spent must equal the amount charged. The implementation of ITFM capability from a TBM Cost Model output can be managed in several ways by the Finance team. The decision on which of these to use will depend on specific circumstances, audit regimes, and so on, but include

- The Cost Model output being treated as a weighting factor rather than an absolute value, such that 100% of cost is always allocated even if the Cost Model has been unable to deliver that level of completeness.
- Taking the values in the Cost Model output as being accurate and making manual adjustments for costs which are not allocated within the Cost Model.
- Using a full TBM PxQ charging model (rather than a Cost Model) to be used as the input to the Finance systems, with balancing transactions being used to ensure reconciliation.

The final example above is not going to be a workable approach for all organisations and implies that the Technology organisation is run as a Profit Centre. This style of management is most likely to be applicable to large organisations with high levels of management independence around organisational and financial decision-making.

Implementing a Budget or Actuals model first

One of the earliest choices to be made about the implementation of a Cost Model is around what data is going to be in the input. You are always going to be reliant on financial, technical and reference data and will need to build ongoing relationships with all the data owners to supply that on a regular and reliable basis.

The first input that is required to build the model is finance data, so the decision on whether to start with Budget, Actuals, or both at the same time needs to be included in the earliest discussions of scope, and with the Finance team.

There are specific benefits and complexities to each approach, and the initial answer may end up being affected as much by the timing of the decision within your financial calendar as by technical reasoning.

Starting with a Budget Model

A simple benefit of using a set of budgetary financial data for a Cost Model is that it is expected to be static. You would expect the budget to be available near the start of the financial year, provide a full twelve months data and not to change, short of major organisational changes such as divestments.

This may sound simplistic reasoning but it leads to a common variation in the building of a Cost Model for Budget, due to the requirement for other similar 'forward looking' financial views. Many organisations require updates to their financial forecast on a twice yearly or quarterly basis, and some update their annual forecast monthly. As a basis for modelling, these are relatively straightforward variations of a Budget Model, as they are likely to be at the same level of granularity as the budget, and provide a consistent annual view.

As long as the commonality of budget and forecast models can be established, this is a positive reason to implement the Budget Model first, as the data will be static rather than regularly updated, and allows modelling to proceed without some of the complexity of ongoing data management.

Another benefit of building a Budget Model first is that the level of granularity of Finance data is often lower than for Actuals, so the process of modelling is simplified. This may apply both at the organisational level with costs being consolidated to organisational nodes rather than individual Cost Centres, and at the Ledger level. In both cases the mapping of consolidated data and its subsequent modelling is simpler than for fully detailed Ledger inputs.

The availability of other data required for a TBM Cost Model is more complex to analyse. Once financial data input is modelled, all other data sources in the model need to be chosen with care for their accuracy and availability.

Within the financial sphere there is likely to be a reasonable degree of accuracy in Run The Business costs, but budgetary information on Investment and Project spending is often limited in terms of both detailed descriptions and scheduling.

As discussed later in this Chapter, it is possible to approach the issues related to Investment and Change forecast modelling by choosing only to model them at a very high level (or not at all) within a TBM Cost Model.

From a technology perspective, the current point-in-time inventories can be used as a basis for Cost Modelling but will be increasingly inaccurate over time. Both technology and business led initiatives are likely to be available as broad volume projections rather than with inventory detail.

For technology inventories, the decision needs to be made about the best available approach for each technology on an case by case basis, dependent mostly on the rate of change within the inventory.

For an inventory with limited change, it is probable that the previous year's end of year version will be available and useable; you may even choose to use a more recent data set, so that your model is more current and closer to a forecast view. The downside of this is that when you prepare the next year's Budget Model, you will only be able to use the data that is current at the point of the Budget, so you are effectively using the current data for a point in time fifteen or sixteen months in future.

For more volatile inventories, such as where the industry or technology is driving significant change, the modelling of cost and inventory is significantly harder. It is unlikely that any detailed inventory or a Cost Model which uses it will be usefully accurate, so the replacement of an inventory with an agreed projection is often the best alternative.

The creation of projected technology inventories sufficient to build a Cost Model can be informed by the requirements of the TBM Taxonomy but should also be based on the actual current inventory. Technology details such as individual server names will not be available in a projection, but groupings by equipment type and value, alignment to customer (whether by Application, Service or Business) and the like, will need to be created and agreed.

Much of this type of information is usually requested from the Technology and Business organisations as part of the budgetary process run by the Finance department, so the implementation of a consistent process which will feed both Finance and TBM requirements is possible.

While the creation of a Budget Model is a goal to achieve, even with the extension of this capability to delivering forecast models it will not deliver all the ways in which TBM can show business insights and help with business decision-making. The implementation of a TBM Budget Model should only be considered as a phase of a TBM implementation rather than the end point.

As previously mentioned, the timing of an implementation in the financial year can also be a significant factor in the choice of which scenario to build first. For an implementation starting several months before the financial year-end, building a Budget Model provides a defined target date for completion.

Starting with an Actuals Model

The initial business driver for implementing TBM is often to understand and control technology costs, on the way to delivering broader business value. Within that context, a static view of the budget projection is limited in capability, and even its extension to providing updated forecast views may not be sufficient.

Implementing a TBM Cost Model based on the financial Actuals expenses brings some additional complexities in terms of the process of modelling and the operational requirements, but both of these are commonly implemented and well managed.

As in the implementation of a TBM Budget Model, the first input is going to be the financial data and, similarly to the Budget Model, this should be expected to be available from the start of the financial year. As will be discussed in the next Chapter, you should also expect that financial data is available regularly and that there is a period 'close' at which this becomes fixed, which will become the schedule by which the TBM model should be updated, rather than on a more occasional basis.

Other data inputs, such as technology inventories, should also be aligned to this schedule whenever possible. There are times when inventories do not need to be updated as regularly, but inaccurate inventories will become more directly visible to customers with TBM, so need to be treated carefully.

Bringing in each month's data to an Actuals Model provides the ability to see trends and outliers, which are a useful basis for measuring achievement and setting targets.

A negative implication of the same capability is that exceptions, outliers and errors can all impact the Cost Model. If there is a ledger entry which is booked incorrectly, or an inventory showing costs against decommissioned equipment, there will need to be careful management and communication surrounding what responsive action will be taken.

The availability of an Actual expense based TBM Cost Model is the main source of information for TBM value driven decision making, so should not be overlooked in any plan to implement TBM.

Implementing the next TBM scenario

Whether initially implementing either a Budget or an Actuals Model, it is often expected that the other scenario be created afterwards to give a comparative view.

Benefits can be seen through both approaches so, again, the best decision on the approach and phasing is open to interpretation and business prioritisation.

When the first implementation has been of a Budget Model, the actual mechanics of the Cost Model will be relatively simple compared to an Actuals Model due to the data granularity being lower and with few or no exceptions. Bringing the equivalent Actuals data sets into the Budget Model requires either that the additional granularity is lost or that additional modelling is created.

The approach of consolidating and grouping Actuals into a Budget format is quite straightforward within the context of Finance data, as the Budget organisational and financial hierarchies should be well documented and easily accessible. This will mean that detailed Ledgers can be consolidated to the same level as the budget.

The loss of granularity that this brings needs to be accounted for or it can lead to unexpected results, particularly if the organisational hierarchy used for the budget is not sufficiently granular to deliver expected TBM Cost Model detail. Within the Budget Model this can be manually adjusted for, such as by splitting servers and storage manually within a budget node although they are in different Cost Centres. When the data is provided for Actuals at the Cost Centre level, the Cost Model should be adjusted to enable that granularity to be directly accessed rather than assumed or calculated inaccurately.

Implementation of a TBM Budget Model second, after the implementation of an Actuals Model, can bring the reverse issues related to loss of granularity of data, but a more frequent concern is the previously identified need to create and manage forward looking technology inventories and similar data.

Often there is no formal mechanism within an organisation to create technology demand plans and identify how technology usage will grow or shrink. In the absence of such data the choices for what inventory data to use are either to use current data, or to create a proxy for modelling. Whether there is a technology demand plan creating the budget inventory, or when a proxy is created, there is a clear demarcation between that and the Actuals data.

A specific further issue with broad impacts occurs when using current inventory as the basis for budgeting, both on the grounds of its relevance in the future and its separation from its primary use. If a Budget Model is being built three months prior to the start of the financial year, the data being used must be kept separately from its source. This is a common situation and not always well managed, which can result in later changes to Actuals data causing the Budget Model output to change unexpectedly.

Implementing Budget and Actuals Models simultaneously

The main benefit of building both Budget and Actuals Models simultaneously is that the issues relevant to each individually are treated consistently. This brings the clear implication that a longer timeline is required for implementation, and the requirement for knowledgeable decisions to be made where alternative implementation choices are available. These are usually the same decisions which need to be taken separately for each of the individual scenarios but will require capable financial and technical skills to be combined to enable a sustainable implementation.

Although the decisions may be specific to one scenario, they can be more fundamental choices about how to build a Cost Model. The modelling of technology infrastructure has become significantly more complex with the commoditisation of various architectures delivering Technology as a Service, Private and Public Cloud, and Converged Infrastructure. This has significantly increased the range of choices on how to model technology costs appropriately so as to enable both technology management and business management. Those decisions will need to be taken for either Budget or Actuals scenarios as well as for a simultaneous implementation, but the impact of slow decision-making will be clearly higher when both scenarios are affected.

Is your Technology function seen as a Cost Centre or a Profit Centre?

Real Estate, Finance, Human Resources and Technology are now commonly grouped into 'Shared Services' organisations, or treated similarly by businesses on that basis. The implication of this is that they are a cost of doing business but don't independently provide revenue or value to the business. From a business management perspective this is sometimes see as meaning that the costs in a Cost Centre can be reduced until something breaks.

Even for businesses providing one of those functions, such as banks providing Financial Services as a business, there is still going to be a separation between the provisions of services for internal management and those provided to customers.

In many organisations, although the Shared Services functions are identified as Cost Centres, their costs are then allocated to the revenue producing Profit Centres. Without TBM to provide context this is often a mechanical process and so the value provided to the business can not be recognised or managed.

The contextual information that Technology Business Management provides enables segregation of the Technology function from other Shared Services by giving the ability to identify business value alongside the cost. The accurate calculation of the cost of Technology Services, tied to rules on how that cost is allocated to business users, gives Technology a Profit Centre capability, even if not fully realised.

When the costs of Shared Services in an organisation are held and reported separately from the costs in Profit Centres, this can lead to awkward situations. Unallocated costs of Shared Services will show in the books of the organisation as a loss, causing the net position of the Profit Centres to be accordingly overstated. This is bad financial practice, but is seen occasionally when analysing the financial reports of organisations.

Treating your Technology organisation as a Profit Centre can bring the formal recognition of improving the value of technology and increased efficiency of the delivery of Technology Services. There is a requirement for Technology management to understand and work within the capabilities and constraints of this too, which can be a slow process to develop but is part of the maturation of TBM.

Within a Profit Centre for technology, the level at which a profit or loss is measured must be clearly defined and targets set, or individuals will take actions that do not benefit the organisation. A Service Owner who believes their job is to maximise the profit of their Service may reduce their costs at the expense of service quality, attempt to increase the price unreasonably, or fail to invest in necessary capacity to account for business growth. All of these behaviours can be predicted and accounted for by setting a target range of profitability, and educating Service Owner on their role within this context and the impact of their actions.

How separate is the cost of Change and Investment from the cost of Running your business?

A business metric which is often taken as one of the measures of the health of a company is the priority and value expended on change compared to that required to run the business. This takes multiple forms with phrases such as RTB (Run the Business), KSOR (Keep the Show On the Road), KTLO (Keep The Lights On) being used to recognise the role and cost of core functions, while CTB (Change the Business), Project, Investment, Growth, and similar terminology is used to differentiate forward looking activities.

For Technology Business Management implementation, the choice of which costs are RTB or CTB should drive the decision of how a Cost Model reflects them. This direction is likely to have already been taken, but the way in which the business then wants to see this information modelled and reported will have a larger impact and should be identified at the start of creating a TBM Cost Model.

The choices for answering this range from excluding classes of cost from modelling, through to fully integrating all classes of cost into Services, something we see by example in everyday interactions.

The fully integrated costs of running and changing a service are what we see most frequently in normal life. When we buy a meal in a restaurant, we are paying for a complete service including the costs of not just the ingredients of the meal and the labour of the staff, but the equipment in the kitchen, and the restaurant itself. When the restaurant needs redecorating, we would not expect to see a separate surcharge on the cost of the meal to cover this. The restaurant may decide to raise the prices to cover the cost, but we do not have a choice in this.

An example of where surcharges for Change are partly integrated into a service cost is in the purchase of long-haul plane tickets, where a basic ticket without the possibility of change is priced lower than one where alternative flight times can be booked. This premium exposes the additional costs that are born by the airline for processing changes, along with some additional element of cost related to the risk that their flights will be over-booked or under-booked as a result.

The complete separation of Change costs from the base service or product is something we see less frequently, but certainly occurs in the 'aftermarket' for cars. Once we have purchased an original specification, we can separately buy additional parts and upgrades at a later point, changing the original into something new. Interestingly, similarly to some technology changes, these will not usually be seen again as separate from the overall product and become fully integral to it.

All of these can be translated into options for how to represent costs in a TBM Cost Model and there are multiple further variations. Returning to the question of which approach to choose for a business, the two aspects which need differentiation are what is required for internal management of cost, and what is required to be shown to the customer?

As a company matures in its use and integration of TBM disciplines, the choice of approach may vary. This does not exclusively suggest than any one option is specific to a stage of process maturity, but helps demonstrate the ways to answer the two questions above.

Internal management and customer visibility of Change

Early implementations of a TBM Cost Model can exclude the costs of Change. These costs are regularly seen to be well-managed through project and portfolio management practices, with clearly defined sponsors and customers, budgets, progress and performance tracking, together with tightly managed financial control and visibility. This answers both the questions of internal management and customer view of cost clearly, but may not give the customer the best view for them to manage the business.

If an upgrade is required to a system, replacing an old version with newer equipment, the process around this may be treated as a project. The additional costs of purchasing and implementing this needs to be charged to customers, and in this instance they would see their cost for the normal service through the TBM Cost Model, plus an additional cost for Change on the same components through the project charge.

This generally leads towards a more mature TBM model where the costs of Change are still kept visible for internal management, although they become integrated into the total cost and are not made separately visible to customers.

Following the same example, the integration of the Change costs into the core TBM cost would mean that the customers see a single charge inclusive of both Run and Change. This charge would be effectively shown as the volume consumed and either a Unit Cost or Price.

There is an implication in this that the Unit Cost for storage would reduce over time, which would also be able to be fed back into the process of generating a Business Case at the start of the project, and help to justify the initiative.

This might appear to be the ideal outcome and suggest that all Run and Change costs be integrated into a TBM Cost Model and not made visible to customers. The problem with this is that it is not uniquely correct and can also generate bad behaviours in some customers who gain the benefits of change without paying for them.

In instances where a change will benefit specific customers and not others, the full integration of the cost of Change into a Service will provide an incentive for those customers who will benefit to request the change to take place. The customers who will not benefit may object, but are also likely to request at the same time that the changes which benefit them be prioritised. With a limited budget for change, the full integration of these costs into a service may be insufficiently accurate, leading to a requirement for Change costs to be at least partly aligned directly to a sponsoring customer.

Costs of Application Development are an example of where this type of situation can occur; where multiple departments using a single application may need to decide how to split the cost of their changes equitably. It is possible to model each project separately, or to include them all into the total cost of the application and charge that out, and both can be implemented with a TBM Cost Model.

This example also leads in a full circle to the situation where a new department wants to start to use the same application. They can be seen as gaining the benefit of all previous development without having to pay for it, unless all previous Change cost is fully integrated.

These examples are particularly seen in large and cost-sensitive businesses, and agreement on the approach to them are beneficial at an early stage of TBM development.

Who owns and manages Products and Services?

The governance processes surrounding a TBM Cost Model extend to ensuring that the Taxonomy and the Cost Model are both actively managed, and maintaining these are vital to a TBM implementation and its ongoing success.

The TBM Taxonomy provides a structure to target in a TBM Cost Model implementation, suggesting a range of IT Towers, Infrastructure and Business Products and Services to which cost can be assigned. The Taxonomy provides an outline level of detail on each of these levels including definition of Products and Services.

The definitions at the Business Services level of the Taxonomy are the most extensible and least likely to be a perfect fit to an organisation's structure and pre-existing processes.

This is one of the 'destinations' discussed in Chapter 3 as being a critical identifier for the outcome of a TBM Cost Model. The business users of the Cost Model's output must recognise the grouping of cost at this level as relevant to them, with this being consistently and clearly defined, and backed up by technology Service Owners who have the authority to manage them.

A consistently useful way to ensure that these requirements are met is to turn this part of the Taxonomy and Cost Model into a formal Catalogue of Products and Services. The governance of the Catalogue is aligned closely to the provision of cost information about the items within it.

There are multiple approaches to managing a Catalogue, and multiple Catalogues, within both technology and business environments. The definition and governance of some specific Catalogues are available as part of the ITIL specifications, and extensions are included in the CoBIT framework. Neither of these extend significantly into the TBM view of cost management and modelling, so this will be further discussed below.

At what level of a TBM Cost Model is a Catalogue required?

It is possible to create a TBM Cost Model to identify and manage costs for part of the TBM taxonomy as well as end-to-end. As an example, organisations have chosen to model the costs of the IT Infrastructure only. They use this output to align costs to separate business Application Development groups without modelling full Application or Business Services. As another example, it is also possible to model the costs of Business Applications without modelling the cost of Desktop Services, such as in an environment where those Services are outsourced.

In both cases the customer, who is going to see the cost, will want to know what they are paying for, how much, and how they can manage those costs.

For the example of an IT Infrastructure level TBM Cost Model, the Catalogue therefore needs to show the business customers each of the items that is being provided, with a level of specificity about what is included in the cost. Starting at the TBM Taxonomy IT Towers level, the structure of the Catalogue can follow the TBM Taxonomy, although additional detail may be required depending on business requirements and scale. More information about Catalogue creation and governance is detailed in Chapter 10.

To gain value from the Cost Model, the customers will query how their actions can affect their cost of technology, such as whether they will be charged less if they use fewer resources. The ability to put a Unit Cost or Price on each item in the Catalogue, and give the customers control of the quantity they demand, provides a strong incentive for their efficient use of technology.

If the TBM Cost Model is going to provide a higher level of abstraction when shown to the customers, such as the total cost of all Business Applications, the Catalogue needs to list all the Applications. It is often significantly harder to identify a chargeable Unit of Measure for an Application than for a component of IT Infrastructure, so this style of Catalogue may need to serve a different purpose. Consolidation of applications into Business Services, sometimes with individual applications providing functions into multiple Services, provides a more relevant business view of IT Cost. Consequently the catalogue function at this level is less related to technology and more specifically to a taxonomy describing business functionality.

Who owns the Catalogue and what are they governing?

Regardless of the level at which the Catalogue exists, the impact of its implementation and changes to it have the potential to impact business decisions on where to invest or exit.

A challenge to business in defining the owner of the Catalogue is that the function is clearly important but not aligned to any one item within the Catalogue, so must be somewhat independent of the Products and Services management.

There is an argument that this role is closely tied to the TBM Taxonomy so should sit with the organisation responsible for managing the TBM Cost Model, but that authority must be explicitly given rather than assumed. It could similarly sit in another central administrative function or be aligned to pre-existing structures where management of a Business Catalogue is required. The roles in large enterprises of Chief Operating Officer, Chief Administrative Officer and Chief Risk Officer often have these responsibilities and they can also help align multiple Catalogues where they already exist.

The level of detail that requires governance in a Catalogue should not be underestimated. Particularly if the Catalogue is tied to business financials (using the TBM Cost Model as a sub-ledger or as the basis for Chargeback), incorrect specifications or changes can affect business profitability. Change in IT is constant, so examples of this impact are readily available.

In an environment where new technology is being used to change how business is done, such as the implementation of Robotic Process Automation (RPA), it is often replacing a mechanism that has involved manual intervention and may have been measured as such. A Product or Service which was previously measured on the amount of changes processed, based on the staff effort involved, would require a different metric once it was automated, as the staff would not be providing the Service. Changing to a different metric, such as charging a simple percentage to all users of the automated process, would move the cost between users and be likely to advantage some while disadvantaging others. In an extreme example, a user who used the system once might find themselves seeing a massive increase in their cost.

This example can be used to show the importance of Catalogue governance; to the detailed description of each item in the catalogue, to its accurate expression within a TBM Cost Model, to the customer understanding of the cost of the Product or Service and how to manage it, and to the communication of any changes to the Catalogue to all customers.

Chapter 7.   Don't do it

Having set out some necessary and positive choices surrounding TBM Cost Modelling, this chapter is more prescriptive and suggests some areas where actions should be limited or proscribed.

The reasoning behind each of these and possible impacts of missteps are identified, but in each case you may look at these and decide that they do not apply to your situation or organisation.

Using a TBM Cost Model as an Accounting system

The initial input to a TBM Cost Model is financial, in the form of accounts from one or more Ledgers. This can give the impression that cost is part of the accounting process and, as discussed in the previous chapter, can be somewhat correct if there is an expectation that TBM will also be acting as a sub-ledger in an IT Financial Management (ITFM) context.

While the formal requirements for accounting are regulated, the integration of non-financial inputs from TBM are not, so even when TBM is designed to work as a sub-ledger it is unlikely that TBM will be fully integrated into the accounting systems.

From that point we can derive the recommendation that a TBM Cost Model should not be implemented directly as part of the Accounting system, due to the lack of formality and regulatory controls of the non-financial inputs.

This gap is seen in multiple areas of a TBM Cost Model, and particularly clearly in the management of assets from both a financial and physical perspective.

An example is in identifying where TBM should interface with finance systems during the acquisition of a piece of IT equipment, such as a server. This system will pass through a procurement process with multiple financial controls, prior to it being delivered. Once it is delivered and paid for, the cost will be put into the financial system and the "asset" will be added to the Fixed Asset Register. The server will be technically commissioned by being put in a Data Centre and being connected, switched on and having software installed, with the relevant information about this being added to server inventories such as a Configuration Management Data Base (CMDB). At the relevant point in time the finance team will then define that it moves from being 'work in progress' to being fully commissioned, and they will capitalise the cost and move the asset to being depreciated.

There will always be a requirement of the Finance system to maintain a description of the financial process for Capital Expenditure (CapEx), with procedures for capitalisation and management of a Fixed Asset Register. There is still a choice about whether the CapEx detail also needs to be included in a TBM Model or if the output Profit and Loss (P&L) Ledger data is sufficient. This cannot be answered prescriptively, as the management processes around these costs vary significantly between organisations, however management of a TBM Cost Model can be simplified by taking financial input that is the P&L view rather than the Cash view.

There is a danger in implementing the CapEx and capitalisation process within a TBM Cost Model if the process appears to replicate the finance system but the result is not identical. This is a likely occurrence, as there are multiple rules and exceptions that are managed within financial systems that will need to be replicated, including manual processes and communication between people and systems. Any such loss of accuracy or mismatch needs to be planned for, whether through corrective processes or by being accepted (within limits) in advance.

For Cloud environments, this particular concern is minimised when related to the purchase of hardware, but a similar concern can apply to the management of software assets and projects so should not be ignored.

A second gap between the financial and technical management of Assets is often seen due to the differing expectations about what an asset is and what it is used for. Financially the question is whether or not an Asset is in use, while technically the question is what its specification is and what it is doing. This is often seen through gaps existing between the finance Fixed Asset Register and the technology inventory.

Within the TBM Taxonomy and a TBM Cost Model, the costs of servers are consolidated at the IT Towers abstraction layer. To calculate the cost of an individual server, the relationship between the financial view of the server and the technology view need to be reconciled. Specifically for a server, this reconciliation requires that enough information is available to identify the same server in both the Fixed Asset Register and the technology inventory.

There are multiple reasons why this may not be accurate enough for the technology inventory to be treated as a proper financial input, such as:

- Multiple servers being purchased at the same time and listed as a single asset in the Finance system. As there is a single purchase, inaccuracies can occur if the Finance team are unaware of the nature of the purchase.

- Lack of a common 'key' between financial and technology lists. Servers have a serial number provided by the manufacturer and (usually) physically visible on the equipment. This is part of the information stored in the Finance system but is regularly not included in technology inventories as it is not used by or useful to the technology function.

- Changes to a server not being notified between Finance and Technology. The reuse of a server, with the operating system software being reinstalled and rebuilt, often results in a different system name being created. Even if there was an original linkage available between the server name and the Fixed Asset system, it can be broken through this type of event.

Whilst this section has looked at one specific aspect of modelling for which it can be difficult to provide accurate integration between finance and technology systems, there are others which can be similarly or even more complex. For large multi-national organisations, the management of cross-border cost flows and the associated tax implications can be a material cost of doing business. A TBM Cost Model may contain significant amounts of information about these cost flows, including their source location and the location in which services are delivered. The definitive answer on how this is managed is a function of the Finance processes rather than the Cost Model. The relationship between the two and the use or management of this information with the Cost Model needs to be carefully and formally defined, if it is to be used at all.

The overall guidance that should be taken from this section is that a TBM Cost Model should not be fully integrated into a financial system. At one particular level, the General Ledger input to the TBM Cost Model is more straightforward on the basis of P&L rather than Cash accounting.

Beyond this, the role and value of the TBM Cost Model both as a consumer and supplier of information to the financial system needs to be clearly defined.

Quarterly, Bi-Annual and Annual modelling

At a minimum, most organisations have a regular monthly accounting cycle and an annual budgetary cycle. In various business sectors the year is split in to thirteen periods of four weeks, and in sectors which have highly variable demand and supply there may be even more frequent calculations of the business financial status. Similarly, some businesses look at their future financial outlook more than once a year, with mid-year, quarterly or sometimes monthly rolling forecasts.

The balance needs to be found between the cost to a business of processing the financial data, whether of actual cost or a forecast, and the business value that it brings. This is separate from the delivery of a TBM Cost Model.

There is an additional overhead to the business of processing the TBM Cost Model which also needs to deliver value. To a greater extent than for the delivery of financial reports, the processing of a TBM Cost Model requires input and engagement from multiple Technology functions, in terms of providing inventory information and technical knowledge.

The involvement of the Technology functions in the processing of the TBM Cost Model must be efficient in order for the modelling to function and, further, must be well understood by them in order to be able to use its output to deliver business value.

These simple requirements develop into a practical evaluation; that people are generally not capable of efficient involvement in a process when it is on an occasional or irregular basis. This, in turn, leads to the second prescriptive point of guidance for implementing TBM, which is that your main TBM Cost Modelling process must be run on a monthly basis, not quarterly or twice-yearly.

If you are only implementing a TBM Cost Model to deliver an annual Budget view this might appear impractical as guidance, but that cycle also limits the likely level of understanding of the Cost Model and the value to be gained from it, and in turn ties back to the need to ensure that TBM is not only used for budgeting.

Reuse of common terms

Some terms which are used in finance, technology, business and TBM become specialised in their own context. Particularly for TBM, this becomes increasingly important due to the overlaps between the areas, so the issue of ensuring clear communication comes to the fore.

The guidance for this is simply to avoid using common terms in a TBM context, although the examples below will show that there are multiple approaches to achieving this.

One specific example of common terminology which is regularly seen in the Banking and Finance business sector is the use of the word "branch." This may mean a business location with tellers to a Banking employee, a point within the financial hierarchy to a Finance employee, or a group of application development changes to a Technology employee.

It appears straightforward to differentiate the use of the word according to context in this case, because there is little practical overlap. However, if the Banking employee above were involved in a discussion about development of a TBM Cost Model for intercompany charges to trading offices, they could easily be using all three contexts simultaneously.

It is generally impractical to change the terminology in these cases, so the practical advice is to train people to be very careful about the use of these 'key words' and contextualise them wherever possible. Using 'Branch Office', 'Company Branch' and 'Software Branch' may appear inefficient, but reduces the risk of misunderstanding.

A higher risk comes in the reuse of a common term from one discipline which has not been fully or correctly understood. Within the TBM context, this applies particularly to financial terminology such as Direct and Indirect costs, and to Fixed and Variable costs. Accounting texts give definition to these which are not always reliably followed and their use within TBM is best avoided, or kept to cases where the terminology is clearly and independently defined and agreed by everyone.

Part of the challenge with these terms comes from how the same cost can be classified differently according to time and context. As an example, if you are working in a Finance department as an application developer delivering software, the cost of your staff will be 'Direct' to the Finance department whilst the cost of your computers may be an 'Indirect' allocation from the Technology department, as shown in the diagram below.

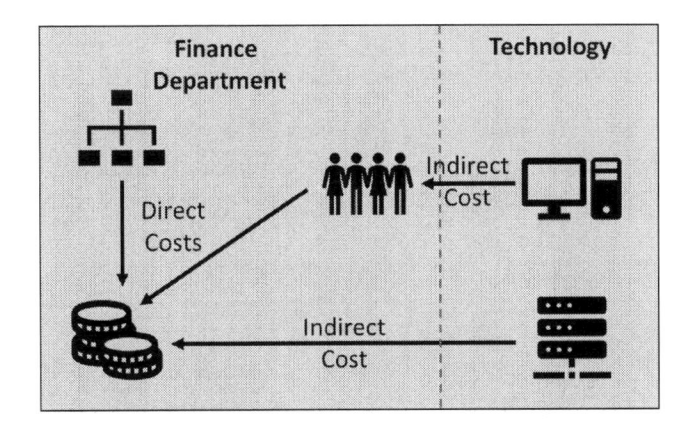

[Diagram: Finance Department and Technology boxes. Direct Costs flow from Finance Department org chart down to coins. Indirect Cost arrow from staff figures (in Finance side) to coins, with Indirect Cost label near Technology computer. Indirect Cost arrow from servers to coins.]

If a change in the organisation moves your Application Development team into the Technology organisation, the cost of your staff to the Finance department is now seen by them as an 'Indirect' allocation, while it is still a 'Direct' cost to you, as shown in the next diagram. Conversations between you and your customer in the Finance department about the cost of Application Development, and how they see it, will now be significantly different, which both parties need to understand.

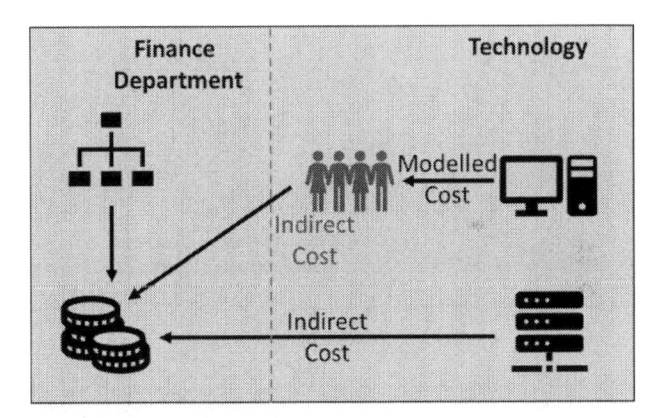

[Diagram: Finance Department and Technology boxes. Modelled Cost arrow from computer to staff figures (now on Technology side). Indirect Cost from staff to coins in Finance. Indirect Cost from servers to coins.]

As noted in the diagram above, this change can be further complicated where there are Indirect Costs associated with the organisational change (such as developers' PCs). These need to be accounted for, as the final cost alignment to the Finance department and will now need to include both the Application Developers staff costs and their previous Indirect technology costs. In this example, those are shown as becoming part of the TBM Cost Model, which is one possible approach.

This example may not cause too much trouble, as a Finance department and Finance Application Developer might be expected to understand these changes.

Within a TBM Cost Model there is an expectation that cost will be owned and managed in several different ways depending on the layer of the Cost Model. The cost of a Data Centre will initially be owned by a Cost Centre manager, but part of that cost will then be aligned to the cost of a server. The total cost of the server will be the responsibility of a Service Owner, who is providing it along with storage and other services to Application and Service Owners, and ultimately on to a Business Unit.

Wherever a TBM Cost Model is not causing financial transfer in the ledgers, the use of 'Direct' and 'Indirect' terminology is not likely to be following formal financial definitions. The advice in this context is to not use these terms within TBM except where they are required for their financial context, and to replace them with terms that you will use specifically for the TBM context.

The choice of words might already be obvious in an organisation, but a few alternatives are below:

Direct	Indirect
Owned	Received
Controlled	Influenced
Managed	Provided
Primary	Secondary

Each person with a role in managing costs within a TBM Cost Model then needs use this common terminology and understand that their 'Secondary costs are someone else's 'Primary costs. Often they will also need to know who their main provider of 'Secondary cost is, so that they can work jointly on delivering improvements in efficiency and value.

Recursion

The situation regularly exists that Services provided in one part of an organisation are consumed by another, which provides Services back to the first. One such example is that an Email Service requires Storage Services and storage administrators use Email Services. This occurs frequently within technology departments providing Infrastructure and End-User related Services, and also where Infrastructure-as-a-Service (IaaS) or Platform-as-a-Service (PaaS) capabilities are being provided for Application Development and delivery.

When calculating the cost of any of these Services, a view needs to be taken on whether to enable the costs to flow with this recursive, or circular, logic. The clear advice on creating a TBM Cost Model with recursive logic is not to do it, and the TBM Taxonomy suggests a more straightforward modelled cost flow. There are cases where a recursive model might be appropriate, generally outside TBM such as in manufacturing environments, so the reasoning behind this guidance is worth understanding.

The main argument for enabling recursion is that it provides a higher degree of accuracy in the calculation of the total cost of each Service. With the previous example, if the cost of an Email Service does not include its cost of Storage, it will be significantly under-represented. Adding the cost of Email Storage back to the Email Service, the total cost of Email will increase significantly; say by 500%. With this additional cost of Email Storage included, the cost that needs to be allocated to the Storage team for its use of the Email Service will increase by a similar amount, so total cost of Storage will increase and this will need to be reflected in the cost of the Email Service.

Breaking out of the recursive logic above, which could logically continue indefinitely, is not complex and a sensible number of cycles can be chosen for a technical implementation.

The difference between this example, where recursion is seen as a bad practice for TBM, and a manufacturing process where recursive cost modelling would be better suited, relates mostly to the necessary degree of accuracy of the results. For a Cost Model where the result is going to be used for setting the price of a Product or Service in a competitive environment, the most accurate assessment of cost is an important factor. Generally in a TBM Cost Model, the expectation is that the majority of Services are going to be provided for internal use within an organisation, rather than provided externally and competitively. These allocations are part of a larger flow of costs towards Business Services and internal customers. The loss of accuracy through a single direction cost flow, rather than a recursive one, can be assessed on the basis of how much cost would flow recursively. In this example, while the cost of Storage to Email Services is a high proportion, the reverse is not the case, so there is a limited impact to the final outcome.

For businesses assessing whether or not to outsource a Technology Service, or to use a commercially provided alternative, the argument could be made that recursive model accuracy is needed to be able to compare internal costs to the market. This argument is limited in its validity, as the commercial margin will generally outweigh the impact of the recursive costs.

Other challenges with implementing a recursive model are that the logic would need to be applied to a large number of relationships simultaneously, and with each cycle of logic the possibility of being able to trace the source of costs becomes less feasible. While it is not technically complex to build a scalable recursive Cost Model, the loss of transparency due to recursion is much harder to overcome. The result of a recursive model is harder for a Product or Service Owner to understand, and also harder to explain to their users, if the basis of the costs is challenged.

Is any type of recursion a good idea to implement?

Recursion in Cost Modelling is comparable to a 'circular argument' in a spreadsheet; try to avoid it! Having said that, recursion describes a way to use multiple cycles to approach an exact answer, which is a valuable tool to consider 'offline' but as an input.

In a business which has implemented a 'Chargeback' allocation mechanism, with internal allocations charged to consumers based on their volume of usage at a fixed unit price, it is quite possible that an element of recursion enters into the modelling of cost.

In the Storage and Email example, if Storage is charging the Email department and vice versa, the mechanism used would be of real allocations taking place in the financial systems based on the volumes used and the prices set. Using the terminology from the previous section, the net result would be that the cost of the Email department would be its 'Primary' costs, spent externally to the organisation, plus its 'Secondary' costs allocated from other Services including Storage. The reverse logic would equally apply, with the Storage department seeing 'Secondary' costs for their use of Email.

This does not follow the TBM Taxonomy directly, and two significant differentiations between this situation and Cost Modelling need to be recognised.

The first is that this description is not actually of Cost Modelling at all, but a financial implementation of an internal Chargeback method. This can work in a relatively mature environment, but accurate cross-charging in this manner requires both the price and the volume being charged to be accurate. It is also likely to require an underlying Cost Model in order to be able to work out the base cost of each Service and set its price.

The second differentiator is that the level of recursion in use within this approach is integrated into the price of each Service, so will only change when the price is updated. Integrating these charged costs into a Cost Model is possible, but brings a level of inertia to the price setting process, as the pricing does not change in the same way as the costs. This could possibly be described as more of an iterative approach than recursive.

Managing Fixed and Variable Costs

There is a broad range of management metrics which can be managed and tracked within a Cost Model and which have varying degrees of granularity.

The organisational question that usually starts a discussion on Fixed and Variable costs is what actions can be taken to save money. The implication is that Fixed costs can't be changed, while Variable costs can, so the answer is always to make the savings out of Variable costs.

The differentiation between Fixed and Variable costs when looking at an organisation's financial health and direction is one that is often chosen when there is limited other information available, but can become less valuable as a tool when more targeted management is possible.

Where a savings target has been set for the year without review of the make-up of the cost base, analysis of how to achieve those savings from Variable costs can sometimes suggest that the target is unreachable. As an example, if a 10% saving is targeted for an Application with 80% of Fixed costs (e.g. capitalisation shown as hardware depreciation and software amortisation) and 20% of Variable costs (support and service level), the savings required are effectively a 50% reduction in support and service.

A deeper look at this shows that the definition of Fixed and Variable is usually tied to a time-frame, where Fixed costs are just harder to change quickly, rather than impossible to change at all. Some of the formal definitions of Fixed costs suggest that the costs cannot be changed for one year, or for the budget period. In both those cases it is possible to take strategic actions to reduce the Fixed costs of an organisation over a longer period.

Instead of looking at a single Application over a short period, a target of reducing the cost of a suite of Applications over a longer period can enable reductions of Fixed costs through application consolidation, virtualisation and Cloud processing, active license management, and multiple other actions.

Measurement and reporting of the mix of Fixed and Variable costs then become a useful tool for long term management at an organisational level, but remain less valuable for shorter term action or low level granularity.

Focus on just one measure, whether it is Fixed and Variable or another measure, can imply and drive decisions that go further than is immediately obvious. When considering the value of moving applications to Cloud environments, particularly Public Cloud, part of the value to an organisation is that the underlying costs move from being Fixed (through the purchase and depreciation of hardware) to being Variable. For an organisation looking to increase the level of variability in its cost base, this is a clear advantage. If the same organisation has clear technical, service or risk drivers which point in a different direction, the balance between these requirements needs to be understood. A similar argument can be followed for many outsourcing approaches, where one of the benefits is often the introduction of increased variability in the cost of IT provision.

Another reason which is sometimes used to justify tracking Fixed and Variable costs separately through a TBM Cost Model, is that this enables the costs to be modelled using separate rules. One potential outcome of this is in enabling separate charges to customers for the Fixed and Variable cost components.

The perceived advantages of this approach are generally that customers will be given a more accurate view of their costs and their ability to influence them. They will not expect that reducing their demand will cause a purely proportional decrease in the cost or charge, and this is a more realistic simulation of the actual state of the expenses.

The management of customer expectations related to cost will be reviewed in some detail in Chapter 14, on Changing Behaviour. A few aspects which reduce the value of making the split between the Fixed and Variable cost components visible are that

- You are reducing the customer's ability to affect their cost base, so reducing their incentive to change.

- It is rare that the variable component of cost is so purely tied to a metric that its increase or decrease matches the model.

- The arguments about Fixed costs not reducing when volume reduces do not necessarily apply in reverse, or not equitably, when volumes increase.

The guidance here, with all these factors, is not to focus on a Fixed and Variable cost split as a significant source of value within a TBM Cost Model.

Transparency

In a book on the practical implementation of Technology Business Management, which has sometimes been described as delivering 'Cost Transparency', it will seem an obvious oxymoron to suggest that you should not be providing transparency. As with all generic descriptions there is additional detail required for this to make sense, which in this instance is that not all costs need to be transparent to all users. Planning from an early stage for which roles will have access to which data in a TBM Cost Model is always good practice, however the general suggestion is not to provide all information to all users. The choice will be dependent on an organisation's working practices and particularly affected by both size and structure, and some businesses take a clear and deliberate decision that full openness of TBM Cost Model information is the best approach.

The structure of the TBM Taxonomy has several clear points at which data structures and costs are consolidated and can be viewed holistically, which provide a basis for defining role-based access.

Financial information

Using General Ledger input as a starting point is clearly of direct value to the Finance team who provide it. The finance systems will also be the source of information used to identify and model Labour, Assets and Vendor costs at the Cost Pool level, so they require visibility to this section of the Cost Model. The later areas of the Cost Model are defined by technology and business drivers which are not expected to be areas of expertise for the Finance team, so their access to this is not required.

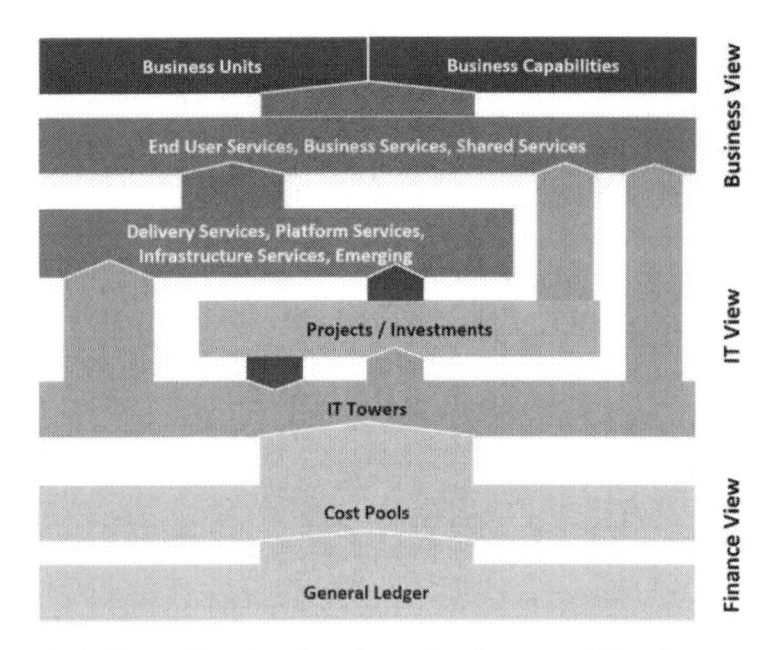

Figure 2: The TBM model translates from a finance view of costs to an IT view of towers, projects and services and then into a business view of costs (from the TBM Taxonomy v3.0, Appendix p2)

There is a separate and more intrinsic requirement relating to transparency of financial information which must also be carefully reviewed and addressed, which is the management of privacy and confidentiality. While information on salaries, job roles and individual names could be included in the data sources of the TBM Cost Model, exposing this in reports is generally not viewed as best practice and, in some jurisdictions, its misuse may be illegal. This is more of an issue with a TBM Cost Model than may be immediately appreciated when data is being collected initially from a finance department. Although the data is managed in that organisation, it will be tightly controlled. Exposing data in a Cost Model means that some of it will be visible to users who would not otherwise have had access.

The implications of this are not just about the immediate visibility of confidential information in the Cost Model. Loading and reporting information about Labour costs at a consolidated level must also be reviewed. Taking the step of consolidating Labour costs at a Cost Centre level may make it impossible to work out any individual's salary within a Cost Centre of 40 staff, but will still effectively expose the information in a Cost Centre with just one staff member.

While multiple strategies can be employed to conceal confidential personal information in a Cost Model, reducing the access to both detailed financial reports on this data and managing its granularity must be considered.

Technology information

Within a technology function both technology and financial accountability is often assigned to a Technology manager through their ownership of a Cost Centre or a role of a similar level. Although these accountabilities may be split when working at a large scale, TBM Cost Modelling brings them together at the IT Towers and so an individual's ownership of the cost of one or more IT Towers is expected. This Technology manager requires visibility of relevant Finance View reporting, as they will also be accountable for ensuring that the costs in the IT Tower are correctly modelled from the General Ledger through the Cost Pools.

The further modelling of IT Towers to the Services layers in the TBM Taxonomy is again owned and driven by Technology management, but not necessarily in the same way. Some Technology organisations separate out the provision of technology infrastructure components from the provision of End-User, Application and Business Services. This effectively matches the TBM Taxonomy separation of IT Towers from Infrastructure and Business Services. From a TBM Cost Model perspective it can also introduce a Technology Service Manager role, separate from the Technology manager role previously noted. The minimum requirement of a Technology Service Manager for visibility of the source of their costs is that they should see them at the IT Tower level. Whether this needs to be extended to visibility of the Finance View is likely to depend on whether they are also a Technology manager with accountability at that level.

An example of this is a Technology Service Manager providing 'Private Cloud as a Service.' The cost of their Service, which would be shown in the TBM Taxonomy as part of 'Platform Services' is largely going to be made up of the costs of Compute, Storage and Platform IT Towers. The costs of Compute and Storage IT Towers will often not be in their direct control, so they only require the ability to review these to the level of the IT Tower. This gives them the information to interact with the managers of those IT Towers, to understand the source of their costs and manage them. The costs of Labour and Software which go into the "Platform" IT Tower may also be the direct accountability of the Technology Service Manager, in which event they also act as a Technology manager. Depending on the organisation design, these costs may equally be owned separately, with a Technology manager for the "Platform" IT Tower completely separate and accountable for that financial view and management.

Business information

In reviewing transparency and how much information should be available to any user role, the focus so far has been on the source of costs. This is still true when looking at what cost information related to Business Services will be made visible to business users. The additional complexity in this case comes from both what is relevant and what will be understood by a business user in terms of the 'IT View' and 'Finance View' within the Cost Model (as shown above in Figure 2).

Business users will be receiving information on their costs from the Finance organisation, which will include both technology and other costs. Isolating the technology costs and ensuring that they understand the relationship between the total they see through Finance and what they see via TBM is a basic level which must be reached.

The implicit understanding is that these numbers will be the same, which means that the TBM output at a Business Service and Business Unit level is reflected in the financial systems. It is likely that this will not be the case in the middle of an implementation of TBM, and not always one of the goals. If these numbers are different it is best not to share information until that is clearly understood by all involved. Ensuring that a business user understands the progress and target status of a TBM implementation is a minimum requirement.

It is also important, particularly when a TBM implementation is moving towards a Chargeback model, of Price times Quantity, to decide what level of detail to show to the end customer and what value that brings. If a customer is being shown the price of computing per month, they will usually have no particular basis to compare that to. If they are given the breakdown of IT costs in terms of Cost Pools, such as Labour, Hardware and Outside Services, they may feel more justified in challenging them.

There are business users with sufficient knowledge to challenge costs on this basis, at a detailed level. More often than not the role of managing those costs is owned by the Technology organisation and is part of the overall cost and price management, from where it does not need to be exposed.

Delivering total transparency and access to all TBM information for all users, particularly in this context, is more likely to be harmful than helpful. The negative impact comes from losing focus on the value of the TBM information 'relevant to someone in a particular role, and the time taken up accessing information irrelevant and of little practical value to them.

Replacing Finance functions

Returning to the first section of this chapter, the advice was to avoid using or expecting Technology Business Management and a TBM Cost Model to be effective as an accounting system. One specific area which it is particularly useful to reinforce this for is drawing a boundary between the information that you can expect to manage within the less formal TBM disciplines and those which require a higher and more specific level of formality.

While TBM Cost Models and their underlying systems may vary, there is a certain level of knowledge and consistency that is required to deliver complex information. The specific example of Transfer Pricing, and calculation of costs and taxes across borders and other boundaries, is an area which needs very specific levels of detail to enable. Integrating this level of financial knowledge into a TBM Cost Model is possible, but potentially subject to a wide range of regulations and rules across multiple jurisdictions.

The challenge to implementing this within a TBM Cost Model is less to do with the input and modelling of relevant information than the extraction and evaluation of this information followed by its integration with relevant financial systems. As an example, it is possible within a TBM Cost Model to identify the country which costs occur within, and the country or countries in which those costs are charged to customers as part of a Service. If the cost is seen as crossing a border, this is easily identifiable, but if there are other costs for Services going in the opposite direction, the knowledge of which can be balanced against each other and which cannot is complex.

In most instances, TBM Cost Modelling does not require you to understand or manage this level of detail, and this type of modelling is often best avoided as it will require regular review, update and management, detracting and distracting from your core TBM capability.

Chapter 8. Gathering information

Unlike a jigsaw puzzle, a TBM Cost Model requires you to spend time and effort on trying to build a picture when you do not know whether all the pieces are available or where you'll find them, cannot be sure how they fit together until you have them in your hand, and could even find that you have some duplicate pieces. This is an apt description of the data sources and information that you will be using to build a TBM Cost Model, along with the expectation that some of the pieces also change over time, occasionally coming back with a different shape and colour but expected to fit in the same place in the picture.

This chapter will mainly focus on the requirements associated with data management for TBM and how to identify, value and process the differing characteristics of it. Some aspects are generic while others are specific to the type of data.

Collecting and managing data

Collecting data for the first time

As covered in earlier chapters, there may be two or three hundred data sources required to build a full TBM Cost Model. However, this does not mean that they are all equally valuable. Starting with a standard structure such as the TBM Taxonomy, there are clear pieces of information which are required to create a model that matches the taxonomy. Lack of availability of this information will lead to a gap in the modelling which is readily visible and measurable, so can be tracked and managed as part of an implementation process. This approach is a good practice to follow, as it will enable clear communication of progress against both the steps of an implementation and the value being managed in the model.

In large businesses, the correct identification of a data source can be challenging due to the management having been distributed across multiple functions. This brings the challenges of building a consolidated data set from multiple sources, particularly in ensuring commonality where required and ensuring completeness.

At the same time as collecting the data, the longer term governance of the data sources needs to be addressed.

We can take as an example a situation where different customer-facing businesses in an organisation each keep their own list of applications; with some kept in a database, some in spreadsheets and one which is not actually kept anywhere since "everyone in the business already has that knowledge". The collection and collation of the data from these sources is going to be required, along with tracking that gap to be documented of "what everyone knows". The process to achieve this needs to be iterative with the data providers, ensuring that the quality of information they provide is adequate and with a plan in place for resolving issues. The types of basic data quality issues that can require action at this point range from required information being missing entirely, partial information within existing data fields, through to apparently trivial issues such as misspelled names.

Consolidating multiple data sources into a single complete version also brings issues of deduplication. Using the same example, there is a likelihood that there are shared applications which will appear in multiple lists, requiring an exercise to ensure that duplication is recognised and managed. This is not necessarily as simple as saying that "these applications have the same name, so they are the same" and may require particular knowledge and expertise to complete accurately, rather than being effectively automated.

> *For any major supplier such as IBM, Hewlett Packard or Microsoft, there are likely to be at least five different spellings of their name across different data sources, and sometimes even within one a single data source.*

A useful method to approach this type of consolidation exercise is to ensure that the people contributing information maintain control of their own data, while improving its value for central use within the TBM system. Where it is possible to move all the contributors to using a common key, such as adding an 'Application Code' to their data set, comparisons and duplications are able to be more easily identified and tracked. A further benefit is that the final consolidated view built in the TBM system is likely to be accepted by all the contributing sources as directly related to their input.

The technical aspects described above are generally considered to be part of an 'ETL' (Extract, Transform, Load) process, about which there is a wide range of knowledge and skill available. The requirements for TBM Cost Modelling are not unique but require understanding of both the technical and organisational impacts relating to managing data, particularly when working across a wide range of organisational groups.

Preparing for changing data

The best practice for a TBM Cost Model is to update the data frequently, usually based around a monthly financial schedule. The preparation of financial data is generally already managed in this way, but other data often will not be. For a TBM Cost Model to be well managed, the management of all its data sources needs to be controlled, which starts with tracking information about those sources.

Depending on the background of the person running a TBM Cost Model, the type of information kept about data sources may be significantly different. Application developers and managers tend to look at data in terms of its type (characters, numbers, format, length), Finance in terms of its value and provable accuracy, and data managers in terms of those previously mentioned plus volume and volatility (among other measures).

Simple characteristics need to be tracked for every data source in the form of an index, including for every source of data

- the name that the data source is known by,
- who provides it,
- what is the data they are providing,
- how often is it updated,
- in what form is it delivered,
- how is it delivered.

From an operational process perspective, each of these then needs to be backed by information on what to do in the event of an exception. This can be as simple as knowing who the backup is if the person who usually provides information goes on vacation.

Formalising this as an index or dictionary of data sources is a one-off exercise during the initial collection of data. At that stage the information has often not been previously collated, as it is well known. It is best to create this index early, since the need to gather the information at a later stage does not scale well when a full TBM Cost Model might include hundreds of data sources.

In some instances, organisations have gone significantly further, by supporting the index of data sources with a dictionary of the detail within each data source. This can be a valuable source of reference information when building a TBM Cost Model but is not recommended. In many cases the information collected as an input to a TBM Cost Model has already been consolidated from multiple sources for other purposes. A focus on the original, authoritative (or 'gold') source of information is of much higher value to ensuring quality and consistency than an index of the derived data.

Many fields in TBM data sources are blank, and not used for modelling or reporting. A useful addition to a data source index, and one which goes part way towards managing a full data dictionary, is to make sure you know which fields from a data source you're actively using so that you can validate the data, or know where to look for errors and exceptions when needed.

Validating changes within data sources

The purpose of bringing data into a TBM Cost Model on a regular basis is to enable visibility of trends and exceptions within the data and its results. This requires the inputs to be correct and consistent, which is a state that must be validated rather than assumed. The alternative is the traditional 'GIGO' status (Garbage In, Garbage Out).

The inputs to a TBM Cost Model will generally already be owned and managed by their provider, as they are using the same information for their own operational processes. This does not prevent errors from being included, so there is always a requirement for some basic validation of data to take place within the operational processes for a TBM Cost Model.

The level at which this needs to be done will be dependent on multiple factors, including the potential impact of an error in the Cost Model (discussed later in this chapter in the section on the value of data), whether the data is provided manually or automatically, and the volatility of the data. The simple choice to be made between how data is provided is that automation of data provision is almost always preferable to manual, with the validation expected to be part of the automation process and not required to be repeated.

The validation of highly volatile data sources is problematic; where there is significant change in the value, volume or base data from one period to the next. This is usually limited to a small number of data sets, as most businesses and their costs change slowly over time, so these sources need to be reviewed regularly on an individual basis.

Dealing with changing sources of data

There is an expectation that a TBM Cost Model will provide consistent outputs over time, built on the consolidated data from a large number of sources. From the perspective of governance of the TBM Cost Model, any changes to the underlying data sources then needs to be made transparent to the users. A TBM governance function needs to keep track of where its data sources are due to change, and ensure that any such change does not cause breaks in the Model.

Technically, changes in the data sources can vary from changing the order of columns, through changing the names of columns, to losing an input entirely as the source system is decommissioned. Although TBM systems can often be built to easily or automatically react to some of these, the complete loss of a data source requires additional planning, and the replacement of this data with an alternative source or model.

The process to ensure that changes to data sources are managed can be made simpler by ensuring that data providers are engaged with TBM and see the value of their input reflected in a TBM system.

This relationship is also important when data, or a data source, needs to be changed as a result of TBM outputs. For these changes, sometimes there is nothing you can do except work hard. Some data sources are so vital that they have to be reviewed and changed line by line, but do assess how far you can simplify that task before taking time on it.

When a data source in a TBM Cost Model is annually updated Reference Data or similar, a TBM Office needs to understand both the data and the timelines for change. This includes understanding both changes that will be provided to TBM, and changes that TBM need to request e.g. to the Finance Service Catalogue.

The value of data

The perception of the importance of a data source often relates to its owner or to historic expectations, rather than its impact to an organisation. This can lead to significant effort being put into collecting and managing data that has little impact within a TBM Cost Model, but is sometimes only possible to recognise after it has been used.

A material part of the cost base of many organisations relates to its staff, as salaries and related expenses. The staff costs are included in the financial and organisational hierarchies, which are at least broadly aligned and often tightly aligned. The tracking of what those staff are doing is an important general management tool, but only in some cases captured at a level where the information is relevant to TBM.

Where staff are working on projects, in many financial jurisdictions their cost can be capitalised and spread (for financial management purposes) across the lifetime of the project's deliverables. For that purpose, tracking the specific hours spent on a project is valuable information to bring into TBM.

The same logic does not necessarily apply to the situation where there are a large group of cross-functional technical staff in one team, whose time may be tracked to identify what technology or what type of work they are performing. Although this detail may be highly valuable for staff management purposes, the impact of it to a TBM Cost Model allocation of costs may not be significant. This extends to managing the geographic location of staff, which is usually a level of detail that is harder to maintain consistently across an organisation, reducing the value that is likely be derived by its modelling through a Cost Model.

Another area in which the value of data needs thoughtful management is that of IT infrastructure, which brings to light the importance of understanding the relationships between data sets and their granularity.

In a business where Private Cloud services are being implemented, companies are purchasing servers and storage with a view to providing Infrastructure, Platform and Software as a Service for their own users, and extending this to development contexts such as Containers. This delivers a situation where a TBM Cost Model needs to manage multiple layers of cost which did not exist historically. While an application might have previously been directly associated with a server and its attached storage, the relationship may now be that the application runs in a Container, which in turn runs on Infrastructure as a Service, which is part of a dedicated cluster of servers and storage.

This multi-layered set of relationships and association of costs from one end to the other is likely to be highly complex, so the value and materiality of the components drives questions about how and when to put this into a TBM Cost Model. 'Value' and 'materiality' are distinctly separate in this instance. The reason for this is partly non-financial and can relate to business efficiency, business advantage, risk or other factors. This applies to any similar direction that an organisation takes with new technology, Prioritisation is then based on business needs, rather than being purely financial.

The materiality impact is still significant to a TBM Cost Model, particularly where there is a high initial outlay (CapEx) on creating a capability, but with a slower expected uptake. The choice of how and when this should be put into a TBM Cost Model will relate to decisions on how the costs are to be aligned to the users of the system. If the upfront costs are aligned only to the early customers, no one will choose to use the Service first as they will receive the full set of costs, but a business must account for its unrecovered investment at this stage..

Once answers are available for both value and materiality, the actual data required for modelling these environments becomes a logical extension of pre-existing IT infrastructure. There is a requirement for new layers of abstraction to be provided between physical servers, logical servers (Infrastructure as a Service), logical servers with software (Platform as a Service), and applications (Software as a Service), but all of these can be modelled in terms of one Service sitting on top of others.

Filling in the gaps

In building a TBM Cost Model, a certain level of expectation will exist about the availability of data sources and the quality of data relationships, which can be overly optimistic. The reality of data being unavailable as a source to use for modelling, or turning out to be missing sufficient detail to be useable, is something that needs to be managed.

As mentioned previously, a TBM Cost Model should not be expected to be a data warehouse, where data is held and maintained, but should be a point at which data consolidation occurs, and data sources are connected and used. When it is necessary for a data gap to be filled by a temporary source, or for temporary logic used to align costs based on a different weighting factor to what is known to be correct, this should not be treated as a failure or reason to stop modelling. It can be the case that this temporary approach is adequate and the effort to replace it with a more accurate source will add no material value.

An example of this is in tracking time and activity for staff working on 'Business as Usual' (BaU) activities. While the accurate tracking of time worked on projects is a regular and required activity, many organisations do not put the same processes in place for infrastructure management and support functions since the requirement for the same granularity does not exist for financial management or other purposes.

When the requirement exists within a TBM Cost Model to align these Labour costs to IT Towers, the choice exists to extend project time tracking into BaU areas, or for a onetime assessment to be made by their managers about how to weight their time. In one specific instance where this transition was being made, the alignment provided by management before time tracking was 95% identical when compared to what ended up being shown by the final time tracking system, with the difference traceable to movement of staff between functions in the period between the measurements.

This does not mean that time tracking data would be less valuable to the model, and the effort to manually collect and collate the initial weighting data had a business cost, since the data collected could not be easily updated without repeated equivalent effort. The detail available from the time tracking system can also provide a range of other data points which are not of use to TBM but of value for other purposes.

In other instances where data sources appear to be missing but parts are found to be available, the question is more about whether to use the partial source or how to fill the gap until the full data is available. Included in this discussion with the data owner is the question of whether they can provide their data in a standard format or if they have a preexisting format or report that would be useful.

At a practical level, the first data that is usually provided to a TBM Office when building a model is incomplete and prefiltered. A question will have been asked of the data owner about the availability of specific information. They will answer with either the output of a preexisting query or with a customised response built to answer what they believe was the specific request. Both of these cases are likely to include filters to remove exceptions that the data owner understands and assumes to be implied, rather than delivering everything that is available or might be useful.

An example is if a request is made to a server administration team for information on all servers and the applications that they run. The reply might be expected to include all servers, but it would be quite possible for the data to be filtered to only include the servers which are known to run business applications, leaving out the ones running infrastructure applications (e.g. backups, security, domain management) and those where the application isn't known.

This response is not a failure but will start to highlight where gaps exist and knowledge isn't complete. A continuing conversation with the same group can lead to both the provision of more complete information and a better understanding of where there might be real gaps in data or knowledge.

Ensuring that these types of gaps in required data are filled is one of the roles of a TBM Office, but should not become a major activity. The ability for temporary data sources to proliferate during an implementation, and the challenges of replacing them with more structured sources, needs to be tightly managed. Failure to do this will eventually show up as incorrect outputs from a Cost Model, traceable to temporary sources not being updated when necessary.

The correct level of granularity at which to collect data can change over time due to the economics of technology and other factors. In an IT environment where costs are still largely related to physical servers and storage, a large amount of information can be available to a TBM Cost Model about the cost of an individual server. This is often not at the level of the costs of its components such as memory (RAM) or CPU cores. This was historically not important to the calculation of the cost of a server, as the entire cost could be simply aligned to one, or a few, applications. The growth of Server Consolidation, Clustering and Cloud technologies has meant that component level costs have become visible once again to the users of the same technologies.

This does not mean that it is necessary to calculate the cost of each physical server in terms of its memory and processing, or to compare cost at that level to the nominal price shown for those by Cloud providers. However, there is more value in being able to aggregate that information for physical servers than there historically was, in order to enable a comparison to be made to Cloud services.

With this approach to consolidated costs, rather than using the full granularity of data for shared or consolidated servers, alternative approaches can be considered. One such approach is to create a 'standard unit' of compute provision which includes a fixed amount of CPU and memory. This enables a more straightforward comparison of costs between the sources of compute capability, without requiring the full granularity of Cloud pricing to be delivered by every TBM Cost Model.

The level of granularity of cost information available is not a problem for businesses using Public Cloud technologies, as this is the level at which the providers invoice. The issue in these instances is more in the reverse, in terms of consolidation and management of high volumes of data.

Improving data quality

There are multiple factors by which data quality can be measured and the ISO 9000 standard (also known as BS5750) includes completeness, validity, accuracy, consistency, availability, and timeliness.

Failure of any of these counts can affect the output of a TBM Cost Model, but failure of all of them should be expected to be possible. Establishing quality checks on data sources is a baseline activity which must be implemented before running a TBM Cost Model, but is easily overlooked during an implementation.

The focus of building a TBM Cost Model is often seen as ensuring that the relevant data is available for calculating and validating an output. This focus may well include all of the ISO 9000 factors listed above except consistency, which is regularly the difference between building a repeatable TBM Cost Model and building a single-use model. Replacing a data set on a monthly basis within a model brings a level of complexity and requirement for consistency that is not apparent with a static data source.

For a static data source, understanding how it will change over time is not an issue. Once the data is being updated, the ways in which the change can occur are myriad. In an inventory showing workstations and laptops this could be as simple as changing a case-sensitive field from showing that a PC workstation is treated as a 'KIOSK' to being 'Kiosk' or 'kiosk'. While this is easily handled by appropriate logic, the logic is unlikely to be recognised as necessary until after the change has occurred for the first time.

As covered in the previous section on 'Filling in the gaps', completeness can also prove a challenge in the earlier stages of collecting data for a TBM Cost Model. Most requests for information are not requests for the type of raw data that a TBM Cost Model will be able to take most value from, but for processed information aimed at providing an answer to a question. There is more value to the development of a TBM Cost Model in gradually improving the completeness of data than in waiting for perfection, although the risks of incomplete data can be harder to identify.

Managing data quality improvement

Running a regular month end process for a TBM Cost Model includes the collection of all relevant data sources. The processing of that data then relies on high quality input, so a TBM Office must be clear about who is responsible for ensuring the quality of the input, validating it, fixing data quality issues, escalation and alternative provisioning.

A multi-layered approach is usually best here, with more than one check on the quality of both raw and processed data. As shown with the example on case consistency above, it is unlikely that every possible data quality failure can be anticipated within a large and varied group of data sources. While this is easier when data is held in formal databases, some sources for a TBM Cost Model are likely to be informal and held in spreadsheets or similar tools where the fields, formats and data can be easily changed without control.

Ensuring that the organisation and individual owner are known for each data source is a minimum step towards TBM data governance. Following this, setting expectations for all aspects of data quality management including timeliness is also needed, particularly for data that is due to be updated monthly. The process around this can be implied from the first paragraph in this section:

- Data provided to the TBM Cost Model should be quality checked before it is sent by the data owner, particularly for completeness, validity and consistency.

- The TBM Office will separately validate data on receipt, either by manual checks or by the impact of the data on test output of the TBM Cost Model.

- Issues with data quality will be returned to the data provider to be fixed and then reinput to the process.

- If data is not provided in time, or fixed in time, the process for communicating this, escalating, and using an alternative data source will have been identified in advance.

The last actions in the above list also become relevant when, as discussed in the section on 'Preparing for changing data' towards the beginning of this chapter, a data source is decommissioned and a replacement is not available. The ability to reuse data from one month to the next is sometimes possible, for example with the list of applications in an organisation. This is less likely to be acceptable when data changes significantly from one month to the next, such as with the amount of time booked to projects.

Within a TBM Cost Model, one area that is consistently affected by multiple factors of data quality is the relationship between data sources. While each standalone data set may be identified by its owner as 'correct,' when building the data relationships within a Cost Model the quality of the consolidated data may be reduced in terms of either source's completeness, validity, accuracy or consistency.

This brings aspects to data quality management which are new to the data owner. Identifying to a data owner that the Operating System of a server is not listed, so it cannot be shown with the relevant costs, is a simple fix for them to make to their data. Similarly, identifying that a server is not associated with any application, so that its cost cannot be passed to business users, is another straightforward data fix.

Measuring and reporting data quality within a TBM Cost Model can be a useful approach to highlight its importance and drive improvements, but this is often a highly manual effort and its benefits must be realistically assessed before putting too much time into it.

Data and time

Cost Transparency is usually a point-in-time based calculation, meaning that separate calculations are made for each period (month) based on the associated data collected for that period.

This brings a number of implications that may differ from peoples' expectations of financial reports and systems, and from technology inventory systems.

Restating historic costs

In the Finance section of a TBM Cost Model, and in Finance systems generally, there is often a requirement to make changes to the organisational hierarchy to match real organisation changes. How this impacts into a Cost Model and is reported can be highly variable, and this is an area where it is important to understand the implications of changes and the alternatives to including them in a model.

An example showing the range of activities that can be required is the impact of moving an IT Helpdesk function from being centrally managed to being part of the End User Computing organisation midway through the year.

From the perspective of a TBM Cost Model this drives a need to understand how to reflect that change, whether it affects the costs in the Cost Model, and from what point in time that should impact. At a basic level, it can easily be argued that this change should not affect the costs, as the same function is being provided by the same people for the same purpose before and after the change, but that may not be the intent behind the change.

The impact within a TBM Cost Model can be straightforward, such as where rules exist to define how Labour costs are aligned to IT Towers based on the organisation structure. In this example it could potentially be seen as moving the modelled alignment of these costs from all Services to be only applicable to End User Services. Alternatively, there might be no impact in the Cost Model if the alignment of the Labour costs to Services was based on their department rather than organisation.

The same change might alternatively only be required to be shown in terms of reporting the cost managed by the End User Computing organisation. This would offset their customers cost, and the choice may be whether this is reported on a go forward basis, or restated from the start of the year.

There is a requirement for clarity and consistency between the output from TBM and the equivalent Finance reports. If it is defined that there should be no impact of the change to Service cost alignment, the TBM Cost Model might need to be updated to realign the Labour costs to their original modelled route.

It is also possible for these two decisions to be combined, and it may be required that the alignment of the Helpdesk costs be fully reflected in the End User Computing Services from the start of the year. This type of change is equally possible within a TBM Cost Model, with the main warning being that it is very important to understand in advance at what point in time it is possible and allowable to make changes to historically reported data.

This is one further reason why it can be challenging to use a TBM Cost Model as a Financial System directly, and why it is recommended not to do this in the previous chapter. It is nearly impossible to guarantee consistent output from a TBM Cost Model when allowing or requiring changes to core data sources (such as organisational structure).

Historic data availability

A further difference between a TBM Cost Model's data and its original sources can occur due to alternative mechanisms to manage data over time. While some systems keep historic records, many do not.

This is generally not a concern for a TBM Cost Model as the data used for a model is expected to have been stored as a point-in-time copy for this specific purpose, as otherwise a Cost Model will not be functional.

This can become a challenge if there is a question about data that is no longer able to be recreated in its source system. This can be the case across all types of data source, from data managed in spreadsheets to those in ITIL Configuration Management Databases (CMDBs).

The requirement to validate or reproduce data from a prior period is not a regular occurrence and can be managed on a case by case basis, but the limitation on verifying historic data completeness and correctness is useful to keep in mind.

Chapter 9. Modelling vs Reality

The question of whether we are really living or we are just figments within a simulation has a long and varied history within philosophical thought, across multiple eras and geographies. Let's assume that we are living, and that we need to build a simulation called a Cost Model, but keep that thought in mind.

There are several reasons for starting this chapter with a somewhat abstract thought like that, but the main one is that it is very easy to believe that a Cost Model is a true reflection of reality, when in fact it is based on a significant number of simplifications and choices. Challenges to the accuracy of a Model can be well-founded and correct, so the need to understand what TBM is for and the limitations of an implementation need to be factored in to all related work.

There are some specific areas where choices within a Cost Model are more frequently required, and these will be looked at in more detail in this chapter, including

- At the Finance layer, how to manage Labour costs and how to capitalise projects.
- At the Technology layer, the relevant abstraction and metrics for networks and shared storage.
- At the Services layer, metrics and drivers for business usage.

For some decisions, there is a level of guidance and standardisation of the approach available within the TBM Taxonomy, while for others the choices are more open. Even where standards are available, there can be reasons to choose an alternative approach due to the specific needs of an organisation.

There will always be competing drives to add granularity and function to a Cost Model, or to simplify and keep it able to be explained. The tenet to keep to on this is that the advantages of simplifying a Model are undone by oversimplifying. That changes the Model from being defensible to being incorrect.

Centralised and federated models

When implementing a central TBM Cost Model in an organisation for the first time, the discovery process will frequently identify that there are pre-existing models that have been put in place for specific purposes. Managers can often see the value of these for meeting their own targets and for building business cases for investment and development of their function. The manager also has a level of knowledge of the structure of their costs which will frequently be highly detailed, and the ability to model that. The challenge of creating a centralised model is to include all necessary detail without losing the value derived from these smaller models.

Reviewing the capabilities and value of standalone models before including them in a centralised capability often shows two areas of difference; the completeness of the costs in the Model and the granularity of the data used to align cost.

It would be highly unusual to find a standalone Model which includes costs that are not part of the central cost base and overstate the total cost of a Service. The reverse, underestimating the total cost, is likely. With multiple separate but 'federated' models this can result in costs which are unclaimed in any model as the owners of the individual models either do not claim responsibility for them, or do so inconsistently. An example would be the cost of office space for staff, which is clearly a cost of business but not always visible to, or recognised by, standalone Cost Models.

The approach of bringing in all costs to a central model, rather than subsets of cost to standalone models, is usually one advantage of a central model as it becomes easier to identify if any costs are unaligned and why.

This advantage is extended by also avoiding some of the challenges in the reintegration of multiple models to a whole. The biggest issue with doing this is inconsistency, so ensuring that there is common scope of costs being managed is helpful even to federated models.

Different models for different purposes

Large enterprises, their technology departments, and even individual technologies, are sometimes seen as going through long term cycles of organisational design; regional to global, centralised to distributed, growth to consolidation. A TBM Cost Model needs to exist within this changing business framework and be created to account for it.

In the context of a large enterprise, a very early decision point for TBM Cost Modelling can be whether there is a single global model or multiple regional versions. There are intermediate options available, such as including regionalised data within a central model, but the decision may also be made, or limited, due to the operating model of the organisation.

The benefits of aligning a Cost Model to an organisational design come from the clarity and consistency of the boundaries of the organisation, along with statements of the goals and value expected to be delivered. As long as these benefits are realised, the judgement of whether one model or multiple are developed becomes a question of what the additional cost is of running multiple models and consolidating them, against the cost of running a single model.

At the scale of a large enterprise, running separate regional models may provide all relevant tools for improving the efficiency of technology expenditure in each region. The management of central or other non-regional costs needs to be separately handled and those costs distributed to the regions for modelling, but need not reduce efficiency. This approach can also deliver comparison capabilities between the regions, assuming that they all have points in their models which use standard Catalogues.

This approach, despite its virtues, is however likely to be implemented rarely. The administrative cost of managing multiple separate models is that each relationship, modelling step and data source needs to be managed multiple times, on top of which the management of central costs and their distribution need separate administration, and a process to consolidate the models will be required.

For these practical reasons the separation of Cost Models on a regional basis is not a good practice.

Similar logic applies to the choice of whether to run separate models for centralised and decentralised technology organisations. Some separation of technology functions is built into the TBM Taxonomy, such as the alignment of IT Towers to End User and Compute. This is largely independent of the organisational design, and whether or not these functions are managed under a single manager or not does not require additional separation in the modelling. Some additional requirements may be seen in the initial collection of financial information, which will now come from separate sources and may need to be kept apart through the modelling, although this should not be an issue technically.

As with the global or regional design decision, the advantage of bringing multiple organisations into a single model is with the capability to model and manage central costs, inter-organisational costs, and to show a single view of the overall costs.

One area where the different characteristics of the model may make it viable, and even preferable, to separate models is between IT Infrastructure and Business Services. This is the point at which there is a transition from the alignment of technology costs with technology inventories, to the alignment of costs according to business drivers and usage which may have no direct technological equivalent.

A separation of models at this point is also aligned with the potential to expand modelling beyond TBM's usual scope. Costs related to business processes can be treated in a similar manner and alongside TBM-based costs at this stage, giving a view of Total Cost of Ownership (TCO) which is more complete and relevant at a business level. The justification provided by TBM, for Technology costs and value, becomes the expectation of what other business functions also need to deliver.

A standard model has exceptions

Before the creation of the TBM Taxonomy by the TBM Council there were similarities in how technology managers understood the structure and relationships of the 'technology stack', but not one clear and obvious structure. As is hopefully clear from the earlier chapters of this book, there are still a large number of choices to be made during an implementation that uses the TBM Taxonomy, and there are still instances when an organisation may choose to take an alternative approach.

Going back to the initial premise of this Chapter, a model is a simulation of reality and not an actual reality, so we must expect that even when we are following a standard model we will need to expect exceptions. The danger of accepting this is that we need to not only expect those exceptions but to manage them and ensure that they do not overwhelm our model. Implementing a standard approach and exception management process at the same time reduces this risk, as well as highlighting points where the standard approach may have been wrong in some specifics.

Do not be concerned if you aim to use a 'standard' and it doesn't fit perfectly for what you do, but be concerned if you believe the 'standard' doesn't fit at all.

One area that can generate a significant requirement for managing exceptions in a Cost Model is investments, or projects. For financial management reasons these are often managed as a separate financial structure from standard expense management. There are particular requirements to identify project cost, capitalise the relevant part, and to tie this back to detailed project activity and time tracking. These need specific additional focus with TBM, as the financial controls are often already in place and managed in detail by many organisations before TBM capabilities are introduced.

The simplest approach to modelling project cost in this context is to not try to replicate work that is already being done elsewhere. If it is not necessary to use your TBM Cost Model to align project costs to projects, use the pre-existing project financial data as an input.

If the information needs to be modelled, particular care and attention must be paid to ensuring that the TBM Cost Model is consistent with the financial reality.

As an example, one aspect of Project Financial Management can be that a fixed daily rate is used to calculate the cost of people working on projects, with this being a combined value that includes a level of non-project (e.g. holiday) time. This daily rate, combined with time recording data, is used to calculate the cost of work done on a project and as part of the cost of capitalisation of the project (spreading the cost over the project's useful life).

There are multiple challenges to a TBM Cost Model in taking this approach including, in the area of project staff costs and time recording, that

- It may not refer to Cost at all, as the project financial calculation uses a fixed daily rate rather than salary information .

- It may have cyclical variances due to cost and time recording data being unsynchronised, causing staff to show as booking time in months when they aren't working, or vice versa.

- It may cause negative values to be shown where project capitalisation is calculated at a higher value than the actual Cost.

These types of exception can all be modelled, and in a financial reporting context will all net out to provide a correct result for formal reporting, but would not be usefully reflected in a Cost Model without significant effort.

With this group of exceptions, the decision-making process about what approach is best should include consideration of the organisational cost, and benefit, of including this in the Cost Model. The requirement to replicate financial processes within a Cost Model can require both standard financial processes and financial exception management processes to be replicated. This level of complexity is likely to introduce inconsistencies between financial and Cost Model outputs.

Particularly where there are pre-existing formal exception management processes, the best practice is likely to be to use the transformed input as a feed to a Cost Model, rather than repeat the process.

Exceptional events

While creating a TBM Cost Model, the focus is on the design of the model and integration of a variety of data-driven exceptions, but rarely on the management of time-specific exceptions. Trying to plan for these types of exceptions is not good practice, and frequently isn't foreseeable either, but becomes more of a factor in an operational TBM environment.

The most frequent exceptional events that need to be adjusted for are financial. Where the expectation for a TBM Cost Model may be that costs will be applied steadily over time and trends used to help manage a business, the presence of large variances in the Ledger will stop that from happening. These changes may have a physical basis, such as receiving a large invoice or credit from a supplier. Exceptions can however also be down to structural or accounting practice, such as managing write-offs in a specific part of the organisation or managing an organisational change by 'journaling' the movement of costs between functions.

The working practice of TBM on a large scale and the integration of previously separate datasets into a Cost Model actually brings to light how often these take place, so a practical approach to them needs to be implemented.

The first stage of this is to expect these types of occurrence and to put in place checks to identify them. This will usually take the form of validation processes, both on data inputs and on model outputs, to look for high value and high ratio changes taking place from one period to the next. It is sometime possible to work proactively with data providers so that these cases are identified in advance, and this is particularly true of the financial inputs; a finance manager will have already taken actions to create the data, so can provide information on what caused the change and why they have taken a particular action.

Once the source of an exception is known, the approach to its management can be reviewed. This stage often requires discussion with multiple stakeholders and careful thought, because the decision on whether an event is managed exceptionally in a model may be defined by organisational rather than technical priorities.

An example of this is when the outcome of a software audit delivers an unexpected and backdated invoice. Should this entire cost be included in the cost of Services going forward, or only the portion that relates to future use? Is Finance able to amortise the charge, or only part of it? Which Service or customer is it equitable to align these costs to and on what basis?

The choices range from accepting the data without any change into the TBM Cost Model, through filtering out the data so that it is not used at all, to a variety of changes to the Cost Model, and there is not a single correct answer for all.

Depending on your implementation, particularly in an environment where the Cost Model is a sub-ledger for the company's finances, these choices may be limited. A useful baseline approach is to consider how much of the cost is legitimately a continuing component of the Total Cost of Ownership of modelled Services, and to aim to include that in the Cost Model as standard.

As with standard modelling exceptions, the management of event-based exceptions should not become a burden to managing Cost Modelling, and if these are a significant part of the operational management of the system then it is likely that other steps should be taken to identify the cause and actions to reduce the impact.

Limitations of modelling

A number of choices will be required during the process of building a Cost Model for which there isn't necessarily a single correct answer, and some are reviewed in this section.

Consumption and Capacity

When purchasing technology, there is often a choice to buy directly and manage it yourself, or to buy a managed service. An aspect of buying directly is that you need to purchase more capacity than you use, while buying a managed service can provide you with more flexibility to increase and decrease your consumption over time.

There are multiple additional perceived benefits, challenges and risks of buying a managed service, and businesses have shown that there is demand for this for all types of technology provision; from Data Centres, through Infrastructure, to Software. One reason that these capabilities are not used by all organisations is that, at sufficient scale, it may be possible to deliver your own equivalent Services at a lower price, since you do not need to deliver the profit that a Service Provider does.

For an organisation that has purchased and is managing its own technology capacity, a TBM Cost Model can help understand and manage the cost of it.

Using Storage as an example, assume you have two Storage frames, each with 500TB capacity, which cost $10,000 each per month and are 80% utilised, as in the diagram below.

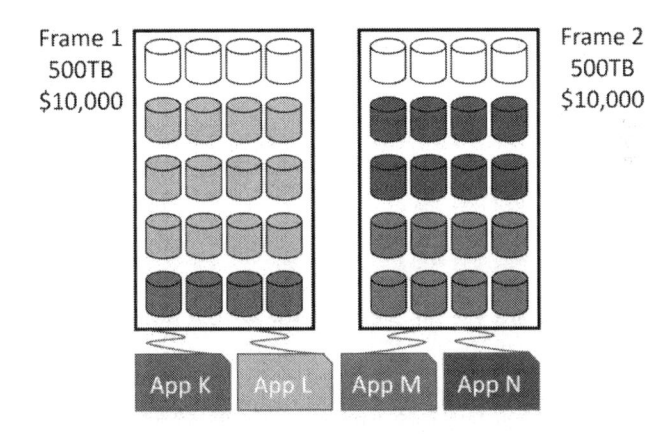

There are already choices of how much cost should be aligned to each Application, so for both frames

- Cost per TB consumed = $10,000 / 400TB = $25/TB

- Cost per TB capacity = $10,000 / 500TB = $20/TB

The second of these choices would not align the cost of the unused capacity to any customer, which would be unusual for a Cost Model. If a 'price' of $20/TB was charged to each application according to its usage, only $8,000 would be charged in total and $2,000 would need to be separately managed.

If Application N is then decommissioned and the space is returned for use by other applications, the choices become wider. Although the calculation of

Unit Cost in Frame 1 is unchanged, we now have only 40% utilisation of Frame 2 and the costs in that frame become

- Cost per TB consumed = $10,000 / 200TB = $50/TB

Even if the two frames are treated as a single cost base, we now are only at 60% utilisation

- Cost per TB consumed = $20,000 / 600TB = $33/TB

so the loss of consumption would cause a modelled increase in the cost to all remaining applications.

The same challenge in determining what should be charged applies when there is growth rather than shrinkage. If the expectation is that new applications will require additional storage a third frame may be purchased.

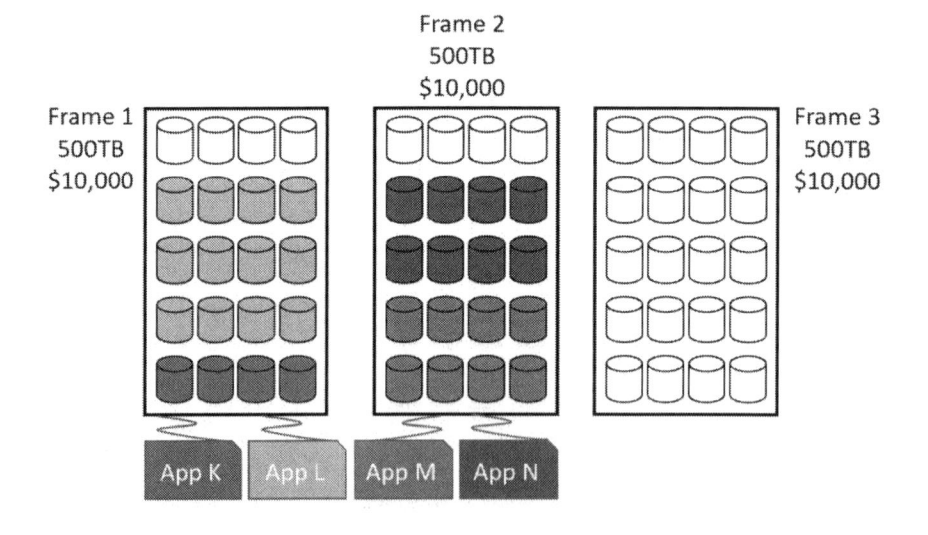

Until additional applications fill the new frame to an equivalent capacity, the average cost of consumed storage will be significantly increased.

The choice of how to model this reality most equitably to the customers is one that applies to many technologies, not just storage. At least in part, this is a challenge which is significantly mitigated by scale. The addition of a third frame and 50% additional capacity in this example is actually more realistically going to be a much smaller percentage e.g. the addition of an 11th frame provides only 10% more capacity and cost.

The perception of application owners or customers relating to this issue is often that the cost impact to them of buying capacity is more material than is actually the case. This perception can be addressed through the logic above and showing the overall trends for consumption, capacity and most importantly the trend of overall Unit Cost ($ per TB).

Where there are truly low volumes, the need to manage this type of impact is considerable. Costs to an organisation of both adding and leaving Data Centres are less likely to scale, so central management of the cost of empty space may be required. Similarly, if you spread the cost of a Data Centre to all the servers in it and then start to exit a Data Centre, remaining servers will increase in cost, in a parallel situation to the retirement of Application N above.

Granularity of data

The level of granularity of data which is used for modelling cost can be significantly different to what is used for management of a technology or service. This is particularly the case where there is a very high volume associated with the technology such as with Cloud based capabilities or, more traditionally, data backups.

To successfully manage backups, a technology manager will need to know every System or Application that they are connecting to, information on the type of backup, how often it is to be made, the quantity of data stored and that the backup has (hopefully) completed successfully. They may also track the number of times that the data is restored from backup, particularly as this is a less frequent but often higher cost activity. Not all of this is likely to be used as input to the modelling of cost, although it can be if the data is available. A more regular view is that the cost of backing up and restoring data is tied to a single metric, such as the volume backed up, so the only information required is to know how much data has been backed up for each System or Application.

When moving into a Public Cloud environment, some of these questions become more relevant to managing the cost of an Application, and the additional detail is available to allow that granularity to be used. The difference in cost between backing up data and restoring it, or between backing up data within the Cloud and keeping a local copy (just in case) can be material.

There is no absolute answer as to what level of detail is required in a TBM Cost Model, so the question of what to implement relates more to ensuring that both the Service can run efficiently and effectively, and that the costs can be modelled to enable business value to be managed. The use of data in a Cost

Model should not cause a reduction in the level of detail used to manage a Service, but nor should there be an expectation that every single detail available should be used as an input to cost modelling.

Low volume is hard to model

There is an intuitive assumption that it should be simpler to model a single object than many. This is certainly true if the level of accuracy of the modelling is identical in both instances, but that assumption does not hold true for most TBM Cost Modelling. Failing to differentiate between situations where you have a low volume passing through a model, relative to those with a high volume, can lead to challenges being made about the overall quality of the model.

The example that we have just used about storage can be extended to demonstrate this. The standard model that was shown is that the ownership of disk storage frames is shared between customers using them. If, instead, a customer requires that an entire storage frame is dedicated to them, there are several changes that must be made to modelling the cost.

The first change is that both the cost and the capacity of the frame (rather than the consumption) must be associated to the customer. This means that they will be charged for the whole cost of the frame regardless of their level of consumption. As they have specified this requirement, it could be assumed that they have no issue with this, but it is best to check that it is correct.

The second change is that the customer must accept that the cost is their responsibility throughout the lifecycle of the frame, and will not be variable if they stop using it. Although this is less of a financial risk when common components such as storage frames are considered, the purchase of specialist equipment which cannot be reused is an area where this is particularly important to manage.

The third change is that the costs of providing services associated with the storage within the frame will need to be agreed, and may be different than those for standard frames. The justification for a dedicated frame may be that there is less cost involved in managing it when compared to the cost of managing a shared version, but equally the argument can be made that there is a higher cost to managing a bespoke service than a standard one.

As with many such discussions, there may not be a single correct answer that covers all situations, so the implementation of a model for this standalone or bespoke service must be added to the list of modelling exceptions to be managed.

A further abstraction of this approach is the suggestion that it should be possible to manage the individual cost of each inventory item in a TBM Cost Model and to combine these to give a precise Total Cost of Ownership of Services. The implication of this is that there is no standard service or component used in IT and that everything is customised. While this might make customers of IT feel important, the reality is more likely to be that the Technology department is delivering a range of standard components and Services, so the level of detail required to enable this is not available or relevant.

Some Technology departments have taken this approach directly, specifying the Technology Services that they provide and communicating that they will not provide additional bespoke options. This enables them to focus more directly on ensuring the efficiency of their core services and the value they provide to the business, but reduces their technical flexibility to some degree.

Evolving technology and markets

The principles of Technology Business Management and Cost Modelling provide a mechanism to enable clear visibility of the cost of technology services. This can allow an economic assessment of the cost of local provision of those services against their equivalent in the market, sometimes even when it is in comparison to a new offering.

In the recent developments of the technology market, this description could cover services ranging from IT outsourcing, through Converged Infrastructure, to Cloud and various 'as a Service' capabilities. Using a TBM Cost Model to enable these comparisons can be a valid approach, with the specification of the Services providing like for like costing against the market.

Some technology suppliers and some technology directions and pricing structures make this comparison difficult, so this should be treated with care. To ensure that the TCO calculated in a TBM Cost Model is a useful comparison, steps must be taken identifying how accurately these services are represented, and where definitions differ.

As examples

- IT outsourcing contracts often separate a baseline cost from cost of variability (Additional Resource Cost / Reduced Requirement Credit) and may also have exclusions or separate services which make comparison difficult.

- Converged Infrastructure consolidates a wide range of capabilities at a single price, but will need to be redivided between customers on a consistent basis. There is not likely to be sufficient information to work out the correct division of the cost of Converged Infrastructure to enable adequate comparison against separate technology components and services.

The impact and challenge of new technology and how to model it within a TBM Cost Model is particularly acute when it comes to the comparisons of Cloud and 'as a Service' provision.

The creation of Cloud Compute and Storage provide a very straightforward comparison for businesses when looking at traditional technology ownership. Having the ability to interactively vary capacity, along with only paying for the specific amount of compute consumption used, enabled business case justification with ease.

The wider implications of risk together with financial structures for Operating Expense against Capital in budgets, ability to migrate, service levels and reliability, all meant that Cloud migration was not an immediate choice for every business, and many larger businesses still provide their own Private Cloud capabilities.

Modelling these with TBM requires a higher focus on the relationship of one technology component with another, as the historically stable layers for IT infrastructure from Data Centre, through Network, Hardware and Software are now augmented with multiple abstractions and additional layers.

The TBM Taxonomy provides a clear standard for the separation of technology at the IT Tower layer which is then augmented at the Products/Services layer with Infrastructure and Application services that enable those costs to be consolidated as needed. As an example, Compute Server costs at the IT Tower layer may become part of the cost base of 'Infrastructure Services' Virtual Compute Service, and then part of the 'Platform Services' Application Hosting Service.

This flow of costs in a TBM Cost Model must adequately represent the physical and logical relationships between technology components and be backed up by inventories that show these relationships. While it would have been adequate in a physical IT implementation to simply associate the costs of storage with a server that they were attached to, clustered and virtualised IT components need to be defined to match the additional layers of abstraction.

The main capability required for this is that the parent/child relationships for each layer of technology are understood logically and then modelled. In general the logical layering is additive, in that each additional layer is clearly based on a prior capability. The logical relationship between 'Infrastructure as a Service' (e.g. Virtual Machine), 'Platform as a Service' (e.g. Database), and 'Software as a Service' (e.g. Application) is very similar to the physical equivalent.

This can be complicated by the apparent re-use of technologies within layers and the potential for several of these to be used by a single Application, particularly with the range of services at the 'Platform as a Service' layer. As with the discussion in Chapter 6, recursive alignments are not recommended for this. These need to be reviewed to understand what cost, impact and business value will be affected in the Cost Model, but can generally be shown in a hierarchical relationship without material loss of accuracy.

Technology challenges

Challenges in modelling changes in technology can be broadly split into those related to standard evolution and those which relate to revolutionary change. Even with well understood technologies which have developed and been implemented for decades, ensuring the best modelling of cost can throw up some interesting questions. For new technologies the initial choices for modelling and comparison can need some quick thinking and more than one iteration.

Networks

There is probably more variety in the way that network costs are managed and charged within organisations than any other major technology. This extends even further when telephony and storage replication are included within the scope of networking costs.

The previous sentence provides a part of the answer as to why there is such a large range of ways in which organisations look at their network costs, as there are multiple technical disciplines involved which often have a broader range of attributes than technologists expect. The need to manage network suppliers, physical connections, wiring throughout buildings and Data Centres, switches and router hardware and operating systems, security and intrusion management systems, wireless connectivity, and more, is a complex combination which is no longer needed for many technologies.

The outcome of any model of networking cost must be designed to match the overall requirements for a TBM Cost Model; to equitably align the cost to its consumers. The consumers of networks cannot be expected to understand this detail, so the definition of what is included in each Network Service become a key point of reference and target for modelling.

What will a user or non-technology manager understand as the cost of networking? Their main point of reference is likely to be their telephone and internet provider at home, so they do have an expectation of being charged separately for different types of service. They most likely will accept that there is a fixed charge associated with the provision of their connection (whether telephone or network) and a further charge related to some, if not all, usage. Some companies now also provide chargeable security, so the separation of those costs may also be accepted.

A technology manager or application owner can be shown additional Network Services, but most are not likely to need to understand all the detail. The cost of server connectivity in a Data Centre, possibly with higher charges for faster connections, and for connection to firewalled networks for specific security, are generally going to be the only relevant levels of detail to output from a Cost Model.

To a network manager, the simplification of their domain to fewer than ten Services can be difficult to accept. The ability to create a model of all of their costs that groups down with reasonable accuracy to this level is challenging, but for a large proportion of their users, this is all that is required.

Storage

When the cost of Storage in an enterprise is calculated in a Cost Model and made visible to an organisation, the usual response is that someone looks at the cost per Gigabyte (or Terabyte) and says "How much? I can buy that much capacity for my home PC for less than you're charging me each month!" It is interesting to note that this is likely to be true, and that the comparison also applies to the cost of storage available from a Cloud Storage provider.

By way of an example, as of April 2020, the cost of Amazon S3 Standard Storage was $0.023 per GB per Month up to 50TB, equivalent to $23 per TB. The cost of a 3TB Hard Drive on Amazon store was as low as $47.50 which is over 30% discount.

Storage pricing	
Region: US East (Ohio)	
	Pricing
S3 Standard Storage	
First 50 TB / Month	$0.023 per GB

WL 3TB 7200RPM 64MB Cache SATA 6.0Gb/s 3.5" Desktop Hard Drive (For Server, RAID, NAS, DVR, Desktop PC) w/1 Year Warranty

★★★★☆ ~ 104

Electronics

$47.50

Figure 3 :Snapshots of online comparative pricing of storage

There is quite a long list of reasons why this is not a reasonable comparison, many of which need to be understood as part of the context of Cost Modelling for technology generally, although particularly relevant for Storage.

One of the largest differences between the cost per GB of storage within an organisation (or as provided by a Cloud company) and the cost of a hard drive is the efficiency with which it is used. In a home computer with a 1TB disk, there is a high likelihood that less than half of the capacity is used and many users can easily use only 10%. If you have paid $47.50 for a 3TB disk, as above, and are only using 100GB, your comparison is actually against $2.30 per month online. Reversing the logic, you have just paid $47.50 for 100GB which over a projected three year lifespan of the PC is $0.40 per GB per month.

Storage within an enterprise also provides a higher degree of performance and resilience than is understood by home users. Most enterprise storage will be implemented in a RAID (Redundant Array of Inexpensive Disk) configuration, which is designed so that that the failure of any individual hard drive does not have any impact on data availability. It does have some effect on the price though, as there is a need to have 'raw' capacity available to achieve this. This capability is much more efficient than having a copy of every piece of data, so does not double the cost of storage capacity, but is an additional factor in the cost.

Why is this important to Cost Modelling? As with networks, there is a hierarchy of technologies which are used to deliver storage capacity to users and applications, and that hierarchy needs to be modelled so that the management of the cost of storage can be shown to be efficient, both in terms of delivering relevant service and cost.

The calculation of Storage cost must include provision for increased growth through maintaining unused capacity, but should keep sufficient granularity to be able to model and allocate cost separately for higher levels of resilience.

The TBM Taxonomy has changed between versions to match how the market has matured in respect of this differentiation between technology, resilience and service. The removal (in versions 2 and 3 of the Taxonomy) of differences between either the storage technology or "tier" leaves a simplified view which is closer to how storage is perceived by its users, although there is flexibility to extend this when needed.

Servers and Computing

An early driver of the development of Technology Business Management as a set of disciplines was the move to server virtualisation and clustering, which was the precursor of the core Cloud technologies.

Value came from Technology Business Management systems in providing the ability to model individual standalone servers, which varied from desktop sized to those able to process at similar capacities to historic mainframes, alongside clusters of servers providing multiple virtual machines.

Multiple approaches are still available within TBM to manage privately owned system and Data Centre costs alongside Cloud, but some of the comparisons now become harder to make as the variety of Cloud services do not match with classic Compute Service descriptions.

An example of this challenge is in defining the proper unit to measure servers with. Before virtualization, it was relatively easy to count servers and to group them by size into large, medium and small. With sufficient information, it was sometimes possible to extend this to the component level within a server and measure the cost of processing per CPU core or per GB of memory, but this was not a realistic level at which to manage any large volume of servers.

With virtualization and Private Cloud capabilities, particularly when comparing to Public Cloud services, the need arises to enable comparison, which means enabling your own costs to be broken down in a comparable way to the Cloud providers. This is a complex activity, as the number of price points that Cloud providers allow you to choose between is in the tens of thousands. It is not realistic for a TBM Cost Model to work in this way.

One of the simplest approaches to this is to start with a comparison of server costs against dedicated Virtual Machine costs. Logically, the provision of a Cloud service on a full-time basis ('Reserved Instances') is comparable between Private and Public Cloud versions; as the costs are the same whether it is in use or not. Similarly, it is realistic to split a Private Cloud capability into a specific number of Virtual Machines of a particular size in order to make this comparison.

The result should be expected to show that it is cheaper to run this specific capability in-house rather than online, as this comparison to how Public Cloud Services are provided is inaccurate even before the normal commercial markup on price of the Public Cloud providers.

A more realistic comparison can be built from this starting point, by looking at the cost per minute of Virtual Machine provision, rather than the cost of a dedicated server. This comparison enables several additional factors to be taken into account in comparing Private and Public Cloud costs, including the expectation that not all computing will be running simultaneously so that more servers can run in a Cloud than when the space is dedicated.

The results of this level of comparison may be useful for understanding the cost of providing a Private Cloud service, but the main limitation of any comparison of this nature is that Cloud Services extend significantly beyond the simple provision of Virtual Machines. With the availability of pre-provisioned Cloud Services for database, web, development, security and multiple other options, enabling equivalent comparisons for all Cloud Services is again unrealistic for a TBM Cost Model.

While it is possible to create TBM Cost Model capabilities to compare specific infrastructure and business capabilities delivered through Private Cloud and compare these to the equivalent Public Cloud Services, it is unrealistic to expect to compare every alternative.

Modelling the future

Compared to all previous challenges in understanding the difference between modelling and reality, the requirement least likely to deliver accuracy is modelling the future. This does not remove the requirement to create budget and forecast views of finances within a TBM Cost Model, but it should be recognised as being limited by the need to layer one assumption on top of another.

Within this limitation, as described in Chapter 4 about "Where can you go?", Technology Business Management disciplines can help with the development and delivery of regularly updated information useful for forecasting and budgeting.

The process of developing this level of maturity starts with creating the ability for a business to see its use of technology through standard TBM Cost Modelling. The availability of historic and trend data can be used as the basis for projecting future demand, with the TBM Office helping Service Owners to use this data to identify the cost impact 'backwards' through the TBM Cost Model.

The most basic approach to this should be able to be verified by rerunning the Cost Model and seeing the Total Cost of Ownership and Unit Cost of Services reflecting the changes demanded by the business. Slightly more complex approaches may provide a level of logical separation between the collection of business drivers of technology volume and the preparation of IT budget costs, but the expectation of validating TCO and Unit Cost would remain.

An assumption in the previous paragraphs is worth noting, which returns to the relevance of granularity in the data sources for modelling the future compared to those for real data. Where a TBM Cost Model for actual financial data can be built using real inventories, a projection of the future might need to account for the commissioning and decommissioning of services, infrastructure and components, changing of vendor relationships and changes in business structure. It is unrealistic to expect detailed inventories to be available for these future changes, so a Budget Model will need to use parallel or proxy information instead.

These data sources should match the structure of the real data, but only hold data at the level of granularity relevant to enable the most limited modelling that achieves a comparable result. A test of this is to run a set of actual data through a Budget Model and compare the output to the main TBM Cost Model. Perfect accuracy should not be expected, but major differences should not be seen.

This approach also enables modification of the budget inventory and other data sources to account for the changes in demand from the business, raising the level of confidence in the process of modelling the future state.

Chapter 10. The mid-point(s)

Up to this point, this book has generally focused on the technical and practical decisions which will affect a TBM Cost Model implementation. These encompass understanding of the scope to be covered including your starting point, the Cost Model structure you are going to follow, and some information on the general destination you are aiming for.

Before moving towards a more complete TBM Cost Model, it is necessary to look in more detail at the later stages of building a Cost Model and particularly how to list and manage the target Products and Services. This can be where businesses compare their own structure and deliverables to a standard such as the TBM Taxonomy and see a wider gap than applies to technology.

This chapter will also start looking at some operational processes that you will often need to start implementing during the course of building a Cost Model, enabling the sections that have been built to start delivering regular updated outputs and value.

The location of this chapter, while logical in a number of ways, should not imply that the review of the later parts of the TBM Taxonomy and an organisation's Services should be left until Cost Modelling of finances are complete and technology is underway. Having a target for the latter stages of the Cost Model provides early and constant guidance on what is important to build throughout a modelling process.

The structures around which this is based are one or more Service Catalogues, where a non-technology user interfaces with the Technology department and needs to be able to base their interactions on something that they can understand.

While the TBM Taxonomy provides a degree of standardisation to the structure and detail for this, most businesses have a more firmly established and unique view of their organisation as a whole than they may do for the lower abstraction levels of a model. The organisational design of both Technology departments and Business units need to be brought together to agree lists of what Technology is providing.

What is a Product and what is a Service?

The TBM Taxonomy shows this as two inter-related layers of capabilities under the title of 'Products and Services' (see Appendix p16). This neatly side-steps the question of how these might differ in definition and is a realistic way to handle a question where there is no fully agreed answer. As was advised earlier about avoiding using financial 'key words' such as 'Direct' and 'Indirect', the best approach is probably to set and stick with your own definition, or to use whatever terminology already exists with this meaning within your organisation.

It is an interesting comparison if you look at how many of your non-business purchases you would describe as a 'Service' rather than a 'Product'. You would usually call food bought in a supermarket a Product, but if you buy online and have them delivered have you bought a Service?

Defining what you provide

This book uses the following categorisations, which are relevant to Technology Business Management but are also relatively generic:

Component	A unit that could have a price, which is only provided to other Products and Services and only consumed by other items in the Cost Model e.g. Storage for Applications.
Product	A unit that could have a price, which can be consumed both within the Cost Model and by business units e.g. Virtual Servers used for Application Development and for Application Delivery.
Service	A unit that could have a price, which is mostly consumed by business units e.g. a desktop workstation.

These definitions all start with the same base statement and differ on the basis of their target consumer. Both of these sections of the definition could be understood as describing purpose and usage, and up to this point do not include any description of attributes which are sometimes used to differentiate a Product from a Service.

The first part of each definition states that 'a unit could have a price' which ties together with the previous Chapter's review of how to model a cost of one unit, the 'Unit Cost'. The definition does not require that a price is set, but is suggesting that at this level there should be a standard definition with measurable units. That the total cost should then enable units to be shown with a Unit Cost, for which a price can be set if that is the business process.

Even without setting a price, identifying the Unit Cost of anything takes it from being abstract to manageable in many cases. It allows you to show your customers how many units they are using and receiving the cost of, and enables you to set up systems that they can interface with to increase or decrease their consumption.

There is often a demand to look at the TCO of applications :- "How much does Application 'J' Cost?" is a question that realistically should be answerable, but the cost of one application in isolation does not provide a useful measure. If you have 2000 applications, you would not expect them all to be the same cost, or that you could save 50% of your cost by cutting the number of applications in half. Asking a similar question in terms of "How much does each transaction delivered by Application 'J' cost?" is a better basis by which to manage.

The second part of each definition statement is more effectively a differentiator based on whether something will be used only as a technology, or has a direct business value. This is much more clearly going to be affected by the scope of a TBM Cost Model, and the definition is written with the assumption that all costs will eventually be aligned to Business Units. The main point to take from this is that you need to segregate the costs which you are using inside your Cost Model from the costs that you are showing your customers.

Product and Service Catalogues

One description of the genesis of a Catalogue is that it usually starts as a list and is then extended with details that make the list useful for reference. A list of applications turned into a database showing the business owner, development manager, creation and decommissioning dates, is just such a Catalogue, and many of these can exist in an organisation.

How many Catalogues are needed?

TBM will not be the only management discipline that requires a Catalogue and the purpose of any Catalogue needs to be kept in mind when it is being developed. A Catalogue should be a reference point containing organised and relevant information. The definition of relevance in this instance is that the consumer of any Service, Product or Component in the Catalogue must be able to see and understand the information they need. From this we return to the question of who the consumers of the catalogued information are, in order to identify how many Catalogues are needed.

The three core stakeholder groups for TBM; Finance, Technology and Business, are all going to need to use a Catalogue, so their requirements must be met.

Finance will already have 'Catalogues', although not given that name, which are the Organisational Structure and Chart of Accounts. On top of this they will often also have a Service Catalogue of their own, which is used for allocating costs to consumers, and is part of formal financial reporting and calculation of tax liability. A TBM Service Catalogue should be very similar to Finance's Service Catalogue so that the real allocation of costs by Finance can be seen to match the costs identified in TBM. The Finance Service Catalogue can be less detailed than the TBM Service Catalogue and does not need to have every TBM Service separately listed but can group some together. As an example, within a TBM environment it might be possible for the Finance Service Catalogue to have a single Service for Technology's End User Services, while additional granularity would be needed for that Service Type for a TBM Service Catalogue. This would make the TBM Service Catalogue an effective superset of the Finance Service Catalogue. This only applies for Technology Services, as the Finance Service Catalogue will also include a wide range of Services for other business functions.

For the most part, Technology Services can be divided into an End User Catalogue and a Technology Catalogue based on their customer profile, although these are often consolidated to one Catalogue without issues being caused. Relating this to the TBM Taxonomy classification of Service Types (Appendix p16), the separation can deliver one Catalogue combining End User Services and Delivery Services, and a separate Catalogue for Platform Services and Infrastructure Services. The main reason to keep separate Catalogues is that there is no need for most customers to see anything except the End User and Delivery Services. This can also be achieved by just showing relevant portions of a Catalogue to the relevant users, as the attributes that need to be collected for Services in both catalogues are nearly identical.

As well as the differences in granularity between Finance's Service Catalogue and the Service Catalogues used for TBM, there can also be a difference in the level of granularity of Services that a Technology function wants to provide to their customers compared to the level which a TBM Catalogue will cover.

Taking an example for End User Services, the TBM Taxonomy defines a Service Category of 'Client Computing' and a Service of 'Computer', with an option to add a further level of Service Offering granularity such as the examples in the Taxonomy of having a 'Standard Desktop' or 'Development Workstation'.

Category	Name	Description
		Type: End User Services
Client Computing		Client Computing includes all the physical and virtual devices and associated services that enable a user to interact with the enterprise's technology systems. This includes desktops, laptops, mobile devices and virtual desktop environments.
	Computer	A selection of IT-provided computers, workstations, laptop or tablet configurations. Each type may be ordered with additional memory and storage. Standard corporate image will be loaded on each device. Requestor may order optional software through the Productivity services. Includes network and remote network access. Standard support package including security, back-up, antivirus, updates and patches, remote access, centralized service desk.

Figure 3: End User Services descriptions (from the TBM Taxonomy v3.0, Appendix p18)

Within the description for this Service, both the Technology Department and its customers may legitimately ask how they should manage extensions or removals to the Service, such as enhanced support or removing remote access. There are multiple ways in which this can be achieved, with the choice being driven by factors such as the size and complexity of the Catalogue as well as

When looking at the Services that will sit in a Business Catalogue, there is a lot less clarity than exists for the Services in Finance and Technology Catalogues. While some other 'Shared Services' functions that work across an organisation can create a Catalogue like those for Technology, the dimensions that a business measures itself on are often less amenable to being classified in a taxonomy.

It is possible to step back from looking at all the individual Catalogues and try to identify the relationships between them. A layer of abstraction covering multiple dimensions such as Organisational, Financial and Risk/Resilience allows this to be visualised, placing each Catalogue on a chart with axes such as the ones shown below.

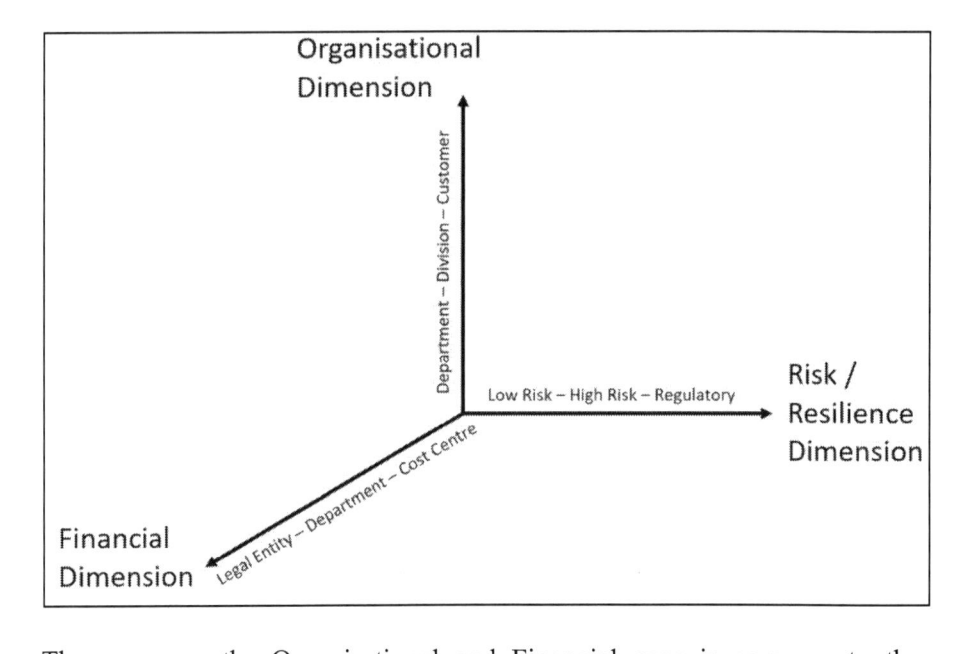

```
                    Organisational
                    Dimension
                         ↑
                         │  Department – Division – Customer
                         │
                         │
                         │        Low Risk – High Risk – Regulatory        Risk /
                         ├──────────────────────────────────────────────→  Resilience
                        ╱                                                  Dimension
                       ╱  Department – Cost Centre
                      ╱
                     ╱  Legal Entity – Department
   Financial       ↙
   Dimension
```

The range on the Organisational and Financial axes is common to the information that is required for TBM Modelling. The Risk / Resilience dimension is additional and not generally required for the alignment of costs in a TBM Cost Model, but is frequently required to collate and report on that output from the Cost Model.

For many business sectors, classification of business functions according to their functional capability and risk, either to the business or to the market, is a legal and regulatory requirement. While this is sometimes aligned to the organisational or financial structure, more often it is an additional view which overlaps into one or both. These requirements generate either additional information in pre-existing Catalogues or, in many cases, cause the creation of new Catalogues to meet new requirements.

Examples from the Banking and Finance sector of why Risk and Resilience is a useful axis to include are the requirements to classify Applications according to their level of risk (e.g. Sarbanes-Oxley), regulatory requirements for separation of various business functions (e.g. German Bank Separation laws and Ring Fencing), and the collation and reporting on Applications according to their business functionality (e.g. for the UK Payment System Regulator).

This does mean that Risk and Resilience is the only possible additional dimension for classifying Catalogues, and it can be replaced by another range which is relevant to a particular business context. The practical treatment of the relationships between Catalogues follows a common set of approaches, whatever dimension is used for this purpose.

Catalogues, hierarchies and process lists can be plotted against the axes as a basis to understand the organisation and flows of information around TBM.

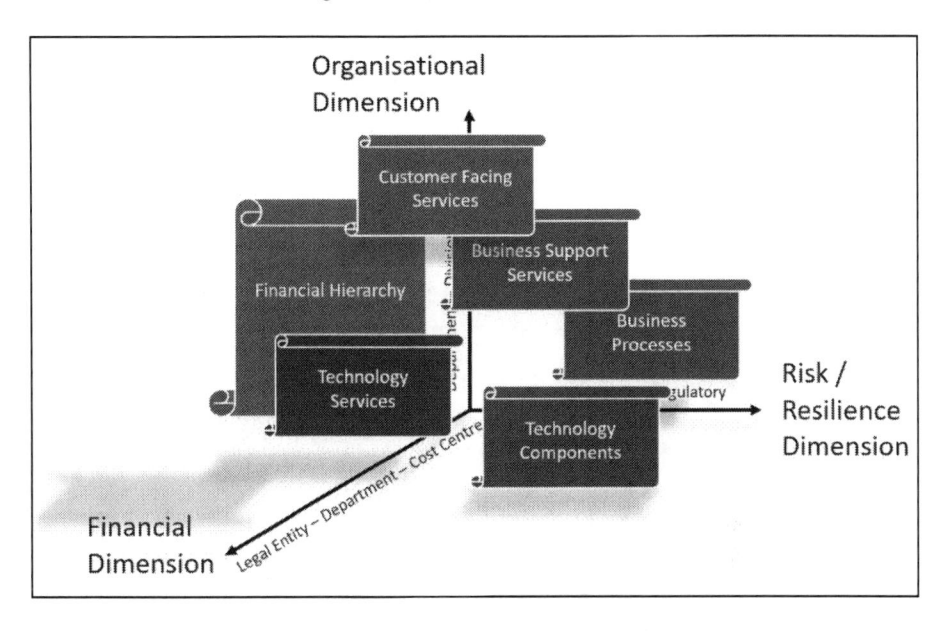

Many of the Catalogues shown above should not be administered by a TBM function, although the alignment of Technology Services to them should be, either by setting a common key or by establishing the cost relationships.

For general Business Management purposes, the benefit of this comes from the ability to look for how the financial information generated from the TBM Cost Model can be used to align across all three axes, as shown below. This extension takes the capabilities beyond Technology and into wider organisational strategy and management.

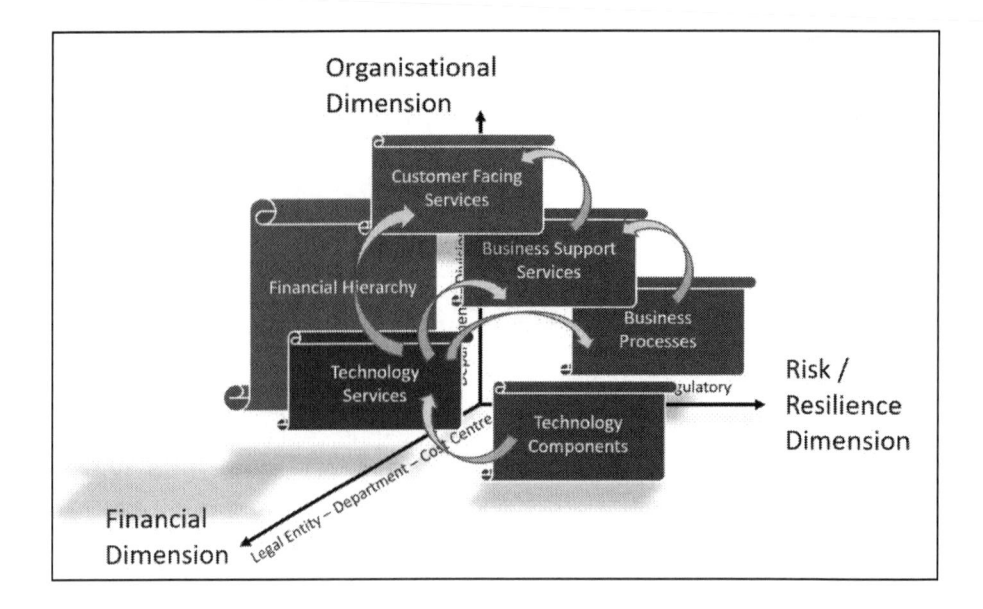

[Figure: Diagram showing Organisational Dimension (top), Risk / Resilience Dimension (right), and Financial Dimension (bottom-left), with interconnected blocks: Customer Facing Services, Business Support Services, Business Processes, Financial Hierarchy, Technology Services, Technology Components, and labels including Regulatory, Legal Entity – Department – Cost Centre.]

Following the flow from the cost of Technology Services it is possible to build a view of how Technology Services costs affect broader business processes and services, right through to an external customer orientation. The main limitation of this is that only the costs explicitly included within the TBM Cost Model will be shown, and any more complete view of the total cost for the rest of the business will need equivalent modelling.

What should be in a Catalogue?

When creating a Catalogue to be used with a TBM Cost Model, whether based on the TBM Taxonomy or on a pre-existing Business Catalogue, useful perspectives to measure against are who is going to use the Catalogue and how.

Without properly noticing, we regularly have experience of multiple catalogues, both offline and online. Our use of the catalogues is as consumers of the information in them, and we often use them without thinking about our role in the relationship or what the company providing the catalogue is trying to sell to us. Without thought, we may not differentiate between two different catalogues from the same company which serve very different purposes and relationships, and may confuse them in ways should be avoided with the catalogues we create for a business purpose.

An example of this is the relationships we have with large IT companies such as Amazon and Microsoft. If we wish to make a purchase of an item; a book or some software, we will be looking for a Catalogue which shows us that specific item with its description and price, possibly augmented with alternative sources, delivery options and related products. If we look to purchase 'Infrastructure as a Service' from those companies, we may find a Catalogue with large numbers of options around locations, sizes, providers, service levels, software providers, and many other factors.

The differences in the Catalogues are based on an expectation by the provider of what we, as the consumer, know about the products and need to be able to choose between. They also allow the provider to set separate prices or service descriptions to help guide us to particular choices, such as whether we want next day delivery.

Within a business context, it is similarly necessary to consider which choices we wish to provide to our customers, and it is often at this point in the creation of a TBM Cost Model that the opportunities occur to help define formal interactions between Technology and Business functions. The Technology Catalogues should show business users, from the Technology perspective, how to spend their money most effectively.

This also leads to an alternate perspective on the use of Catalogues, which is about maintaining interactions over time. The governance of the Catalogue must account for customers' usage throughout the lifecycle of using a Service. Catalogue governance must account for growth and shrinkage in the use of a Service, the lifecycle of each Service, and the need for customers to receive a bill for their ongoing use.

Information in a Catalogue

The types of information that you would expect to be in a Catalogue for a retail company is a useful guide for what you should see in a Business or Technology Service Catalogue. If you consider how you make buying decisions in a non-work environment, both online and offline, the common elements and the levels of detail that you look for are the same that you need to rely on and deliver in a business context.

Name and Description

The most obvious characteristic of a Technology Catalogue is that everything in it should have a name and a description which is clearly understandable. What you expect to see in an online catalogue or marketplace is a good example; there you can usually start with a basic description, and then be given additional detail if needed. It is worth noting that online catalogues do not show you all the information available at once.

Beyond the description that you might expect, a Technology Catalogue should also clearly state when there are specific exclusions to the scope of a Service. If a customer is going to need to add other components in order to obtain a working system, they need to know this at the earliest stage, rather than having to go through multiple cycles of ordering and implementing.

Each item in the Catalogue should also have a 'machine readable' code as well as a name. This is a practical level of abstraction which allows the name to change over time without necessarily affecting other systems. The value of this can easily be underestimated, but an example is the need to change a Service name when a supplier is taken over; the service is unchanged and can keep the same code, but the name will need to be updated.

Cost or Charge

Your customers will also want to understand how they are going to pay for the Services you provide. How this is shown to them will depend on the completeness, strategy and maturity of your TBM implementation, so some choices are shown below.

In an environment where you are showing them a price, you need to state what that price is and what the 'Unit of Measure' is, such as the price 'per GB' of storage, or 'per CPU-hour 'of processing, or 'per PC desktop'. Stating any price implies that you are going to keep it at a stable level for a period, and that you are giving your customers the ability to change the amount they are charged by varying the quantity that they use. This needs to be a deliberate decision and followed up with relevant pricing and governance strategies, discussed in Chapter 15. Defining the 'Unit of Measure' in a Catalogue should be done even if prices are not being set, to help guide people on how to help use the technology efficiently.

If your strategy is to allocate cost based on a formula, the basis of both the cost calculation and the allocation formula should be described. This can lead to a more complex conversation, as customers may wish to know how they can affect either of these factors. Similarly to the situation when showing a price, it is helpful to set the expectation for both how and when it is possible for the customer to affect the cost-base and the allocation factor.

Inventory review, ordering and decommissioning process

Following on from the characteristics of cost or charge, providing information to your customers on how they can increase or decrease their usage of a Service is needed, as this will be their mechanism to control their expense.

The ability to change the level of usage of a Product or Service implies that the customer can see and review and inventory which shows what they are currently being charged for. The inventory itself is not part of the Catalogue, but the ability to review it alongside the Catalogue is a basic requirement so must be described.

As well as the inventory, the processes for changing the level of usage of a Service are not part of TBM, but are more fully developed in other Service Management disciplines such as ITIL.

Service Levels and ownership

Catalogues within the TBM environment do not require information on 'Service Levels', except where they become part of the base description and differentiators of the Service. This does not reduce the requirement to include aspects of the Service Level alongside the other product details, where they are a component of the cost. What the hours of availability for a Service are, and what the response time to a failure or query should be, can both expected by customers to be among the basic attributes of a Service.

As well as including inventory and change process information in the Catalogue relating to Service volumes, information on how to raise queries and issues are core information for catalogued Services. This often extends to identifying an individual 'owner' for each Service, to act as the contact if there is an issue requiring escalation.

How many items should there be in a Catalogue?

The size of any Catalogue might be expected to relate to the size of the organisation that it is used in, but there are multiple approaches that can limit or control that growth. In some respects, the earlier discussion about what we expect from a Catalogue on a personal level apply similarly to Technology Catalogues; we need to be able to look at the Catalogue and find what we need, with sufficient but not excessive detail. That expectation can put a limit on the size of an effective Catalogue and affect choices for how to manage the listed Services.

The structure of Services in the TBM Taxonomy is that there are three defined levels, with a fourth level available for customisation. Looking at the number of items defined in each level of the Taxonomy, from the most consolidated Service Type level to the most granular Service Offering level, we find:

Service Layer	Count of items
Service Type *	7
Service Category *	26
Service	121
Service Offering	Available for user definition

The items in the top two levels, Service Type and Service Category, are shown in the figure below.

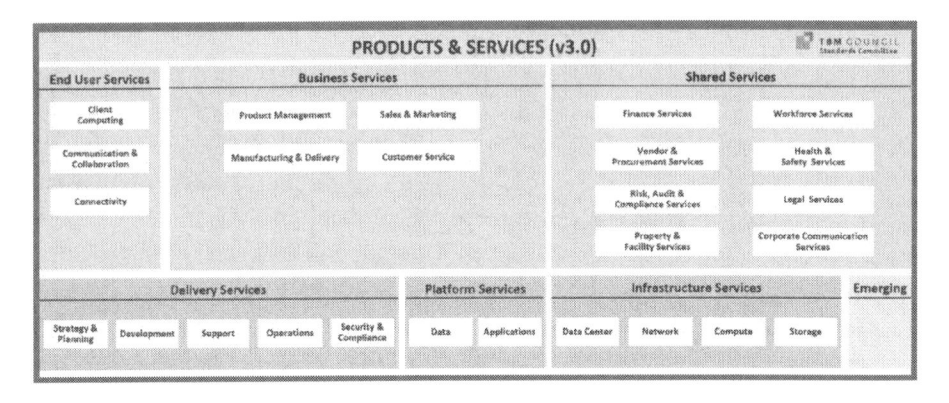

Figure 4: Product and Service Types and Categories (from the TBM Taxonomy v3.0, Appendix p16)

The two ways in which information from a Catalogue will most frequently be used are for ongoing charging, and when there is a change in the amount of a Service being consumed.

In practical terms, this provides an effective limit on the number of Services in a Catalogue. If you consider how many items you are ready to choose between on a restaurant menu, you may similarly see different sections for specific courses, but might generally expect the menu length not to exceed a few pages. At the end of a meal, the bill that you receive will have fewer items on it as you will not be shown a zero cost for things you haven't purchased. You would expect an itemised bill showing how many of each item was consumed (although even then it doesn't show you who ate what).

Considering the TBM Taxonomy Products and Services list and the breadth of what is included, the question becomes whether or not the consumers of the Catalogue will need or benefit from any additional level of detail.

A deeper dive into some of the individual Service Categories and Services may suggest that they do not match business priorities. This is not a limiting factor, since there is already an available Service Offering level defined to enable Services to be split by additional differentiators. Additionally, as described earlier, the base TBM Taxonomy is effectively a combination of three Catalogues; Business and Shared Services, End User, and Technology. It would be realistic to treat these Catalogues separately as they have different customer sets, providing more (but still relevant) granularity to each set of customers. Creating and maintaining three Catalogues with between 80 and 120 items in each is a realistic and achievable maximum, as was also described in Chapter 4.

This view of the size and complexity of a Catalogue can be backed up by setting a practical expectation of the relevant cost of any individual Service in a Catalogue. A useful guideline is that no Service should be less than 0.25% of the Catalogue's total cost base, which usually allows for a range of high value items while leaving a manageable 'tail' that does not trail into insignificance.

How a Catalogue changes behaviour

The detail in a Catalogue can affect both how a Service is managed and how it is perceived and used by its customers. This is a relationship which varies and matures, as well as being an effective feedback loop where both the management of the Service, and customer behaviour, affect each other.

More detail on causing behaviours to change through the active use of TBM are covered in Chapter 14, but some items related to the design of the Catalogue are included here.

Perception of a Service starts with its name

As a Catalogue develops and matures, the users of the Catalogue can start to choose between Services based on their impressions or recollections of what is in the individual Services, rather than reviewing each description. This can mean that something as simple as changing the name of a Service causes confusion, as people can no longer find what they expect to look for.

To help them choose accurately between Services can then become as simple as ensuring that Service names do not change over time and are structured carefully to imply and advise the best choices.

If you are given three items in a catalogue to choose between, named for their quality of service as Bronze, Silver and Gold, your choice may be different to when the identical service levels are named Standard, Enhanced and Critical. Organisations may have different perceptions of value and service requirement, but the medal colours are not associated with implications of increasing cost in the same way as the Service descriptions.

Keep ranges open

Customers of Services often wish to use them in a pre-packaged form, rather than having to identify every detailed requirement separately. One of the most common approaches to providing this is to create different sizes of a Service, such as small, medium and large, but ranges can be applied as easily to service quality, risk and multiple other factors.

Impacts of fixing the size for specific Services or Service Offerings can be that customers request exceptions within the size range, or that they request extensions to the range.

The choice of whether to enable customers to have 'a la carte' access to technology choices not listed in a Catalogue is one that needs to be taken in every organisation. The challenge for TBM Cost Modelling is that these exceptions are less likely to be able to be accurately modelled.

The choice of what sizes to offer might seem straightforward, but should account for the possibility that the provided sizes may need to be extended, at both ends and in the middle. Using grilled steak as an example:-

Basic range	Extended range
	Blue
Rare	Rare
	Medium-Rare
Medium	Medium
	Medium-Well done
Well done	Well done
	Burnt

A further example is in the classification of the impact of various risks associated with Business Services, which might be measured in terms of their financial impact. Two categorisations are shown, but only the 'open' range can be extended sensibly if a new top level needs to be added to the Risk Impact column.

Risk Impact	Closed range	Open range
> $250,000	A	D
$50,000 – $250,000	B	C
$5,000 – $50,000	C	B
< $5,000	D	A

It is unlikely that this range will ever be extended to account for lower values, but quite likely that it will need higher value categories. Choosing the 'closed' range does not leave room for expansion beyond 'A', while category 'E' can be simply added to the 'open' range.

Keeping up-to-date

Part of the ongoing provision of a Technology Service is managing the 'lifecycle' of both the overall Service and its components. A Service Owner running a Database Service may need to ensure that they are using up-to-date, supported software and multiple other components. This leaves a choice as to whether or not to show the different versions as different Services.

Every Service in a Catalogue must be expected to be managed within a lifecycle of its own, from creation through to retirement, but becomes much harder to manage, both within the context of a Catalogue and a TBM Cost Model, if it changes frequently.

It is possible to make changes to components of a Service without changing the Service description. This is a good practice to follow, while continuing to separately identify to customers any items relevant to the lifecycle of the components. In this respect, it is best to leave information on software or hardware versions out of the description of a Service.

Within the example of managing a Database Service description in a Catalogue, it would be possible to differentiate 'Supported' and 'End-of-life' options. These would be identified through their description in the Catalogue, possibly with updates showing specific software versions and the dates on which their support ends. This would be backed up within the TBM Cost

Model by aligning the costs of extended support contracts against the 'End-of-life' Service, giving a clear financial incentive to the users to move off this product.

An enhancement of this is that customers would not be allowed to increase their use of the 'End of life' Service by buying additional instances, and that any database instances that they had would be automatically switched to the 'End-of-life' Service at the relevant time. This interaction would be part of the Service Owner's overall relationship with the customer, providing them a financial as well as Service Management interaction point to help keep software updated.

A useful factor in affecting behaviour within an organisation, compared to within an open market, is that management direction and actions can be significantly more effective.

Managing vendors

It is sometimes necessary but not generally recommended to identify in a Technology Catalogue which vendor provides a Service. The underlying logic is similar to keeping version information out Catalogue entries; that what the customer sees in the Catalogue should be directly relevant to their choice of a Service.

One practical example of this is in the provision of Windows and Linux server capabilities as virtual servers. An identical Service can be provided by multiple vendors, so there is generally no expectation that the vendor would be identified in the Service name. If the Technology department choose to change vendor on the basis of cost or quality of service, this does not need to be exposed to their customers through the Catalogue.

There are occasions when it might be seen as relevant to show the vendor name in a Catalogue, for example where a strategic change from one vendor to another is being made and there is financial or organisational pressure to show the costs separately. This is closer to the issue of managing versions in a Catalogue, discussed in the previous section, than it is related to the vendor relationship directly. It is useful to review whether this information can be provided directly to customers, rather than as a Catalogue change.

Ownership and governance of Catalogues

As Catalogues are critical components of a full Technology Business Management implementation and ongoing processes, understanding their ownership and governance becomes a critical factor in enabling ongoing maintenance of a TBM Cost Model.

While it might seem obvious that a Catalogue needs ownership, within the context of a complex business it is possible to find that the identification of Catalogues and their owners is no more complete than for other data sources. Many separate and partially overlapping Catalogues may exist, creating a requirement for a level of consolidation to be done in order to deliver value from Technology Business Management. While it is generally advisable not to take ownership of data sources as part of a TBM Cost Model, this is one area where delivering clarity of governance and change management may be more important to the practical success of TBM than resolving an underlying business ownership issue.

The Organisational Structure

The easiest Catalogue to identify is the Organisational Structure, which also provides a base for understanding what will be required to deliver governance processes for managing other Catalogues.

Ownership of the Organisational Structure, as a Catalogue, sits most commonly within the Finance organisation, showing the Cost Centres and how these are aggregated to the organisational or management hierarchy. This is not the Chart of Accounts, which is a separate Catalogue owned by the Finance organisation and shows how accounts and ledgers relate to each other.

The ownership of this Organisational Structure is so core to the running of a Finance organisation that the associated governance may almost be a business as usual process. A clearly documented hierarchy of the organisation, from the company level, through various management levels and down to Cost Centres, is a basic requirement for accounting purposes. Other critical information in this Catalogue will be equally well understood and documented, including both the names and codes for each point in the hierarchy, an 'owner' of each Cost Centre (and usually of every other grouping point or node), and potentially other information such as whether the Cost Centre is active, or what currency it uses.

It is immediately clear that this Catalogue is not a single purpose tool just for financial purposes but also reflects the business and organisational structure. Changes to the business must be reflected in a relevant way in the Organisational Structure, so there is a need for business management to communicate to the Finance team what is going to change and when, so that the changes are coordinated.

In an organisation without TBM, there are generally only a few users of this Catalogue outside the Finance organisation and its own systems, so there is little need for further communication and coordination of those changes. This status changes with the integration of this Catalogue into Technology Business Management systems. The Finance team will now have a responsibility to ensure that changes are also notified appropriately to the TBM Office, and that its impacts are understood.

This type of change has to be managed with care and accuracy in all cases, and often in larger organisations it is decided that these changes can only take place on a specific, known, well communicated schedule, such as quarterly or semi-annually. This does not limit the business ability to make organisational changes on a different schedule, but defines when those changes will be reflected in the Financial systems.

The process for this Catalogue change, run within the Finance team, can follow well understood and defined steps from definition, through implementation, verification, approval and roll-out.

Communication and co-ordination will be needed at various times in this, with both the business and TBM Office, depending on the scope and impact of the change. The way in which these changes impact a TBM Cost Model may also take into account the ability and requirement to make historic restatements of the ownership of cost, which the TBM Office must ensure are understood.

The Finance Service Catalogue

The Financial organisation may also own a Service Catalogue. This can take multiple forms and generally provides the list of Services that are used to charge or allocate cost from one organisational entity to another, but sometimes as a 'Work Breakdown Structure' to provide immediate identification and functional grouping of ledger entries.

These Services and 'Work Breakdown Structure' Catalogues can be used to enable different capabilities within a TBM Cost Model. The 'Work Breakdown Structure' is useful as a tool to help map costs to the appropriate IT Tower within the TBM Taxonomy, while a full Service Catalogue should compare more directly to the outputs of the TBM Cost Model.

The phrasing in the previous sentence about where a Finance Service Catalogue maps to a TBM Cost Model is deliberately awkward, as it is one of the scope definitions that will vary between organisations. If any organisation is looking to use Technology Business Management to manage the cost of technology infrastructure but not applications, the Service Catalogue for Finance and TBM Cost Modelling will meet at the level where the Technology organisation's infrastructure costs are distributed to its customers. For an organisation where the TBM Cost Model extends to providing Business Services, this is the point at which the Finance and TBM Catalogues are expected to be linked.

The linkage must also be recognised as not necessarily being like for like, although it will generally be the Service Catalogue in the TBM Cost Model which will be more granular. This will be a Business and Finance management decision, driven by requirements for efficient financial management at both operational and regulatory levels.

Using the list of End User Services from the TBM Taxonomy as an example, the choice may be that rather than list and manage every End User Service Offering or End User Service as separate financial transactions between Technology and the Business, only the three End User Service Categories are listed in the Finance Service Catalogue.

End User Services		
Client Computing	**Communication & Collaboration**	**Connectivity**
• Computer • Mobile • Bring Your Own Device • Virtual Client	• Collaboration • Communication • Productivity • Print	• Network Access • Remote Access

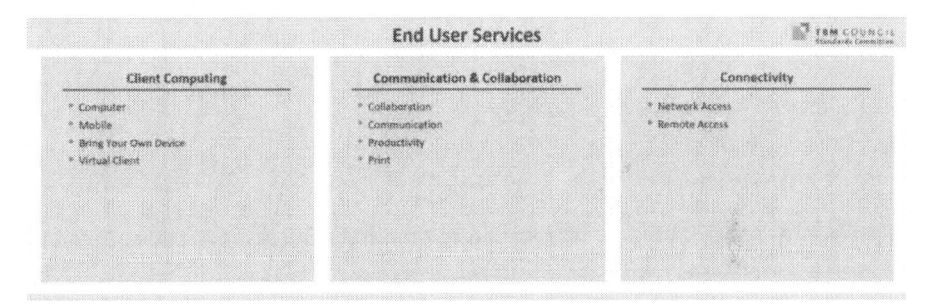

Figure 5: End User Services Type, Category and Services (from the TBM Taxonomy 3.0, Appendix p18)

The organisation receiving these costs as an allocation or charge would see the consolidated amounts for Client Computing, Communication & Collaboration, and Connectivity Services in their financial reports, and then be able to review the detail via the TBM Cost Model.

The implications for managing changes to the Finance Service Catalogue and the TBM Service Catalogue are potentially more complex than for changes to the Organisational Structure Catalogue, so need close cooperation between the Catalogue owners.

The example above is using the TBM Taxonomy as the basis for a company's Finance Service Catalogue, which is not likely to be the starting point in any organisation. It may also not be the relevant end point that a company wants to move to, but ensuring that the specific mapping between a TBM Cost Model and the financial systems exists is a pre-requisite if there is an intention for TBM to provide a Chargeback capability for Technology costs.

With the ownership of the Finance Service Catalogue obviously being with the Finance organisation, they will also own both the change management process and timeline for it. If change to the Finance Service Catalogue is required from a TBM perspective, it is important to understand both process and timeline, and to interact with them effectively. These types of changes may be less frequent than organisation changes and may only be allowed annually as part of a budget process, although they may also be possible in the same cycles as Finance Hierarchy changes.

The impact of these changes is to Finance systems, Technology (through TBM) and the Business (as customers), so communication and coordination need to take all three groups of stakeholders into account.

Changes at this level may also need to be modelled in advance so that cost impacts are understood and approved. Although this requires a level of TBM maturity that should not be underestimated, it can be delivered with a TBM model as part of a budget or forecast cycle.

Technology Catalogues

Identifying what is a Catalogue within the context of a TBM Cost Model can result in identifying multiple options. As described below using the TBM Taxonomy, these may include managing the IT Towers as a Catalogue, and one or more Catalogues of TBM Taxonomy defined Products and Services. It may include a completely separate set of Catalogues based on pre-existing business systems and lists, either consolidated or distributed.

There is a balance is between using an available standard such as the TBM Taxonomy, compared to the accuracy of a pre-existing Catalogue which is already specific to the business. Using the TBM Taxonomy as the basis of several Catalogues is reviewed below.

IT Towers

It is useful to note that the IT Towers specified in the TBM Taxonomy are a broad and generic specification for aligning IT cost, which there is value in using because technology is not business specific at that level. Choosing to use the standard IT Towers in a TBM Cost Model, even if not migrating to this structure for operational technology management purposes, does require that the IT Tower structure is treated as a Catalogue with both some level of ownership and defined governance.

Ownership of the IT Tower structure will generally be held by the TBM Office and changes should be infrequent and mostly only affect the Technology function, so the process can be a less formal than is needed for customer facing Service Catalogues.

The question does arise as to whether there is a need for individuals to be identified as owners of IT Towers (and Sub-Towers) in the same way as there are clear owners of Cost Centres within the Finance layer and owners of individual Products and Services. This tends to be a decision made by the management of the Technology organisation, rather than being a requirement of TBM, although some organisations have restructured their Technology function to align with the TBM Taxonomy at this level.

Infrastructure and Service Catalogues

One or more Technology Catalogues will need to exist for Services that are provided to non-technology users. Where these Catalogues already exist and meet the requirements described at the beginning of this Chapter, the key requirement for their use within a TBM Cost Model is that they are well governed and that TBM becomes a part of their change process.

In the absence of such Catalogues, or in the presence of multiple Catalogues with different capabilities and potential overlaps, choices need to be made on what to use in a TBM Cost Model. This is so critical to the successful implementation of TBM that some level of intermediate ownership should be taken by the TBM Office. This may be to consolidate the current Catalogues to a relevant format, or may require creation of additional material to fill gaps, but it will not be possible to complete a TBM Cost Model without a functional Technology Service Catalogue.

A practical effect of creating such a Catalogue is that it must be shared with technology users. This helps to identify to them exactly what Technology Services are being delivered, reinforcing one of the key impacts of Technology Business Management; that people should be able to understand the value of technology and not just its cost.

> *It is surprising how much value consumers of technology gain from being handed a paper copy of the Technology Service Catalogue, indexed to show its structure.*

In a mature TBM environment, governance and change management of Technology Service Catalogues can become one of the most important parts of managing a TBM Cost Model, as the impacts of changes will be directly received by business customers as changes in their cost of IT. Changes to prices in a Chargeback environment are an obvious factor, but business users can be impacted by the introduction or removal of Services, changes in the description of a Service (such as raising or lowering support levels), or by changes in the measurement of units being delivered.

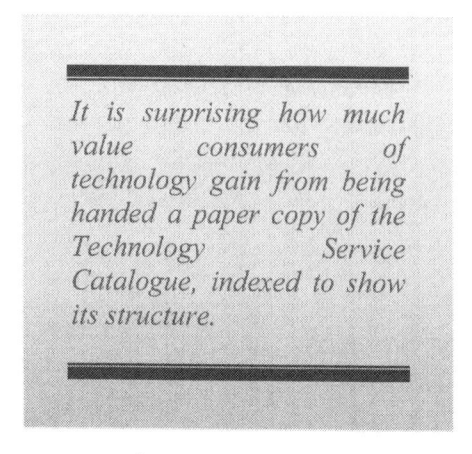

Governance of Technology Catalogues

In Chapter 3, part of the description of the purpose of TBM was that the cost should be equitably aligned to its consumers, so changes to the Technology Catalogues need to be reviewed particularly in terms of their impact on consumers. This is clearly not just a topic that is just about the 'mid-point' for TBM (as shown in this Chapter's title) but one that continues through into a mature TBM environment.

Managing changes to these Catalogues, and in fact to any Catalogue, is the responsibility of the Catalogue owner. As this may be a TBM Office responsibility, it is worth looking at a few specific suggestions for how to do this.

As for all previous descriptions of changes to a Catalogue, changes to the Technology Service Catalogue need to go through formal processes of request and definition, implementation, verification, approval and roll-out, along with relevant communication and co-ordination.

Specifically for these Technology Catalogues, it is useful to set a baseline position that prescribes change to Catalogues as an annual cycle. This allows an adequate timeline, described below, to be applied across all Technology Services. It also ties in with the requirement described earlier in this chapter that the Technology Service Catalogue be linked to the Finance Service Catalogue so that technology costs can be allocated or charged to the business. Although this will particularly apply in a Chargeback environment, it is a useful discipline to apply.

Month	Activity
January	Prepare process for Catalogue Change Management
February	Communicate Catalogue Change Process to Service Owners
March	Gather Service Change Requests for next year's Catalogue
April	Collect full details for Change Requests
May	Validate Change Requests with Technology Management
June	Test Change Request impacts in a TBM Cost Model
July	Final approval of changes to Service Catalogue
August	Communicate changes and expected impact to customers
September	Use updated Service Catalogue for Budget Modelling

The timeline to deliver changes can be worked backwards from the point at which Finance and Technology's Service Catalogue changes are first used, which is the same point in time at which the next year's Budget is created. Prior to this, you need enough time to identify all the changes, ensure that there is sufficient detail about them to work out the cost and how it will align in the TBM Cost Model, build that model and verify that it is working as planned, gain approval for all the changes, and communicate them to customers. This is an extended exercise which can be scheduled over nine steps, from initial planning and communication to final rollout as shown above, in this example with each step scheduled to take a month.

Enabling Operation of a TBM Cost Model

Technology Business Management has operational components as well as analytical and actionable ones. Failure to implement a consistent and smooth operational process will make it impossible for users to rely on the output from TBM.

The main components of this process have already been covered in Chapter 5 in terms of collecting data, validating it as the input to a TBM Cost Model and ensuring that the output is reasonable. The detailed scheduling of month-end processes will be company specific, although there are some topics which can be useful to understand and look at for improvement over time.

Month-end scheduling of TBM operations

Regular month-end General Ledger input is the primary driver for many TBM implementations. The timing of the availability of this data is controlled by the Finance organisation and often measured in terms of 'Working Days' around the start of a month, so Working Day 1 (WD1) is the first weekday of the month (unless that day is a holiday e.g. in January or, in some countries, May).

The Finance department processes may then include running a 'Pre-Close' or 'Flash' calculation of the General Ledger, which they check and use as the basis to correct errors. This may happen on the last day of the prior month, for example on Working Day -1, or early in the new month. They will then move to close the Ledgers for the completed month, at which point there is not expected to be any further change to the General Ledger.

The initial implementation of a TBM Cost Model month end process will use the month-end close General Ledger as its source, as the data is expected to be complete and validated. The challenge with this is that it may take several working days after the start of the month for this to happen, for example, with financial data not available to TBM until WD8 of a month and TBM output not validated and published until the third week of a month.

This cycle needs to be communicated and understood by TBM users. Without knowledge of financial systems, you might be tempted to expect that in September you can review August information. With the timeline above, the most recent TBM data available may still be that for the July month-end, until September 20th when August data has been processed.

While the financial processes cannot be hurried, the option exists in more mature TBM environments to run a 'Pre-Close' process for a TBM Cost Model in the same way that Finance create a 'Pre-Close' General Ledger. The collection of non-financial data sources needs to be planned to work on the same accelerated timeline, but this can make a TBM Cost Model function as a more responsive management information system, with output more closely in line with Finance timelines.

Validation of TBM results

Validation of a TBM Model is a function which is part of an implementation, but then becomes an ongoing process that is repeated with every month-end or change cycle. The validation does not need to be for every logic step and calculation of the Model, but moves to be based on confirmation that the output is realistic i.e. that material changes are based on expected changes to the inputs rather than incorrect assumptions or implementations within the Model.

There are a series of checks which can help with this validation that apply to a full TBM Cost Model but can also be used at a more granular level. One of these is to look for places where cost is not flowing all the way from the General Ledger to the Business Services which are chargeable to customers.

It is a useful practice when building a TBM Cost Model to ensure that all costs flow through the Model, even if it requires some temporary logic, Products or Services to be created to enable this. The process of ensuring that these otherwise unallocated costs are traced and corrected is part of the process of maturing the Cost Model.

With an expectation that no costs are excluded from modelling, their appearance shows clearly where there are gaps in data or logic. The identification of either issue can then be pursued by making one of two types of validation check; that your TBM Cost Model is still working as expected (i.e. no costs are lost), and that changes are as expected (month-on-month changes) and where.

Model Level	Granularity of report	Test	Expected outcome
General Ledger	Cost Centre or higher level in hierarchy	Does the value match the input from Finance?	Values match exactly
		Has the value changed from previous month?	Change is within pre-specified limits or already identified by Finance
IT Towers	IT Tower (possibly IT Sub-Tower)	Does the total match with the General Ledger?	No new or unexpected costs failing to reach IT Towers
		Has the value changed from previous month?	Variances match to the same items as for General Ledger
Technology Service Catalogue	Service Type and Service Group (possibly each Service)	Does the total match with the General Ledger?	No new or unexpected costs failing to reach Services
		Has the value changed from previous month?	Variances match with known changes to inventory or cost

A validation report enabling the TBM Office to analyse this information can be a simple set of tables and tests, such as those above, with the approach documented for whether and how these should be reviewed accepted or fixed. A useful side effect of this report is that it can be used to validate changes to the TBM Cost Model as well as for month-end processing, as the same tests will enable a 'before and after' comparison of changes.

Chapter 11. Reaching the point of 'But …'

Building a Technology Business Management capability, based on a Cost Model or smaller scale tactical implementations, requires as much thought and effort put into building trust and confidence as it does on technical aspects. The consolidation of information into a central repository, and the way that it will be used, can attract negative comment in an organisation. Responding to these types of challenge requires understanding of both the role of Technology Business Management and the technical detail of an implementation.

Rolling out a TBM Cost Model within an organisation, and particularly to one that has not worked with internally priced Products and Services before, requires cycles of education, problem solving and query handling. There is a potentially steep learning curve for people who are seeing the results of a TBM implementation for the first time. This is not about concepts that they aren't used to seeing outside of a business environment, but how they look at Technology cost.

Education and understanding of the principles of Technology Business Management relevant to each user's role can help set a baseline of knowledge. Ensuring that the education is based on how those users have previously received information, and how that will change, can reduce the volume of queries but will never eliminate them.

But … this information is wrong

There are many reasons why people complain that the information they've been given is wrong, including that they are correct and the data is wrong. Particularly with a Cost Model, which is a synthesis of a wide range of data sources, there is regular opportunity for errors to be introduced into the input data and for it to flow through to create errors in the output.

The first response to this is not to claim that the information is correct, but to understand what is being challenged and whether it is being properly understood. Ensuring that you can recreate the information you're being told is wrong, as well as understanding to what extent or level of materiality you're being challenged, opens up a variety of answers.

Ensuring simple data validity

The earliest point in a TBM Cost Model implementation at which people are usually exposed to data, is when the Finance organisation gets to see their initial input replayed to them, grouped into the TBM Cost Pools and Sub-Pools, but otherwise essentially unchanged. Errors at this stage are likely to be limited, and analysis limited to ensuring a simple data match, but this is insufficient for later Cost Modelling.

If a significant expense item reaches the Finance organisation late in their monthly cycle, it can be correct for them to enter it into the General Ledger on a temporary or dummy account code. This enables them to reconcile their records sufficiently for financial and regulatory reporting, and they have the capability to reverse those entries and book them correctly in the next accounting period.

The impact of this behaviour in a TBM Cost Model is that those expenses are likely to appear in the wrong place at later stages (e.g. against the wrong Application) and that any sort of monthly trend reporting which includes the original expenses, and their later reversal, will show as inconsistencies and outliers.

The extent of this specific type of issue is, by definition, unpredictable in both timing and scale; a major cash expense may show up one month and be reversed and booked as a depreciating asset in the next, but neither the Finance department nor anyone else can be sure of that in advance.

There can be mechanisms open to a TBM Office to work with Finance to understand these as they occur, in which case communicating the causes of these known variances with the release of monthly TBM data can be a valuable way to manage expectations as well as build trust.

Differentiating the basis of a question

As you build up a TBM Cost Model beyond Finances and into the IT Towers, Applications and Services layers, the importance of understanding what information is being challenged increases.

In an initial TBM implementation, many queries about the results and the information being presented can be answered by explaining the modelling process and logic. A regular example in an onsite computing environment is that the cost of Servers to an Application Development manager suddenly appears to increase. The explanation for this could be that the cost they used to see was just that of the hardware depreciation and Operating System software license, but they are now also being shown the cost of associated maintenance, system administration, and Data Centre costs.

Further queries about the logic by which each of these component costs are calculated do occur, each of which should have a known answer that is justified by the TBM Cost Model and data. Once this query has been explained and understood, it is worth making sure that it becomes part of further training, a list of Frequently Asked Questions, or similar knowledge base.

This explanatory approach is not limited to traditional IT environments but applies to Cloud deployments too. While each Cloud Service being purchased may be fully featured, it is rare that there is a single component that matches completely with a business or application requirement, so multiple associated services and their costs must be consolidated. Tagging of Cloud Services, so that each instance can be associated with the relevant application or component, enables costs to be grouped. Whether that tagging is complete and how to manage costs of untagged Cloud Services can both impact on the way in which you manage costs within your own Cost Model. This is similar to the issue of how to manage costs of unused storage capacity reviewed in Chapter 9. How administration and management costs are included on top of this also needs to be justifiable and explainable to your customers.

Tracing the source of cost

When a question about the information provided from a TBM Cost Model has been answered logically, but the values are still being challenged, it can be necessary to work back from the perceived error and look at what its sources are.

It is generally advisable to approach this type of analysis on the basis of materiality; starting with the highest value cost sources and working down the list if necessary. At each step, checking for obvious abnormalities in the types of costs and tracing the cause of those is needed, but there is a limit to the point at which this is useful.

At a certain point in this analysis, it is possible that you should decide that there is no business value in continuing. This may actually be at the very start where a query is going to cost more to answer than the potential value to be gained. Before discounting the query it is necessary to check whether you have been asked to look at a single symptom of a wider issue, rather than whether a data point is right or wrong.

An example from a fully mature and large scale TBM environment is a query from a business manager about being charged for equipment of users who have left the organisation. While each item being charged may only be a few hundred dollars within a multi-million cost base, the underlying question is whether the entire inventory that you have used is valid.

Errors do happen

You must not discount the possibility that there are real errors within either the data or logic of a TBM Cost Model and that these are the reason why something is being queried.

At a practical level, most of the logic errors in a Cost Model should be identified as part of the process of building the Model and validating the output, but not all will. Some errors will be created after a Model has been built, by changes in technology or organisation so that, for example, costs which had been aligned to one Service move organisationally and end up aligned to another.

> *Materiality; whether a cost affects a business outcome, varies according to each user's perspective. I was asked by a business administrator about three months of $0.89 charges in a $4 billion TBM Cost Model, because they had been told to query everything.*

Validation of the output of a Model becomes hugely important to the ongoing level of trust that is placed in the data, both during the build phase and during each subsequent data or model update. This validation is not something that should generally be left to the users, but is a responsibility of the organisation running the Model.

Understanding where each material variance is in a TBM Cost Model, every time there is a change, is a first step in this process. Tracing the causes of those variances, and documenting and communicating them alongside the release of the data to users, need to be steps that are taken to get beyond the "But …" stage of implementing TBM in an organisation.

Don't do it ... again

A TBM Cost Model and its data may be challenged from end to end, and there are a few choices for ways in which to build a Cost Model that are made completely impractical by the need to be able to trace and explain the source of costs. One such choice is the implementation of a 'recursive' Cost Model, as described in Chapter 7 – 'Don't do it'. While it is possible to justify logically in some instances, the ability to unwind a recursive cost allocation, and explain the process, is not practical.

If there is a request to implement any recursive capability within a TBM Cost Model, a general explanation of how it limits the ability to trace and explain costs must be part of the education and documentation of the system.

Another situation which will reduce the ability to explain or justify TBM modelled costs is over-complexity. This can either be the introduction of too many exceptions, making it very difficult to tell whether any costs are the result of the standard modelling approach or some additional logic, or simply creating non-standard models without transparency.

It is possible to mitigate for exceptions and complexity by adding in specific transparency on them, for example through additional reports and explanations, but it is easier to manage this by limiting their introduction in the first place.

But ... this doesn't match with other numbers

Implementing Technology Business Management disciplines and tools into an organisation will impact people differently, depending particularly on whether or not they have a pre-existing equivalent approach.

In most cases, regardless of the starting point, some level of Financial reporting will have been available to the managers who will be starting to use TBM outputs, so you need to be able to explain how to reconcile the two sets of numbers.

A manager is likely to query when the cost apparently increases for a Component, Product or Service that they thought they knew. The underlying cause of this will usually be that additional Component costs are included which the manager previously didn't see. Although it is not always practical, there are times when one or more reports can be used to demonstrate the costs that were previously shown alongside the new total. This type of transitional approach is useful in establishing trust in TBM reports, although it is difficult to maintain consistency and understanding between two different reporting approaches for an extended period.

As an example, a manager who was previously responsible for a team developing and supporting an Application may know the costs of their own Cost Centres. Showing them the full cost of their Application, including server instances and storage, can be surprising but easily made visible through TBM reporting. Explaining to them also that the cost of their team isn't just the salaries and benefits but also the cost of office space and support from the company's personnel department, may also be easy to explain but can be difficult to show in detail.

The total's right, so we're talking about details

As previously noted, one basic requirement to help people believe and trust the output of TBM Cost Modelling is to be able to adequately explain the relationship of the TBM reports to the underlying Financial information. If a TBM Cost Model can be described in terms of the value of the Financial inputs being the same as the value shown for Services, people will generally understand that the whole of that cost must be aligned somewhere. The discussion from this point is not about removing costs from a Service and from the Model, but whether or not they are in the right place.

The TBM Taxonomy provides a structure that can be used to help ensure and validate the completeness of a model, based on the core layers of the Taxonomy, as shown in the figure below. The starting point is the total value in the General Ledger input to the TBM Cost Model. The exact scope of this should be clearly identified, as described in Chapter 6, about 'Inputs to the Cost Model', and becomes the baseline value which you are trying to reconcile to at each subsequent abstraction layer.

The first point at which you should be able to validate that all costs are still visible is at the IT Towers. These are defined as individual and separate costs and there should not be any costs flowing from one IT Tower to another, so the total costs at this level should equal the baseline value.

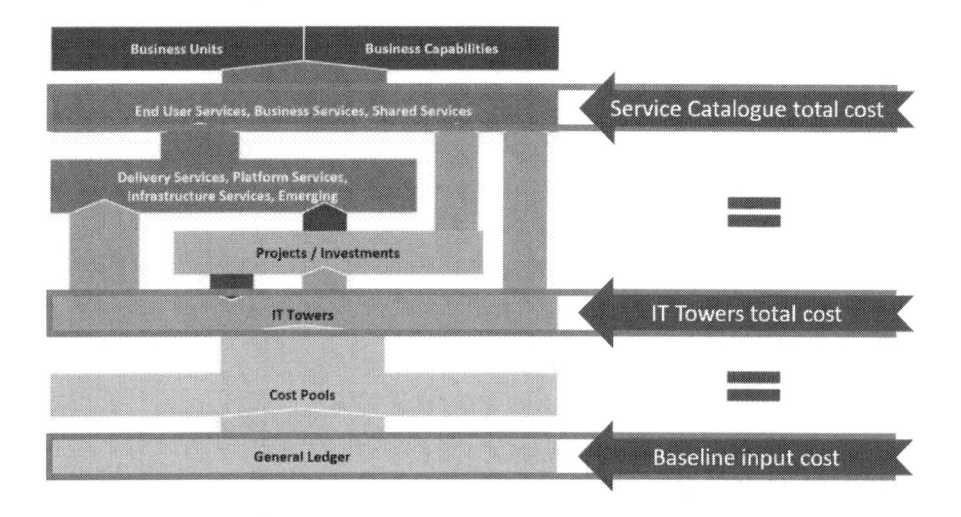

Figure 6: Equal cost points in the TBM Taxonomy (based on the TBM Taxonomy v3.0, Appendix p2)

Once costs have been modelled beyond IT Towers, it can be more complex to define another point at which they are next measurable on a consolidated basis. A generalised approach is to use the assumption that 'someone' needs to pay for all costs of the Technology department, and that will ultimately be the Business Units. From this assumption, the point in a TBM Cost Model at which the Service Catalogue is exposed to those customers becomes the point at which the total costs can be measured for validation against the baseline.

The major simplification implicit in this approach is that it is frequently not possible to accurately model all costs to IT Towers or into the Service Catalogue due to missing data or incomplete modelling logic. It is best to define a general method for managing this when building a TBM Cost Model. This can range between accepting the gaps but measuring and reporting them, through creating an 'Overhead' category into which the costs are placed until they can be resolved, to forcing all costs into Services. The choice of which of these to use, or whether to use different approaches according to circumstances, is not one that will have the same answer for every organisation.

But ... that isn't how it actually works

'Everyone knows ...' is a dangerous phrase when reviewing TBM reports and analysis. It can be heard applied to the descriptions of Services, the metrics used for measuring the capacity or consumption of Technology, through to expectations on the total cost of Services. Where that knowledge or the equivalent assumptions are not in line with what a TBM Cost Model is showing, it can be necessary to provide much more support than just providing additional data to the people who are challenging the information.

A few examples below, across End User Services, Platform Services, and Infrastructure Services provided by the Technology department can demonstrate this depth.

Technology Services are easy to understand

When buying items on the internet, our personal transactions are generally quite simple; we identify a product, put it in a basket and specify how many we want, and then go through a checkout process to pay for it. This is the process that everyone knows, and without specific knowledge they often assume that this also applies to the purchase of Technology Services.

There are times when this assumption holds true, such as when purchasing Software as a Service, when you are more likely to be presented with a single all-in price that includes all necessary underlying components. The same does not generally apply to what are described as Platform Services in the TBM Taxonomy; application infrastructure that enables business-facing Applications and Services.

These transactions often require specialist knowledge, at a detailed level, to understand which Cloud-based components to use and on what basis. A generic assumption that you can buy 'a database service' online in the same way that you would buy a vacuum cleaner is incorrect.

The user of an Application doesn't need to understand this complexity to and level further than the above characterisation. Setting an expectation about how their costs will be impacted by how they use the Application, for example that more transactions will cost more money, is a practical basis for them to understand the complexity being managed on their behalf. A defensible TBM Cost Model will still be able to relate those costs to their source components, if the user still wants all the details of compute, memory, operating system, support, storage, replication, backups, database licenses and so on.

Technology infrastructure is simple and standard

Among the characteristics of Technology Products and Services described in the last chapter, two of the most important are the description, and the 'Unit of Measure'. This is an area with multiple opportunities for a TBM Cost Model to differ from reality in interesting ways.

As shown previously, one of the areas where there can be a gap between people's understanding of the Unit of Measure is for Storage. Although there will be a useful common understanding of what a Gigabyte or a Terabyte is, the use of these terms within a Service Catalogue or to describe the quantity of a Component, Product or Service can easily be misleading.

As an example, let's look at some possible Storage products with the descriptions below, all of which are sold with a Gigabyte Unit of Measure:-

Basic Storage	Data is stored in the Data Centre
Storage Service	Data is stored in the Data Centre and a backup to Tape taken daily
Replicated Storage	Two copies of data are stored in one Data Centre and a third copy in an alternative Data Centres
Offline Backup	Data is backed up to Tape daily

Even for Basic Storage, a Gigabyte of data is probably not exactly as described, but the basic understanding is that you can store 'up to' a Gigabyte of data. You will actually be paying for a Gigabyte of capacity rather than for the amount of space that you use; a Gigabyte of consumption.

If you were using that type of Storage Service, you'd probably also want to make sure that your data was saved in case of problems, so you would also use the Offline Backup Service. How much of that would you use? If you were using your full Gigabyte of disk and it is backed up daily to Tape, that may well be counted as one Gigabyte for each day, possibly around 30 Gigabytes per month. Tape backup options are more complex than that, but the principle remains the same when thinking about the Unit of Measure.

An alternative approach is to use the Storage Service, which combines the Basic Storage and Offline Backup, as shown in the second description. In this case, your Gigabyte of Serviced Storage is defined as including a daily backup of that data. A Gigabyte in this instance includes both a Gigabyte of online storage and its offline storage within the Unit of Measure.

A final example extends the online storage capability by providing redundancy both locally and remotely, meaning a copy is available in case either a disk or a Data Centre fails. In this case the description says that there are two copies of your data on disk in one Data Centre, plus a third copy in another Data Centre. The answer to how much data you have stored is still one Gigabyte, but the amount of disk capacity you need to pay for is three Gigabytes.

Similar issues with the understanding of a Unit of Measure occur in both traditional and modern compute environments, such as for the Mainframe and for Cloud Compute as described below. As with the previous Storage examples, part of the response to questioning on these topics is to rely on having a good description within your Service Catalogue, along with documentation of the logical processes of your TBM Cost Model so that you can defend it.

In a traditional, enterprise technology environment, mainframe computers are provided by IBM. They can be split into Logical Partitions (LPARs) and are generally paid for in terms of their 'peak' usage i.e. if there is one time of the day when they are working particularly hard, that peak utilisation is the basis of the contracted cost. A Unit of Measure that is regularly used for Mainframe computing is MIPS (Millions of Instructions Per Second), and often this is shown in a Service Catalogue as the Unit of Measure for Mainframe, but that is not the true measure of usage, or cost, of the system.

MIPS is really a measure of the capacity or maximum available performance of a Mainframe, rather than its ongoing usage. If you take statistics for what Applications are running on the system, they will be measured in terms that are much closer to the Cloud view of computing; something like CPU-hours (or minutes).

Translating between 'MIPS' and 'CPU-hours' is not going to make any difference to a TBM user's understanding of the source of their cost, so it is often easier to be incorrect in the description in favour of living with something that "everyone knows ..." so Mainframes may stay with MIPS as their measure.

This can be challenging for a Technology Manager who understands the difference and has been communicating it. If they have been successful in changing their customers' understanding already, the Unit of Measure should be based on their accomplishment.

The balance between clarity and accuracy must also not get in the way of helping businesses to make good decisions about the use of technology. It can be possible to save money on Mainframe costs by moving compute processing away from the peak time. This will not be visible with a single Unit of Measure for the mainframe, but can be augmented by splitting the Mainframe product into 'Peak' and 'Off Peak' alternatives. This choice can be about helping to deliver cost and technology efficiencies, and will be further investigated in Chapter 14, Changing Behaviour.

This willingness and ability to adjust to material issues within a TBM implementation is a key discipline.

The cost of a Service

On occasions, TBM modelling provides unexpected outcomes, where capabilities open up for an organisation as well as actions developed from its immediate outputs. One area where this can happen is for projects, where a Business Case is part of the justification for making an investment. An operational TBM Cost Model can be used as part of the validation of a Business Case, which can provide unexpected results when the cost of an investment is not fully recognised upfront.

In starting a project to deliver a business move from Desktop Workstations to Virtual Desktop Infrastructure (VDI), there is a common conception that VDI would be cheaper. This would be included in a Business Case, as a statement that money would be saved by reducing the power consumption in the office, not having to upgrade physical PCs and laptops, not needing support staff to visit users to provide hardware support, and not having to pack up and move equipment every time a desk or office move takes place.

A TBM Cost Model for VDI would support some of that 'knowledge' including the reduced costs for desk moves, reduced office power consumption and fewer desktop visits needed by IT Support technicians. On the other side of the equation, there would be increased Data Centre requirements and costs, VDI server infrastructure and storage costs, and the need to upgrade those on a potentially similar timeline to the replaced physical devices.

The level of scrutiny of a Business Case varies between organisations, but it is useful to recognise that one purpose of a Business Case is to sell the benefits of a project, which introduces the possibility that cost projections will be minimised and benefits maximised. The availability of backing financial data from TBM, to support a Business Case such as this, could limit the gaps in the cost projection.

A TBM Cost Model would not guarantee that all costs would be identified, but within this context would limit the possibility of certain classes of cost being overlooked. The impact on Data Centre capacity of increased numbers of Servers is beyond TBM modelling to generally identify, but the standardised cost for equipment in a Data Centre could not be left out of the project justification.

Items such as this can make the Unit Cost of a Virtual Desktop much closer to that of a Desktop Workstation than originally thought, or even higher, so is this a worthwhile move?

The first paragraph in this book extends the TBM acronym from Technology Business Management to include risk and service as non-financial factors that need to be thought about in measuring the business value of Technology. Often those businesses who look at large scale VDI implementations place significant value on those other factors as well as cost, such as the value to them of maintaining and controlling their data in a secure Data Centre environment.

The calculation of the Unit Cost of a Desktop Workstation can expose unexpected results in a situation like this, which may either be justified or be a potential cause of changes to business decisions. Significant items such as this must be managed with care, as will be discussed in Chapter 14 on Changing Behaviour.

In companies with a high level of maturity in their processes for the distribution of technology costs, and those where TBM is reaching maturity, these questions can also extend into budgetary and operational management. In the example above, if the expense of purchasing desktop and laptop computers starts in the hands of the Business Units, but with VDI ends up in a central IT organisation, this change must also be recognised and managed as part of the TBM reporting of the total cost.

But ... I'm different

A number of subject matter experts and specialists will always need to be involved in building a TBM Cost Model, and their input will need to be actively reviewed to balance between practical and perfect modelling. As was reviewed in Chapter 9 – Modelling vs Reality, there is a level of granularity beyond which there is little practical value in adding to a Model, as the results will not be materially affected.

This must not detract from the ability to recognise and manage the cases where a significant difference from the Model does exist, either during the initial build of the Model or subsequently.

The choice of which cases are significant enough to be treated differently will sometimes return to the question of financial materiality, but may also have other causes.

Financial materiality is a variable measure, in that the value that is material to a senior executive in a company will be different to the value that is material to an individual Cost Centre manager. Recognising this and prioritising accordingly are functions of a TBM Office, as is understanding that smaller values can still be material if they are hugely out of line.

An example of this is if Cloud Compute is being charged throughout an organisation at a simplified standard rate but a new application is being built to use different, highly efficient capability. One case is the use of non-time critical 'spot' processing, where Cloud providers sell their excess capacity at significantly reduced rates for a short time. There may be additional complexity and cost to modelling this with TBM, but it could be the difference between whether the new application is worth implementing or not and, in turn, what business decision is taken.

The other main area where it becomes necessary to accept that a TBM Cost Model may not be fully appropriate to calculate costs is when there is insufficient granularity to make a Cost Model work reliably. Aligning technology costs to Services is most likely to be realistic when there is sufficient volume to be able to say that there is an average cost for each item or unit.

As an example, with a single large software contract which is used for only two or three Applications, you will need to look for the correct level of information to align that cost accurately to the Applications, or risk introducing a gap between the Cost Model and perceived reality.

Identifying large financial transactions within a TBM cost base can be a useful identifier for the areas of a Cost Model which will need to be individually managed in this way, giving a way to identify the key people involved early on, and reducing the need for later exceptions to be created.

Chapter 12. Who's making decisions?

In the previous few chapters the focus has been on practicalities of building and running a Technology Business Management operation and Cost Model. In this Chapter we will break from the more technical disciplines to review the organisational impact of Technology Business Management and how to build maturity in an organisation to gain the best advantage from TBM.

In Chapter 3 – 'Where are you going?' the core objective for a TBM implementation was described as 'To manage IT efficiently and equitably align the cost to its consumers.' To achieve this overall, the question is who is setting this as the target and how do both they, and their staff, understand it. Reaching a point where TBM disciplines and outputs are embedded in an organisation and almost unnoticed due to their ubiquity, is a long but achievable process.

The importance of a sponsor for TBM and their role, active during its introduction and then by example while it matures, will be explored further below. The importance of other TBM stakeholders and users will also be reviewed, as it is their actions rather than those of the sponsor that usually dictate how the targets are met.

Good for me, good for the business

A TBM Office needs to work with Financial, Technical and Business stakeholders, each of whom will have specific targets. Those targets will often include financial elements, but most will have primary targets related to strategy, service quality, risk or other business characteristics.

At the level of a project sponsor, or the most senior management engaged in the use of TBM, all of these targets will be visible. Their decision-making will include the choice of how to prioritise the targets within their team, which can lead to co-operating or conflicting directions.

Even within the business environment, individuals think separately about their own goals and the business goals. A TBM Cost Model does not directly recognise these individual boundaries, as the costs in any one Cost Pool, IT Tower, Product or Service are going to be part of a flow in which multiple managers will take ownership at different points. From that position, a TBM delivery function will usually argue for the approach that is best for the efficiency of the company, rather than the individual.

A regularly identifiable example exists within the TBM Taxonomy at the Services level, between Business Services and Delivery Services. A Business Services Manager is likely to have targets for business growth and development of new applications, while a Delivery Services Manager could have targets for reduced support call volumes and faster resolution.

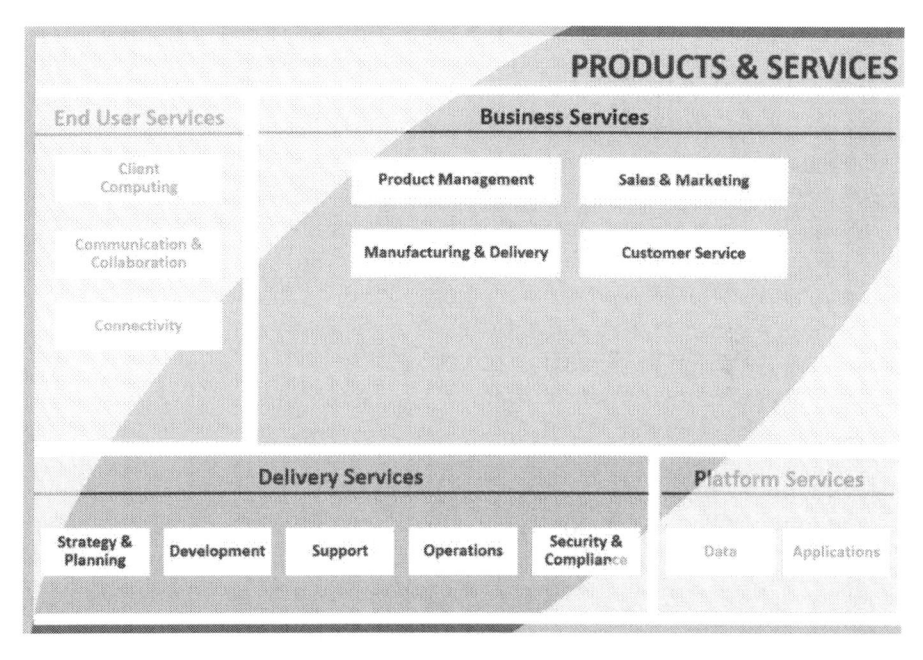

Figure 7: Organisational and TBM structure overlaps and choices (based on a partial extract from the TBM Taxonomy v3.0, Appendix p16)

The opportunity exists for either manager to attempt to reach their targets without co-operation; it doesn't matter to the Business Services Manager if their new Application is crashing regularly as long as the business is growing; conversely it doesn't matter to the Delivery Services Manager if their team is understaffed and do not have the ability to report or support calls for the new Application. Both might still hit their targets but not in a sustainable way.

A Technology Business Management implementation cannot fix this situation but can help identify areas where inefficiencies like this are affecting the cost of a Service. The linkage of Delivery Services costs to Business Services, based on a metric for the time taken on calls for that Business or Application, will help identify one area with problems.

The cost of the Delivery Services function to the Business Services manager may not be their highest priority, but their target for business growth is likely to have elements of both revenue and profitability. Being shown the increased cost of Delivery Services calculated within a TBM Cost Model, and the opportunity to reduce it by improving the Application stability, helps both individuals towards their goals, as well as the overall value to the company.

Who wants what?

The TBM Office needs to understand who is involved in the TBM disciplines in different ways. Stakeholders will include those who are involved regularly, those who are important, those who are engaged, those who are helpful, and often those who show the reverse of each of the prior traits.

In all cases, when a TBM function is delivering information it must keep in mind that this is only part of the user's role. The information should be relevant and self-explanatory for the user's known requirements. It is useful to consider how much time and knowledge each person will put to TBM, such as looking for a Service Owner to put at least one day a month (5%) of their time to managing their Financial and TBM responsibilities.

Senior managers and sponsors

The requirements of the sponsor of a TBM capability are key, but these may be more strategic than immediately obvious. Within the remit of such a sponsor there are likely to be business strategies which cannot be known to their teams, or are delivered over a longer term than is likely to be recognised. These could be related to mergers, acquisitions or divestments of parts of a business, outsourcing, offshoring, or multiple other factors. Without knowledge of these specific directions, guidance from the sponsor about the scope and remit of a TBM implementation must be built into TBM explicitly.

TBM output has been used in the Financial sector and others to enable business planning and decision making in this way. At the time of the 2008 financial crash, information could be taken from TBM systems to understand the technology and business costs associated with markets that were on the point of failing. Financial organisations going through mergers, acquisitions and divestments have similarly taken information to help identify costs and efficiencies, sometimes specifically restructuring their TBM Cost Model to enable this.

As well as their strategic focus, the senior management involved with TBM are often those who are looking at a forecasts and budgets as well as current or historic views. The choices for modelling future costs of Products and Services bring significant additional complexity compared to modelling with real data. This will be covered in more detail in Chapter 15 – 'Delivering Capability and Succeeding'.

Business Users

The requirements of Business Users, and relevant information to enable them to interact with their internal suppliers, can be within the scope of TBM to deliver.

Business users' targets are more likely to appear to be strategic rather than directly operational within TBM. Their requirements are for a broad understanding of the cost and trend of Services, or a high level breakdown within them, rather than direct control of components. Similarly, their view of how costs can be influenced are less likely to be based on Technology Components and Products.

Part of a TBM Office's interface with its customers will involve explaining the relative importance of cost and other metrics to them. Taking the example of a large Financial Services organisation, it is possible to identify Business Units with significantly different approaches to technology cost, service quality and other characteristics. A trading floor will often look at how fast technology can be delivered, with an expectation of immediate support for any issues, but without too much care for cost. A back office or operations function is more likely to be looking for highly reliable technology, with the highest efficiency or lowest cost, but with less urgency.

An additional factor for business users, which is often not seen for other stakeholders, is the need for predictability. This can include the ability to identify and manage variance from a Budget, align cost with growth or shrinkage of their business, or forecast future costs with confidence.

The TBM Office interaction with these customers is likely not to be as direct as it is with the stakeholders involved with Technology management. A Business Relationship Management role may deliver this separately from the TBM Office, adding an additional layer and set of stakeholders. Ensuring that the TBM Service Catalogue is exposed to these users, containing the information relevant to them, is a critical component of this information flow.

For some items in a TBM Service Catalogue, the relationship between business demand and technology cost can be treated as unit based. The description of most End User Services and how the Business can affect their own costs can be quite reliably shown in terms of the number of units consumed and the Unit Cost or price.

For Business Services and Applications, providing predictable costs within a stable demand profile is realistic, with the added expectation that TBM enables technology cost efficiency to be shown to the users.

Following the same model as for End User Services, if a Service is transactional, such as sales in a supermarket, the Unit of Measure for their 'Sales Service' could be 'per sale.' The Unit Cost of a sale would be the consolidated cost of component technologies, products and service offerings calculated through TBM, divided by the volume of sales. For a full 'cost per sale' they would need to add additional costs, such as shopfloor staff, which are generally outside TBM's scope.

If a Unit of Measure such as 'per transaction' is used, which has a range of meanings, its value as a Unit of Measure and for predictability to the Business may be limited. Within the Finance sector, it is possible to look at some Services and say that there is more than one Unit of Measure that should be used.

A 'small business' banking service, for example, might be measured in terms of number of customers, number of bank accounts (as many businesses have multiple), number of transactions on those accounts, account balance, and multiple other metrics. It is quite likely that at least one central Application will exist which contains all of these metrics, leaving the question open as to whether any one of them is the correct Unit of Measure. There may be a purely technical answer to this, but it is more likely that a combination of these metrics will mix together, so that the only expectation that can be set is for directional correctness rather than an accurate prediction.

Resolving this situation can be impossible as, again, there are conflicting targets in pure business management terms. When one department is managing high transaction value customers and another is managing those with low transaction value, the preferred metric for each department will be the one that delivers them the smaller proportion of cost. The high-transaction-value department would like to be allocated cost based on the number of customers, while the low transaction value department would like to use the value being managed.

The ownership of the TBM Service Catalogue, including the definition of the Unit of Measure or other method for distributing costs between Services, is at the core of resolving this type of question, as described in Chapter 10 – 'The mid-point(s)', and is critical to the delivery of a TBM Cost Model that is relevant to business users.

Product and Service managers and owners

For many Technology, and Finance managers, their interactions within an organisation will alter when using TBM tools and disciplines compared to traditional methods. One of the ways in which this happens is a general broadening of their understanding of how their role impacts not just their immediate customer, but those who are further on in the value chain, sometimes right through to Business users.

TBM can help deliver and strengthen the recognition by other stakeholders that the ultimate drivers of demand for their Services are the Business targets and requirements. While on a regular basis they will be concerned with delivering their own Service efficiently, additional focus on the Business requirements can help them prioritise and focus on the most effective way to achieve their individual targets.

If one of a Technology manager's targets is to reduce cost, they may be able to create efficiencies by changing processes, renegotiating support contracts with vendors, or many other actions. If they know that a Business change is going to remove the requirement for an expense, such as stopping the use of a license entirely, their priorities and actions may change to benefit from this.

In a large organisation, there is particular value in aligning targets that are set for Product and Service managers with the targets for a TBM Office. The TBM Office will rarely be seen as a technology delivery function, so its role becomes one of enabling Product and Service managers to measure and demonstrate their own financial efficiency and achievements.

Cost Managers

The role of a Cost Centre manager may sometimes be seen as conflicting with the strategy of implementing and using TBM disciplines. In an organisation with a traditional cost management structure, the 'ownership' of cost and targets related to it are a measure of hierarchy and importance. Within a TBM and Service based organisation, it is possible for a different hierarchy to exist where an important Service Manager is a coordinator, rather than the owner, of a significant segment of the cost and targets.

The change in this relationship is one that lies at the heart of how an organisation uses TBM disciplines, requiring that the senior managers and sponsors of TBM choose whether they look to manage both approaches with the same staff, split the Cost and Service Management roles, or move entirely from a Cost focus to a Service focus with TBM.

The change can bring organisational challenges, as the importance given to a non-traditional function may be seen as detrimental to the original goals and targets. A switch to using TBM Taxonomy as the basis for organisational ownership can appear confusing when some of the responsibilities for cost management appear to be shared rather than simply owned. An example of this is when the costs of a Technology Component are within a Cost Manager's targets and accountability, and at the same time the subject of cost targets and accountability for a Product or Service owner.

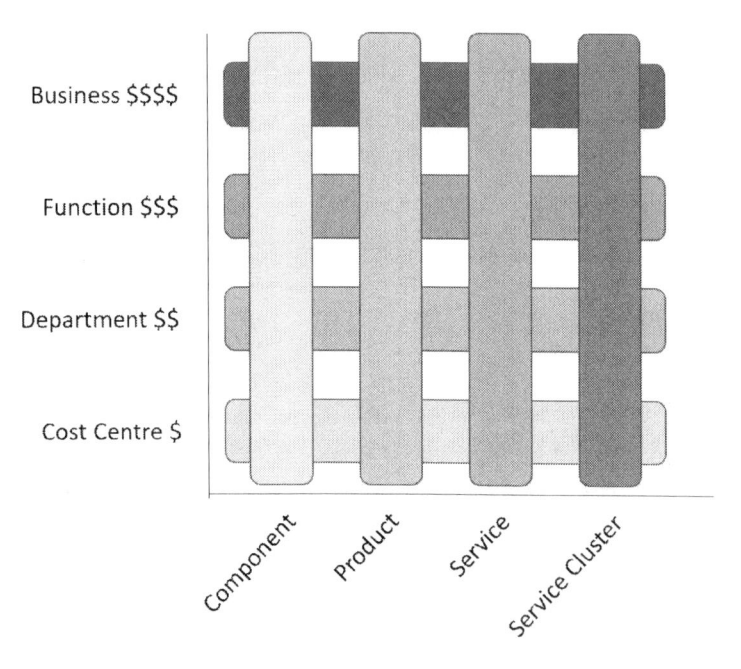

One of the differentiators that can be used to decide between the Organisational and Service approaches is that, while all costs are managed at each level within both approaches, the Service approach embeds joint accountability more evenly than an organisational hierarchy. The choice does not need to be simply one or the other, though a matrix or overlapping set of management roles must be designed not to leave gaps in either dimension.

Whichever approach an organisation is taking, the management structure and targets set for Cost and Service Managers are key to ensuring a TBM Office's understanding and prioritisation.

Service, Strategy, Risk and Cost

The use of TBM to show that Technology is being managed efficiently can extend beyond financial measures, starting with the choice of items in the Service Catalogue. Service descriptions should include information about how the quality of service and approaches to the management of risk are drivers of cost. From this, the value of these to the Business becomes part of their understanding of Technology Service value, moving the focus from just being its price.

Acknowledging that increasing value may cost money is one area that regularly needs to be reinforced in any analysis of Product and Service costs. Targets that are set to improve service quality, reduce errors and control risk will often be at odds with targets to reduce cost, so it is useful to have the ability to understand which costs are for which purposes within a TBM Cost Model. This is not a generic requirement which applies to all areas of a Model, but they should be specifically identifiable and reported where they are important and material to a business's direction.

The TBM Taxonomy has some capabilities to enable this, starting at the IT Tower layer with the Security & Compliance and Delivery Towers, where specific costs are identified by their technical function. These gain granularity with the definitions of Delivery Services within the Products and Services layer, where alignment according to their business use is required.

The specific definitions of the TBM Taxonomy for these Services do not always fit with an organisational construct, and flexibility may be needed to ensure that a TBM Cost Model is relevant to the organisation rather than making the organisation work according to the Taxonomy. This particularly applies where an organisation or industry is subject to specific and stringent requirements and regulations.

Product strategy and lifecycle

Beyond the specific requirements around Service Quality and Risk, strategic metrics reviewed in a business are likely to be related to growth or reduction in scale. These are more directly aligned to the core of TBM disciplines and Cost Modelling, with the alignment of both Total Cost and Unit Cost being explicitly within the outputs from a TBM Cost Model and measurable as the basis for business targets.

The strategic choices when looking at targets of this nature will relate to the lifecycle of Products and Services; whether they are developing, stable, or retired (which goes by any other number of names such as Buy, Hold and Sell or Invest, Maintain and Divest).

The lifecycle of Products and Services will generally be at least five to ten years, so at any point in time most Products and Services should be expected to be stable. The target within TBM should be that there is measurable improvement in efficiency, usually shown as a reduction in the Unit Cost.

During a 'stable' phase for any Service there will be some level of ongoing investment to ensure that the Service stays current rather than receiving increased cost due to 'end of service' charges from suppliers. Both this investment and any increase in volume should be demonstrable within a TBM Model as delivering a net reduction in the Unit Cost.

At both ends of the Product lifecycle, during initial development and when it is being retired, management of cost needs to be much more closely aligned with the processes impacting the lifecycle.

For a new technology product there is often the view, following the logic of the movie Field of Dreams, that 'if you build it, they will come.' This is actually more likely to be correct within a business than it would be in a commercial environment, as internal customers' behaviour can be affected by management action as well as by market forces.

Even so, ensuring that the whole cost of a new Product is not charged to the first customer is not the default way to model. Several approaches can be taken to manage this so that an equitable cost distribution can be achieved. If, however, both Technology processes and TBM are not coordinated in delivering Product lifecycle changes, it is likely that customers will not recognise or accept the costs they are shown.

Similar challenges exist during the retirement of a Product, which were outlined in Chapter 9 – 'Modelling vs Reality' using the example of cost management when exiting from a Data Centre. The challenge of managing reducing Service volumes where there are fixed costs and capacity can be met, but this needs active engagement from both Business change agents and TBM functions.

Prioritisation

A general principle of management and delivery is to understand the difference between important and urgent. Urgency can be imparted by deadlines, levels of interest, or simply someone standing by your desk until you have done what they want. Importance is a measure of the value of the work through either its financial, organisational, or personal impact.

Within Technology Business Management, as within most management and project disciplines, understanding the important aspects of delivery is the first step to achieving targets, enabling planning, and reducing the need to change direction due to urgent activity.

The most relevant of the important disciplines within TBM for this is the understanding of the standard financial cycles of the organisation. Knowledge of when the financial year starts gives a baseline from which the timeline for many other TBM deliverables can be derived.

The timing for developing a Budget within a TBM Cost Model, or using other TBM disciplines in conjunction with the Finance and Technology departments, should not be a surprise. Similarly, the requirements for (often) quarterly reporting should be expected, along with any standard monthly cadence of work.

> *Urgent requirements can be prioritised easily as they will be highlighted by their owner.*
>
> *Important requirements may need to be independently identified as they may be overlooked or affecting stakeholders who are disengaged.*

After establishing the requirements to deliver fundamental TBM capabilities, the prioritisation of other work can follow standard management approaches. Having a roadmap for development, prioritising within it and managing changes to the priorities, can use Application Development or Project Management approaches, including traditional Waterfall or Agile approaches as relevant.

Chapter 13.   Reporting

There is no value in building a Technology Business Management Cost Model if you cannot extract information from it. There is similarly no value in producing information that is irrelevant or is misleading. The purpose of TBM reporting is to enable users to access information relevant to their function and to make decisions based on it.

While there are always likely to be common requirements that can be met by predefined reports within a TBM environment, operational and organisational design can also generate the need for other views.

Although all these comments may seem obvious, the way that they are implemented should not be taken for granted. There is particular flexibility required in building additional reports during the process of building or creating a TBM Cost Model, to help validate that it is working as expected. This approach continues into managing exceptions, and will need to be undertaken repeatedly during a TBM implementation and when it is in regular use.

The decisions about which views of information are required, in what hierarchical or comparative format, will not be the same from one organisation to another, but the common expectations and factors can be generalised. The need for summary, comparison and detailed views must be accounted for, along with relevant hierarchical, time-based and technical factors.

Levels of overviews and details

In large organisations, the provision of management reporting has sometimes been a 'cottage industry' with significant time spent on the collection, aggregation, presentation and development of discussion points associated with each report presented to senior management.

Presentational reports can end up being highly customised and are often inflexible, particularly if there is any outlying or exceptional information which needs further analysis. The reports for senior management are regularly highly consolidated, with limited capability for comparison between levels in a hierarchy. For example, a report showing the ten highest cost Applications in a business, will need to be in a separate table from the total cost of

Applications by Business Unit, even though they are based on the same underlying data.

The general case for this is that a high level summary of data, by itself and without context for comparison, is largely useless. A list of numbers and their totals may be contextualised in many ways, such as by comparison to a baseline such as a budget, over time as a trend, or by a breakdown such as by type of cost. These can also be combined, although this level of detail may mask rather than clarify the information presented.

In defining and building overview reports, the same data and primary context may be used for multiple types of reporting. Using the difference between actual and budgeted cost as the primary data and context, each manager in a hierarchy will be interested in their own absolute result. By specifying who the users of this data are (such as the manager in a hierarchy), we have effectively added a second report context and some additional reporting requirements. Within a management hierarchy, the head of Application Development is then likely to be looking for comparisons between their staff portfolios, for trends over time and potentially for some specific high impact items. Individual managers may be less interested in comparing themselves to their peers, but might want similar information within their own context (if there is another layer of managers), or more depth such as the individual applications or types of cost.

Defining a single report to provide all of this detail is possible but making that report equally useable for every user and requirement less so. The separation of the requirements is, as for the definitions of Services in a Catalogue, often more valuable when based on the ability of a user to access and manage the information adequately. Ensuring that the report is targeted at a user or class of users is more valuable than adding data. This concept is extended further when considering the ways that the users will understand and make use of the information.

The mixture of static, presentation-based management reporting and interactive online backup to it, is one of the capabilities that a TBM Cost Model can help support. The opportunity to use the same raw underlying data for both becomes a basis for common acceptance of TBM. The ability to immediately validate presented data against its source and flexibly add detail can show the quality and depth of a TBM Cost Model, as well as enabling actions to be more directly specified based on the information.

The level to which management action and reporting is data-driven can depend on the quality of the data available. The level of confidence in data and reporting should be respected and made known as part of the context of a report, particularly where there are known inconsistencies or errors.

Consolidation of data, to create a Key Performance Indicator (KPI) is one mechanism used to fix the context of a report and prioritise its management. As with the generic consolidation of data into an overview report, each KPI needs to be understood in terms of how they will be used and by whom. The choices on this start with whether a KPI is going to be used as a passive tracker of progress, or as an active comparison over time or across the organisation.

Definition of the measure as 'Key' suggests that it is more likely to be actively managed and intended to drive behaviour, although KPIs that run across industries or disciplines may be targeted at longer term change.

The decision on how to use KPIs to affect an organisation's behaviour will be discussed further in the following Chapter, in terms of setting ownership and accountability for Services, actions and goals. The choice of whether a single specific measure will help in ensuring that behaviour is for the common good, rather than for an individual, is the core challenge to be addressed.

Relevance and timing

The way in which reports are used can often be characterised as either being for tracking status or for tracking action. Along with understanding who the report is for, this will help with defining the scope and data points needed within a report.

Tracking status

Tracking status is most generally relevant when reporting on an environment which is in a relatively stable condition, where all that is required is a quick analysis of whether there has been a single-period change or if a trend is developing. This type of reporting is easily taken for granted and often not reviewed unless something is known to be changing or going wrong. As a result, the delivery of this information must be done in a way that is easily accessible, showing either that everything is on track or that there is a further review required.

Within a TBM reporting capability, status reporting should mostly be delivered through a limited set of 'at-a-glance' graphics, with set boundaries beyond which further review will take place. An example would be the use of a relevant KPI, measured monthly and shown as a historic trend on a line chart. It is useful and important to support this style of presentation with the underlying data, but not necessary to present all the data immediately.

There is an underlying assumption in status reporting that the data being used is consistent and that the result is not hiding underlying issues. This relates back to the previous section in this Chapter, where overview and detail levels of data were discussed. Ensuring that at least one additional level of granularity of data is available for a status report, and reviewing this for exceptions, is a useful validation. The level of depth required in this review will depend on who the report is for and how they will use it.

The question of who will review a status report or dashboard of this type, and how often, relates to the overall position of TBM within an organisation. The number of metrics on a status dashboard, the level of detail and setting of acceptable boundaries for variance, and the way in which exceptions are identified, reviewed and communicated, will all vary according to the needs of the reviewing manager. The provision of monthly financial updates as the basis for a review cycle would often make this type of report relevant for senior management review. Organisationally however, this may be delegated and quarterly reporting given precedence.

To ensure that this information is reviewed, understood and accepted it is necessary, from a TBM practitioner's perspective, that this type of dashboard be self-explanatory. If the meaning of a metric needs to be discussed whenever a report is reviewed, there is a higher likelihood of exceptions being missed or left unmanaged. This level of confidence and understanding can be tied in to the regularity of reporting, since monthly reviews of status at one level of management should provide the confidence that allows the same measures to be presented at quarterly reviews with a more senior manager.

Reporting exceptions

The reporting of exceptions is significantly more complicated than reporting status but must be relatable to relevant status reports. When an exception occurs, its impacts must be recognised and traceable, which means being able to see both the effects and the item or action which is causing the exception.

The TBM Office's role includes the identification of exceptions, so knowledge of where exceptions occur regularly is a useful place to start reporting from. The idea that exceptions may occur regularly will seem to be an oxymoron but is an accurate reflection of working practice in large and mature TBM implementations.

An example discussed in the section in Chapter 9 on Modelling vs Reality, is of exceptional charges or journal entries appearing in the General Ledger layer of a TBM Cost Model. The Finance department's requirements for accounting and reporting will not be overridden by TBM disciplines, so their need to accurately represent transactions at a point in time, and their ability to then reverse and re-present the transaction more accurately in the next period, are a regular cause of exceptional items appearing as input to TBM.

The requirement for reporting these exceptions is that they are firstly identified, secondly characterised, and thirdly that their impact is reported.

A simple report, showing how many of these exceptional items are occurring and their financial value, is a place to start. Thresholds for both the volume and value of exceptions can be used to mask 'noise' that could be caused if every item was treated as an error, but it is similarly important to also recognise when an exception must be recognised or escalated for action.

Neither a status report nor an exception report, by itself, will cause action to be taken. As previously stated, these are pointers towards where the reviewer of the report, might expect to make decisions on those actions. The creation and governance of report review processes and exception management processes become increasingly valuable as a TBM implementation matures and the data becomes integral to the Business.

Tracking action

The discipline associated with management of workflow and tasks in Project Management can be usefully brought into the context of using TBM reporting to track actions.

Actions to be tracked through TBM may come from an external source such as a management programme of work and associated targets, or be generated from within the TBM discipline through the identification of anomalies and efficiencies. From a reporting perspective, the main difference between these is that the internally identified action will be where the way to measure and report is already identified within the TBM Cost Model.

The main capability that TBM will provide for tracking the impact of actions is the ability to report reliably, consistently and on a regular basis. Action tracking is usually towards a target and is almost invariably based on progress from a baseline status. It is important that any reporting is put in place and the baseline agreed, to ensure that the continuing reporting is trusted regardless of whether the output is on-track to the target or not.

A side effect of implementing action tracking reports into a TBM environment is that they can frequently provide information for periods before a measure was requested. In a TBM Cost Model which has historic financial and technology information, a request to create a new view of that information is only limited by the availability of data. Any requirement for reporting and analysis which does not require completely new data points, can show historic trends as well as delivering a current baseline and future tracking.

Constructive limitations of TBM reporting

TBM reporting is not always practical as a way to measure the impact of programmes of action, particularly where the programmes focus on a limited scope within a TBM Cost Model rather than the overall business.

The unusual description of this as a 'constructive limitation' is due to the requirements that TBM disciplines bring for looking at the overall value of Technology expense, rather than a narrow and blinkered focus.

An example of this constructive limitation is the use of TBM reporting in the context of 'cost reduction' programmes. One of the approaches taken within large organisations when implementing such a programme is to identify a large number of activities which will save cost. These may involve reductions in technology, staff, and vendor expense, such as consolidating to a smaller number of central vendor contracts.

To report on such activities within TBM, it would be necessary to identify how each activity would be visible within the TBM model, create a reporting capability of it, and measure the baseline position.

With no TBM capability to manage and view technology cost and value, a programme such as this would often characterise each activity in terms of the costs removed rather than the overall impact. Taking the example of consolidation of spend from three vendors into one, there is a clear saving related to the removal of two vendors' cost. Outside a TBM Cost Model, it is possible that only the saving might be reported, ignoring the remaining vendor's cost increasing to provide the same capability. This is unlikely with TBM Cost Model as the costs would already be treated together.

This is not to say that it would be unachievable for TBM reporting to be administered in such a way that only the 'savings' were reported in this instance, but it would require a significant amount more effort to do so than it would to report the net saving.

The alternative approach that TBM would bring to this reporting would be in setting the original goals at a more structural level. The 'Cost Reduction' would be recognised in terms of its net impact, rather than specific line items, and would be reported in terms of improved efficiency as well as reduced cost. This allows for management to balance justified business demand for growth with the cost reduction. In a large organisation, if one business unit is setting targets for cost reduction while another is growing, it should be possible to balance these and enable both to hit their targets. If the entire business is set cost reduction targets, it should be possible to demonstrate how this is being achieved and the net position, rather than ignoring the reality of there being some cost increases.

Designing reports

The designing of reports and the user experience associated with them are a further group of disciplines which is highly developed outside of Technology Business Management, but which apply equally to a TBM implementation and should be integrated rather than ignored. The choice of whether and when to use pre-existing reports or create customised versions during an implementation will usually result in a blend of approaches, so it is worth reiterating a few of the thoughts which enable this to happen more successfully.

As identified previously in this Chapter, start by defining what the purpose of a report is and who the users are. This will often be defined by a Subject Matter Expert but should then be validated with other target users. The process must also take into account the level of TBM knowledge available to the users, since they may not be aware of all the reporting capabilities that exist. A simple example from the perspective of an Application owner might be that they have only ever been shown their costs in terms of financial account codes or groupings, so are unaware of the possibilities of IT Towers or cost alignment through technology inventory.

Working through a 'Use Case' as the basis for a report can provide additional structure to some requirements, which is reviewed later in this Chapter. It will help identify who the report is for, what they need to see and what types of actions they should take as a result.

With some report requirements identified, an iterative process of development and review will provide huge value. Initial design of a report is often in the abstract, so can be rapidly improved with the ability to physically see and work through users' interactions with it. Engaging users in the development process also helps them understand how they and you will use the information.

Report descriptions

Particularly when interactive online reporting is being developed, the level of knowledge expected of the report user is a factor that must be accounted for. Within a TBM implementation, as in any other specialist discipline, gaps in knowledge can lead to reports being created which are not readily understood.

The design of reports needs to particularly account for the possibility of the data being reviewed or used by users with a full range of skills; from those who the report is intended for, to those who have reached the report more fortuitously.

It must be made clear what the key points are that a user should be looking at, since even for regular users it may be that they are only looking at the information monthly or quarterly. Enhancing each report with a description of its context and business purpose is a useful practice, which also helps when a new user joins the target audience through organisational or job changes.

Some good design practices

There are several patterns which can be seen in successful implementations of TBM Cost Model reporting which can be used as examples of good practice.

TBM modelling can enable the same cost to be part of multiple different items simultaneously, so avoiding this in reports is critical. For example, the cost of space in a Data Centre can become part of the cost of a Server and the cost of the Server can become part of the cost of an Application. These three separate views of one cost should not be shown to a user in a form where they might try to add them together. This requires that the context of a report is well defined; you are either looking at Data Centre costs, or Server costs or Application costs, but not all of these simultaneously.

When a report is provided online with interactive elements, it should have a readable result when it is first viewed. Although some reports will need to show large amounts of information, this can usually be prioritised financially or sorted by some other characteristic so that this can be achieved. Similarly, ensuring that the summary is the first level of information available is a useful design, with additional granularity that can be added when the user requires.

A point to be learned from 'User Experience' (UX) testing is that most users will not be interested in scrolling through multiple pages to reach the information they want. Although this applies in different ways when shopping online and through search engines, for online reporting it is a realistic goal to deliver a report on a single screen or within a page and a half of vertical scrolling. Information that is not immediately on screen might never be seen. Any report that requires a user to use a horizontal scrollbar is very likely to result in information that will never be viewed.

Sub-totals and totals are used in different ways in online and printed reports. In a printed report, it is necessary to group details with sub-totals and then provide the totals because there is no flexibility to change the level of granularity of data that is displayed. In an online report, it is possible to provide capabilities such as a choice of which level of granularity to report at, so sub-totals are needed less frequently.

When using subtotals and totals for data, the data must be using consistent metrics. This particularly applies in a TBM context where there are mixed measures within a report, such as different Unjts of Measure for different Services. The usual metaphor for this would be of comparing 'apples and oranges' but as both of these are counted as single items it is probably better to describe this challenge as comparing 'kilograms of apples' with 'numbers of oranges'.

Governance and maturation of reports

An organisation's understanding of what is required from TBM Cost Model reporting will mature and become more focused as the system is used. The approach to how to implement and change reports needs to be structured to take this into account, particularly the differences between the period when TBM is being implemented and when it is in regular use.

During implementation

The two starting points when looking at implementing TBM report capabilities are the reports which existed previously in the organisation, and the ones which are part of a TBM tool. The classic arguments about whether it is better to buy or build apply, along with the standard limitations of both, so the usual approach taken is a mix of the two.

As with the building of a TBM Cost Model, the challenges of building reports are ensuring that they are complete, relevant and understandable. This can start off relatively simply, as the first check that will reliably be required is that the output of a model matches the input.

There is immediate value in reporting the TBM General Ledger data with various filters, enabling the Finance team who have provided that data to validate that it is correctly received. This simple capability should not be underestimated, as there can be instances where it is easier for a Finance department to access the data within a TBM tool than through their own tools. The full flexibility of the Finance systems will not be available to them, but within its limitations, the TBM data can be useful.

> *A TBM Cost Model may take multiple General Ledgers as its input and consolidate them for managing Technology cost.*
>
> *This may be the only time that the ledgers are consolidated with that level of granularity across the organisation.*

Taking a general lesson from this example, the ability to replay information that is used in a TBM Cost Model back to the function who provided it is a useful check and balance. Augmenting that with other related data and information from the Model enables the organisation to start to identify value and opportunities for improvement. The added information will usually include a cost component, but even that single item can become a cost trend over time, cost variance against a baseline or towards a target, or multiple other measures.

When giving people access to a TBM Cost Model while it is still being built, there is a constant expectation that progress can be seen through the reports. Managing those expectations is a requirement of the implementation process, so that the people reviewing the reports understand both the information they are seeing and its level of accuracy.

Ensuring that people understand TBM concepts and terminology are part of a standard Project Management approach to the implementation. The process of managing expectations around TBM reporting require parallel focus, without which the report users can end up saying 'But ...' as described in Chapter 11. Particularly during an implementation, building trust in the report output involves communicating when reports will be available, what degree of confidence there is in the data, and what the known issues are.

Governance of this process can start with making sure to validate your Cost Model before you release it to users. The process needs a level of formality in order to reduce the possibility of complacency, and allowing errors to creep in, so should generally involve more than one person making checks.

As a TBM Cost Model grows, the number of reports available increase significantly and it becomes unfeasible to validate every report at every change. At the same time, the number of inputs and complexity of logical interactions within a Model mean that changes are hard to trace. The validation of the model then requires a change of approach, towards ensuring that sufficient checking can be done centrally to provide confidence in the overall output. This style of validation can usefully start by following the approach outlined in Chapter 11 in the section on 'The total's right, so we're talking about details.'

A report that shows, for example, the total cost each month at the General Ledger, IT Towers, Services and Business Unit layers, broken down to help identify where there are material changes from one month to the next, will enable many issues to be identified. Providing that information to users along with details of how and when the issues are likely to be addressed during the implementation, is a practical approach that will also build trust.

Reporting the progress of an implementation

The ability to report the total cost at the General Ledger, IT Towers and Services and Business layers is also useful as a metric for the technical progress of a TBM implementation. These can be integrated into a project plan, as an implementation following the TBM Taxonomy will reach these goals in order, and a report can easily show these as specific and measurable values.

This is not the only way to measure implementation progress, and not all implementations will have the goal of delivering 100% of costs to Services, but this is more readily measurable than many other Project status metrics. A challenge with this can be if tactical modelling is implemented, allowing costs to flow for completeness rather than correctness, but this would be a normal Project Management risk to track.

Steady state

Within a complete TBM Cost Model implementation, the delivery and customisation of reports is quite often about understanding a request for information rather than creating something new.

There are usually a large number of reports available to users, but an individual's knowledge of what data is in each of those reports and how to use it is necessarily limited, as most roles will not require the full breadth of TBM capabilities.

The creation of 'Use Cases' for the roles which have regular interaction with TBM information, and how this can provide a standard path to identify and extract information relevant to a goal, will be discussed below. With reports in place to provide that data, the governance of reports becomes partly that of a gatekeeper ensuring that only relevant changes are made.

The challenge with requests to add information into an online report is in finding the balance between showing that information and making the report harder to use. The comparison can be made to the management of information in a spreadsheet, where you can have a virtually unlimited number of rows and columns of data. The data is not directly presentable as a report, so it would be summarised prior to use, and the same is true of TBM reporting.

An alternative and more realistic comparison is to the presentation of information through a data visualisation tool, where an underlying understanding of the data enables significant flexibility in the reporting interface. The difference is that most business users will be capable of using and understanding information in a static report or spreadsheet, but fewer will be familiar with querying datasets through a Business Information or Analysis system.

From a practical perspective, TBM report users will be a mixture of those who wish to have a regular and consistent reports and those who require significant flexibility. For those whose requirements have been met by specific TBM reports, making changes to those reports must not be done at the expense of their ability to work.

This brings a requirement for control of any standardised reporting interface which needs to be understood. If users are exporting data from TBM reports into other systems, particularly spreadsheets, the simplest of changes can break their processes or cause them more work. These changes could be to the order of data columns or adding one in the middle, changing the format of numbers, or others. Once a TBM Cost Model and reporting system is established and embedded in an organisation, these types of data extraction processes should be expected to develop, so need to be considered as part of the governance and gatekeeping around report changes.

To help understand when changes can be made, or should be made, it is useful to also keep track of which reports are used. Most TBM systems will have a large number of reports created during their implementation or available as a default from the underlying tool, but not all will be part of a business process or have specific users. Tools may also allow users the capability to create their own reports and share them with others, so central governance of what reports are available and used by whom become important.

Transparency and openness

At some stage in the implementation of a TBM Cost Model there is likely to be a review of the level of transparency that is appropriate. This was discussed in Chapter 7 in the section on Transparency, and its implementation when delivering reporting capabilities is core.

There is no single approach to this which will fit all organisations' requirements. There is a level of openness required to build a TBM Cost Model which can be seen as contrary to the need to compartmentalize and control the output. The alternative extreme, enabling complete openness and accessibility of all data to all users, is a position that some large businesses have taken with their TBM implementations, but is less frequently seen.

The data required to build a TBM Cost Model, and its outputs, can include sensitive personal and commercial details, such as salary costs and business profitability.

To the sponsor of a TBM implementation, this is core information that they need in order to run their business so their views on how accessible this should be will be one factor. It will also generally be the case that each group providing data used with a TBM Cost Model will need to understand how that data is used and how the associated costs are managed.

The management of sensitive data may be achieved within these requirements with only limited boundaries, such as keeping sensitive personal data out of the system by consolidation prior to loading it and ensuring that Technology and Business reports do not display it. Implementing report access boundaries between TBM Finance, Technology and Business layers and their users may also be sufficient for many organisations.

With the development of data protection and privacy rules in multiple countries and regions, the control of sensitive data must not be an afterthought in a TBM implementation. These rules may cover the storage and access to data, the use of the data and how it is shown in reports, and can extend to unexpected areas such as whether it is acceptable to produce reporting about user logins and which reports they use. These are specialist areas that need to be actively managed, even though TBM systems will generally be only for use within an organisation and not for public access.

Use cases

A 'Use Case' is generally defined as a set of steps, taken by a person, on a system, to deliver a goal. This broad definition should be able to cover just about every conceivable business activity, and all disciplines of Technology Business Management can be covered by it.

More specifically though, when looking at reporting, a Use Case is a reminder that creating a report is not a goal in itself, nor is reviewing that report. The goal is to use the report for a purpose, which leads back to earlier in this Chapter and the characterisation of reports as being either for tracking status or action. It also helps to widen the understanding of individual reports and suites of reports, to be about how they are used to manage a business.

As part of a TBM implementation, creating broad Use Cases for specific roles can aid in several aspects of training and process implementation. The first phrases in the definition (a set of steps, taken by a person) helps keep in mind that the Use Case should not be too broadly or too narrowly defined; a goal of 'reducing the cost of IT' will not be delivered by a Use Case, nor (usually) will a goal be achieved just by reviewing a report.

The general Use Cases for reports can be understood against the definition, as set out in the table below:

	Status Reporting	Action Reporting
A set of steps	Identifying trends and exceptions, on a regular basis	Identifying change on specific metrics, on a regular basis
... taken by a person	... by the responsible individual	... by the responsible individual
...on a system	... reviewing the relevant report(s)	... reviewing the relevant report(s)
... to deliver a goal	... so that action can be taken to manage against an organisational goal.	... so that action can be taken to achieve set targets.

A core example of a Use Case with TBM would be around the standard financial management of a technology component. As 'status reporting' the Use Case would be along the lines of:

> Monthly and quarterly review of the cost and the volume of technology consumed by the business, to ensure that relevant actions are taken to maintain or reduce the Unit Cost of the technology over time.

This is objectively only a partial Use Case, since the same person would most likely be accountable for the quality of service and risk profile of the technology, as well as the financial management.

Business decisions on both service quality and risk might have financial implications, so a single and ubiquitous Use Case covering all operational requirements is likely to be cumbersome and unusable. Aiming for perfection in the definition therefore becomes less important than ensuring that it is adequate to guide the person performing the activity.

Managing maturity

Part of the organisational value of implementing Use Cases is in reducing the chances of a 'cottage industry' springing up to produce large numbers of reports which are of limited value to the business. The creation of a body of Use Cases associated with the major roles within TBM, such as Finance, Technology, Application and Service management, can help inform and train users on which reports are useful for which role.

With a new implementation, or change of personnel in a role, Use Case based training can also help drive towards achieving the best value from what you have, before making changes

With the wealth of data that is used to create a full TBM Cost Model, there will reliably be 'just one more' request for a different view of information to be added to any report. That one-off request for information in a custom format will often be followed by a minor variation or a request for an update. The identification of the purpose of the report within a Use Case can limit that, but maturity leads to these types of requests being accompanied by a Use Case as its own justification.

These signs of mature use of TBM systems require a TBM team to have their own process for handling requests. The receipt of a request, acknowledgement, qualification of detail, acceptance or rejection of the request, quantification of effort, prioritisation, staffing, implementation, and setting people's expectations for each relevant step, can all be identified parts of modern Application Development cycles and treated as such.

Similar governance processes need to be considered for changes not just to reports, but also to the underlying TBM Cost Model, such as integration of organisational changes or changes to business strategy. This will be discussed further in Chapter 15 on 'Delivering Capability and Succeeding'.

Chapter 14. Changing Behaviour

At several points earlier in the book, reference has been made to how Technology Business Management can be used to deliberately or subtly change behaviour. One of these was the suggestion in Chapter 10 about naming Services in a Catalogue, where people may be guided to choose differently between three service levels based calling them Critical, Enhanced and Standard, instead of calling them Gold, Silver and Bronze.

This Chapter consolidates those points and then looks at how build on them, through various reporting approaches, to demonstrate the value of the changes taking place.

Cost Modelling can be treated as just a source of information, but for business purposes it is better treated as a mechanism to drive behaviour, and preferably should drive positive behaviour. Actions that drive negative behaviour can also be identified and mitigated or avoided. As with any single tool, it should not be treated as the only available method to change behaviour but included in a portfolio of management actions.

Service ownership

Regardless of whether a Product or Service Catalogue already exists in an organisation when TBM is implemented, the ownership of Catalogue items and the accountability for aspects of their management are likely to change from their previous state. The role of Technology Manager does not regularly include financial management or efficiency in their remit, so these are areas which need development.

With a newly created Catalogue that follows or derives from the TBM Taxonomy, the role of a Technology Manager can start to be aligned to the structure and hierarchy identified at the TBM Taxonomy's Services layer, which can be seen in full in the Appendix from p15 onwards. From there, the role may expand to include financial accountability and take more complete ownership of one or more Services.

The role of a Service Owner, as described in Chapter 10 about the establishment of a Service Catalogue, includes setting the detailed definition of their Services in the Catalogue.

Service Definition

The description of the Service within the Catalogue, including what is in scope and what is excluded, must tie to the calculation of cost in the TBM Cost Model, so there is a clear requirement for the Service Owner to understand both the concepts and detail of how this works. This holds true whether a TBM Cost Model will be used for 'Chargeback' to customers, or only as an indicator of cost in a 'Showback' approach.

More simply, when defining a Service, a requirement is that its purpose and cost can be understood by its users or customers. The intended behaviour that comes from this is that the customers should understand when to use the Service and how much it will cost them. The Service Catalogue becomes a tool by which the Service Owner promotes or markets the Service, with the description and cost (or price) being the main factors likely to affect their customers behaviour.

Taking an example from the TBM Taxonomy for End User Services level, the given definition of Client Computing Category and the Computer Service (Appendix p.18) is:

> A selection of IT-provided computers, workstations, laptop or tablet configurations. Each type may be ordered with additional memory and storage. Standard corporate image will be loaded on each device. Requestor may order optional software through the Productivity services. Includes network and remote network access. Standard support package including security, back-up, antivirus, updates and patches, remote access, centralized service desk.

The owner of this Service needs to be able to provide all the capabilities to meet this definition, or change it appropriately in their organisation's Catalogue. They will need to work with other Technology and Service managers to ensure that the components that are not with their direct remit are delivered to the scope, which specifically includes networks connectivity, software, security, backup and service desk capabilities.

The Service description should be checked against the idea that something with zero cost might generate infinite demand, looking at where customers might see opportunities to obtain something for nothing. There are still a number of locations, although reducing in number, where there is a significant cost for internet access and the inclusion of remote network access might bring significant business cost. For a customer who might change their business behaviour based on the inclusion of this capability, the cost of doing so needs to be made clear in the definition or there is a business risk.

The Service Owner also needs to be able to provide an explanation to their customers of the core value of the Service, and its cost. This is not necessarily with full transparency, but with an appreciation, for example, of the customer's willingness to put a value on the management of risk and the quality of service, as well as the basic technical functionality.

Beyond this, the Service Owner needs to be clear about the cost and value of any extensions. The TBM Taxonomy definition of the Computer Service, listed above, specifies that these extensions include 'additional memory and storage', 'optional software', and that a Computer includes a 'Standard support package …' with the implication that there may be alternative support packages also available.

The Service Owner may choose to limit the variability around the core services, for example stating that only standard support is available and that extensions are strictly limited. This is an approach that can be useful to help bring under control something that has previously not been managed as a Service. It brings challenges of enforcement and the need to manage exceptions, but also enables simple efficiencies that come from having a single set, or limited number, of variations within the Service.

Ownership of the definition implies a significant expectation of ownership of the end-to-end Service in a sense that includes technical, financial, quality, risk, managerial and strategic aspects. This also gives the Service Owner the ability to effect longer term change. This type of change is sometimes forced on the Service Owner by changing circumstances or technology, but can also be directly managed.

An example is the potential consolidation of communications technologies with those of a desktop computer. With the improvements in Unified Communications technologies and with increased home working leading to more time spent using computer-based telephony than traditional, there is strategic potential to consolidate these to a single Desktop Environment, rather than the separate Computer and Communication Services currently listed in the TBM Taxonomy.

This level of change to the Services in a Catalogue needs to be managed with care, to encompass both the technical capabilities, project, organisational and financial impacts simultaneously. It brings risks that an incorrect specification of the consolidated Service might cause customers to choose not to follow the strategic approach.

The customer's choice can be driven by as simple an issue as the Unit Cost of the new Service being set higher than the old, or the cost of a period when they need to run both the new and old Services in parallel.

These types of issue and behaviour can be anticipated, particularly as the pace of change of Service Descriptions should be tightly controlled and well-communicated in advance.

Goal driven behaviour

With a Service in place and stable, there are likely to be goals set for the provision and direction that the Service takes. Many of the actions that a Service Owner takes will be at least partially measured in terms of cost efficiency, as shown by the Unit Cost of the Service. This can also lead to specific targets being set for the Unit Cost, and the Service Owner's ability to effectively communicate the value of their Service.

If a Service Owner is set a target to reduce the Unit Cost of their Service, they should look at both the cost and volume factors. They can achieve their goal either by reducing cost or increasing volume, while keeping the other factor stable.

A Service Owner should then look at the components in their Unit Cost and how to manage them. This would be good practice in all situations, but without a TBM Cost Model as a data source is harder to achieve.

If a Service Owner is set purely financial targets that are unrelated to the demand for their Service, their choices for how to achieve the target are limited. They may take some positive actions, which is usually the expectation, but actions and behaviours with negative impacts may also enable the same targets to be reached.

The positive behaviours can include actions such as reviewing vendor and license relationships for opportunities to remove cost. Negative behaviours to meet the target might include simply driving customers to use alternative Services.

Technology Business Management also opens up additional approaches for a Service Owner to look at how to reduce their cost. This might be the identification of costs reaching a Service through a Cost Model which are misaligned and should be in another Service, or costs which are incorrectly weighted between Services. This type of scrutiny of a Cost Model is generally valuable for improving its accuracy, but it only results in moving costs around rather than removing them from the business.

In these instances the TBM team needs to consider whether to change the Cost Model for those costs at all, as they are likely to increase the cost of another Service.

Customer expectations and behaviour

The customers of a Service will read its description in the Catalogue and expect that the Service will be delivered precisely as described, with a standard cost. Based on their normal interactions with non-business services, they are also likely to expect that their use of the Service will be precisely connected to how much it costs, and that if they stop using the Service they will no longer see the cost.

While the value of this at an individual level is usually very low, a department or organisation's growth or reduction in the use of the Service provides the potential for cost savings and affects behaviour.

Although there are occasions when the cost of technology may not be treated a significant factor in its level of use, such as during periods of significant business growth, customers will often look at how their use of Technology Services can be altered to reduce its cost to them.

The most obvious behaviour is for a customer to look at the quantity of the Service that they are using and try to manage this. With the relevant information available, starting with a simple inventory of what is being charged for within the Service, this behaviour should benefit the customer and the Service Owner.

Returning to the example of a Computer Service used earlier in this Chapter, the Service Owner should be able to provide their customers with the list of Computers that they are using, and the cost. The Customer should be able to buy additional Computers or return unused ones, at which point the cost that they are shown for the Service should adjust accordingly.

Similarly, if they are using extensions to the Service, such as a higher Service Level for support, the inventory should show who is using that and the Catalogue should list the process to add or remove people and cost from it.

This approach to Service definition and the customer behaviour it supports is positive and effectively self-reinforcing. Both the Service Owner and the customer benefit from removing unnecessary cost and increasing the efficient use of the Service. There can be a challenge to this behaviour if that linkage is broken, which will be discussed in Chapter 15 in the section on Price sensitivity.

The definition of a Service can also cause customers to ask about the possibility of having a reduced cost version as they will not use some aspect of it. This gives the Service Owner a lever to help affect the behaviour of customers, for example by either removing options and extensions from a Service, or ensuring that the more expensive Services are clearly identified, and the cost differential is justified in their descriptions.

As with several other aspects of managing TBM, the complexity of managing a large volume of exceptions within a Catalogue is something that is best avoided. Providing too many choices in a Catalogue can be expected to cause confusion and inefficient behaviour, such as customers choosing the wrong Service.

Financial Ownership

The question of budgetary ownership of technology can have a larger impact on both Service Owner and customer behaviour than is often recognisable from the definition of a Service. These are factors that sometimes affect an organisation without the active involvement of Finance or Technology departments, but their impact should not remain outside the scope of Technology Business Management or a TBM Cost Model.

In a traditional technology environment there was a clear expectation of central ownership of some core technology related costs, such as the provision of Data Centres, networking, telephony and mainframe computing. For decades, this approach has been augmented with sometimes central and sometimes federated ownership of Unix and Server computing, and the same extensions apply to Desktop computing.

The effects of evolving technology on cost, and the perception of cost, need to be understood by the Service Owner, communicated to their customers as part of a technology strategy, and included in the Service definition.

An example of this is found in the 'Client Computing' category in the TBM Taxonomy (Appendix p18). The definition includes 'all the physical and virtual devices and associated services' and the more detailed 'Computer' definition states this is 'a selection of IT-provided computers, workstations, laptop or tablet configurations'. This can be read ambiguously. Are Technology providing the configurations and the customer purchasing them directly, or are Technology purchasing the computers and including that cost within the Service?

Organisations which have not considered these options may say that this is a spurious difference, but the financial ownership of the physical device is one practical differentiator between the more historic desktop computing model and the 'Bring You Own Device' (BYOD) approach.

Assuming that the available configurations are the same whether centrally owned or with distributed ownership, there should be no difference financially between these to an organisation, but there may be a difference to an individual department budget. If the cost of the Computer Service does not include the cost of the equipment, but only the cost of defining which configurations are available to be purchased, the Service Owner has an easier job in setting a Unit Cost for their Service as one significantly variable value is removed from the modelling.

As introduced in Chapter 11 in the section on 'The cost of a Service', a further challenge to this question of ownership comes with the implementation of another generation of Desktop Computing, Virtual Desktop Infrastructure (VDI). The implementation of VDI means that servers in a Data Centre centrally provide the operating system, environment and software, which are displayed at the users' desktop using a simple, low-cost device.

As this device would be used by whoever sat at the desk, with 'their computer' actually being part of a central service from the Data Centre, they would be unlikely to expect to own the device and would expect its ownership and cost to be with central IT.

As a customer of the Computer Service, if you had paid directly for the physical computer that you used, you would then have little financial impetus to move to a VDI Service as you would see yourself paying for both your own desktop or laptop computer and also for the central computer costs.

With the TBM Taxonomy definitions there is a clear expectation that the comparable costs will be equally included, from which these differentiations can be resolved. The level of understanding of this situation within an organisation will be dependent on both the detailed definitions that are published in the Catalogue, and the organisational practice and maturity.

Distributed and Cloud Computing

Over decades, as computing has become ubiquitous and embedded into organisations, some cyclical changes have been noticeable in the development and use of technology, including the movement of financial ownership between a central Technology function and distributed departments.

Coming from an environment where computing was a centrally controlled and managed function due to the high cost of purchasing computers, many early implementations of 'distributed compute servers' (Unix, VMS, etc.) were enabled by departments finding that computing was directly affordable within their own budget and purchasing processes.

Other factors also drove this decentralisation, including the apparent slow rate of change enforced by central control of technology and the differences in prioritisation of requirements between Business and Technology departments. The positive practical aspects of distributed computing included the ability to purchase a server on a much shorter cycle than through a central procurement group, the ability to place a server in an office rather than a Data Centre, and the reduced time to deliver business changes that came with these capabilities.

Over time, better understanding of the full requirements for technology governance have shifted much of distributed computing to more central control, including the need to manage risk and security, data and backups, together with efficient use of equipment.

In common with the End User Services, where the ownership is split between Business and Technology, it is likely that a balance will be found where parts of the Service can be provided centrally in a standard manner, separately from those which are highly variable and specific to a customer. The provision of a standard Service for system management, engineering, operations, purchasing, and risk, may then be separated from the cost of a physical server.

A similar dynamic has changed the Service definitions and financial ownership for 'distributed compute servers'. Organisations have progressed from all costs being outside a central IT organisation, through many costs except for equipment being centralised, towards all costs being centrally managed.

To capture this, Technology Business Management must bring back into focus the impact of decentralisation on the overall financial position. It is not possible to identify the full cost of Technology unless both the central and distributed costs are included on a like for like basis, although the definitions in the Catalogues can make this more apparent.

The behaviour underlying the move to decentralisation of Financial and Technology management, identified above, can be part of the Technology Business Management discipline to identify, but it is an organisational decision how best to manage, allow or change this behaviour.

The implementation of virtualisation, clustering and Private Cloud environments can be seen as moving the dynamic of hardware ownership back towards centralisation, causing the need to manage the balance actively.

At the same time, but with the opposite impact, the implementation and management of Public Cloud Services provides a push toward decentralisation of financial ownership, with the possibility of departmental budgets (and even credit cards) being used to enable the purchase of computing capabilities.

The financial impact of Public Cloud Serices can differ significantly from the previous examples in two main respects:

- The variability of cost provides a similar impetus towards decentralisation, with the ability to start using Cloud Computing not being limited by immediate budgetary constraints. However, unlike the purchase of a server, it also holds the potential for costs to grow over time through increased usage and lack of active management.

- As Public Cloud Services are not what Finance would identify as a 'Fixed Asset', the processes and controls designed to recognise and manage Fixed Asset costs do not apply, which can make budgetary forecasting harder.

These situations do have balancing factors in a business context. One benefit of Public Cloud Services is that the costs are more directly variable than technology has previously provided, so has the potential to be reduced as easily as increased, which is not the case for Fixed Assets.

The variability of cost applies in both directions and again can escape the normal budgetary forecasting and controls. Increases in Cloud Service usage combined with the potential for Cloud Service implementations to be 'orphaned' if not actively administered, can cause avoidable but unmanaged cost. A TBM function needs to provide relevant input to ensure that active management is put in place for these new behaviours in a Cloud environment, and that the costs are captured and reported through the TBM Cost Model.

Overhead and Orphaned costs

With a primary concern of Technology Business Management being the identification, measurement and management of technology and its cost, it can be surprising to find the amount of activity which appears to not be easily identified or measured. This can be for an activity or cost that is not owned within the Technology organisation, so that there is no clear owner, but can also be found purely within Technology functions.

The presence of these costs within a TBM Cost Model is likely, so the need to clearly identify them, understand the reasons for their existence and the behaviours that they cause, must be managed within the TBM team's governance remit.

Overhead Costs

One of the ways in which such costs can be highlighted is to term them as 'Overhead Costs' or 'Management Overheads.' These terms are generally understood to mean the costs of functions and people which are not directly associated with delivering value to a specific Service.

The reasons that many managers dislike the term 'Overhead' relate both to the source of the costs and the way that they are shared. In the first instance, the term suggests that either no-one knows what the costs are, or that their source is being deliberately obscured. The second objection is that costs of this nature will be arbitrarily shared rather than being in any way controllable.

As the importance of descriptions within a Service Catalogue has already been described, along with the detail that is used to categorise costs within the TBM Taxonomy, the impact of an undescribed category of 'Overhead Costs' is due to the way that it breaks those conventions.

From this, the term Overhead becomes effectively derogatory, immediately causing questions about why the costs are not better categorised. One approach to this is to avoid the use of the term and replace it with something less offensive, such as calling its distribution a 'tariff' rather than a 'tax'.

The base expectation is that whatever it is called, the costs categorised this way will not be a high proportion of the total cost. While there may not be a specific threshold at which Overheads are seen as unreasonable, any use of the term must be expected to bring a query on the nature of those costs and a description of their sources.

This can be a behaviour which a TBM Office deliberately invites, particularly in response to costs being categorised as Overheads which they feel should be more deliberately managed.

From the early stages of building a TBM Cost Model some types of cost may be treated as outside the scope for modelling. These costs may then be treated as some form of Overhead and not modelled accurately.

An example is that, while it is clear that salary costs of technology staff should be in scope and aligned to IT Towers, the costs of desk and office space may be thought to be treated separately. It can be the case that there is no information immediately known or available on how to align those costs, so this might be held back and treated as Overhead. The TBM Taxonomy addresses this directly, identifying the Internal Labour Cost Pool as including occupancy (Appendix, p5).

One suggestion heard within the banking sector about how to avoid the negative associations of the term 'Overhead Costs' was to rename it as 'Executive Bonuses'.

Taking an approach of treating costs as Overhead with a view to aligning them more accurately later is dangerous during the creation of a TBM Cost Model and should be avoided. It opens up the opportunity for Service Owners to attempt to avoid cost in their Service by saying that it is not within their scope, which can be an innocent behaviour but can also be deliberate. It can also cause a rapid increase in the amount of Overhead cost, reducing the real and perceived accuracy of the model and its output.

TBM governance of which costs are allowed to be identified as an Overhead is one part of managing this. A further element is to simply take the cost sources individually and list them descriptively. While the alignment of those costs may still be waiting for accurate information, their cost will remain directly visible to reviewers.

Orphaned Costs

Once costs have been categorised and aligned to IT Towers within a TBM Cost Model, there is an assumption that those costs are understood and able to be modelled further. While a few costs may be treated as 'Overheads' as just described, possibly within the TBM Taxonomy 'Other' Cost Pool or grouped within the 'IT Management' IT Tower, there are other instances where costs will then fail to flow through the model and become 'Orphaned.'

Examples of this can be an Application or Service which has no associated Compute or Storage, or the reverse instance of Compute or Storage cost with no associated Application.

It is technically possible, but unhelpful and probably wrong within a TBM environment, to ignore these instances, filter them out of a Cost Model and allow costs to be fully aligned with the available associations.

Assuming you have $1,000,000 of Server cost made up of 100 servers each costing $10,000 of which 80 have known associations to applications, there are choices available for managing this. All the cost could be aligned through the applications via the 80 servers, or alternatively only $800,000 aligned to the applications where the relationship is known.

The reason to take the second approach within a TBM Cost Model, causing $200,000 to be identified as Orphaned, is to help drive behaviours which are better for the overall business. Highlighting the value which is Orphaned, through exception reports, will identify potential savings or efficiencies. The follow-up actions and tracking, to reduce or remedy the cause of this, can be supported by TBM.

The list of actions which may be taken in an example like this will depend on the cause of the issue, which may not necessarily be obvious from the information so far. This example could be caused by:

- Errors in the inventory where servers exist but do not have the associated Application.

- An incomplete inventory where the applications which are running on some servers are not listed e.g. for technology infrastructure applications.

- Errors in the inventory where servers have been decommissioned but not removed from the inventory.

- Errors in the inventory where the application has been decommissioned but the server has not been decommissioned or re-used.

- Errors in the inventory … simple typographic or data matching errors which mean that associations are not recognised.

The actions to remedy each of these causes are of benefit to an organisation, through both delivering improvements in the quality of inventory data, and Financial and Service quality.

Choosing not to show this as Orphaned cost, but distributing them all, fails to highlight the financial impact of these Orphaned relationships. This removes both the incentive to improve the situation and negatively impacts correct technology and service management by creating a gap between the perceived and actual costs.

While issues with Orphaned costs will usually be due to incomplete processes, it is also worth noting that some can be caused by deliberate negative behaviour, such as the intention to avoid costs being associated within a TBM Cost Model. This specific type of negative behaviour should not be expected, but can occur if the wrong incentives are in place, and if management structures are not in place to penalise them.

What people want: Picture, Purpose, Plan, their Part

Individuals are not all motivated by the same things and from a TBM Office's perspective the means to engage people with Technology Business Management needs a variety of approaches. There are multiple studies and views on how to identify individuals' motivations, some of which have particular relevance in a TBM environment.

Two particular areas which should be noted as having limited effect as motivators in a TBM environment are broad business goals and complexity; both are often looked at as irrelevant, with the first also superseded by individual goals and the second sometimes being demotivating.

Although it is often cited that staff want to know the overall direction of an organisation as well as their position and role in it, it is only at more senior levels where the impact of broad business goals are easily identified as being the same as an individual's goals. For the most part, people are concerned with cascaded and differentiated goals that are part of the whole, so do not feel directly responsible outside that.

This is a gap which needs to be addressed when people are involved with TBM, since the benefit of TBM tools and processes is often spread across an organisation and not just of immediate value to one person. If the person owning a Technology Service has expertise to manage the technology but not to properly understand its integration into the TBM Cost Model, they may not understand that the benefit of a request to improve their inventory is for the whole organisation, rather than just affecting their technology.

Where TBM information can be used as a measure of performance, both individual and organisational goals can be set and measured against, helping to overcome this. Continuing the previous example, the technology manager with an incomplete inventory could be providing a technically useful service already. When given a TBM based target to show their cost and how it varies over time to their customers, they would have an incentive that would be good for both them and the organisation.

The second area where individuals' characteristics and motivation can be seen as causing a gap, not uniquely to TBM, is in terms of complexity. The disciplines of Technology Business Management will only need to be known to those who work on it as managers and analysts, and users to a limited extent.

The specific challenge that this causes for a TBM team is in ensuring that the relevant processes must work without everyone requiring the central team's own range and depth of knowledge. That does not mean that they should be less transparent, but that there is value in having a simple explanation that can be used to mask complexity.

Most people who use TBM also have a regular job, so the introduction of TBM is at best an extra tool, but often only seen as an extra workload. In general they do not need to understand the whole of TBM. What is required is ensuring that they see the value of their input being used, and helping them understand how to use TBM output to show their own value.

For those who wish to understand the detail and complexity of TBM, to challenge and improve it, and for whom analytical thinking and problem solving are direct motivators, it is useful to provide additional transparency.

Although the example has other attributes, one area where simplification is a valuable tool is in the differentiation between the Cost of a Service and the

'Charge' to its customers. In general, the users of a Service will only need to be aware of the Charge so that they can manage their spending. They will not need to be aware of the underlying cause of cost and how it relates to the Charge. If they wish to understand more about that relationship, a first step would be to identify the main cost components, and a further step would relate why those are relevant.

The Business User of a Service might originally see that they are charged for it 'per account managed'. If they query how this is derived, the answer will be based on the Service definition and identifying that the total cost is divided by the number of accounts to calculate the charge 'per account managed.'

A request to break down the cost further is likely to be either to better understand the total cost or to understand a specific component of it, with a potential follow-up to reduce it. These actions and their motivations can be respected and may be beneficial both to the individual and the organisation. The same questions can be more of individual than organisational benefit, so the context of the query must be understood.

This level of analysis is more appropriate to the Service Owner than to their customer in the business, so ensuring that both are engaged is also a useful behaviour for a TBM Office to take. The breakdown of cost might be to show them which Applications make up the Service and to break this down into major technology cost components such as Compute, Storage and Application Software.

Managing change and driving specific change

As with the changes in governance and practice that are needed when managing TBM reports in a mature TBM implementation, changes to people's behaviour need management. As discussed in Chapter 4, on what is possible with TBM, many of the behaviours are positive and self-reinforcing, such as the increased ability and speed to build business cases for project and investment activity based on clear analysis of costs from a TBM Cost Model.

To help establish some of these capabilities, the creation and integration of specific TBM reporting can be useful in changing behaviour. This may include both status and action related reports, and should generally be created before the changes are implemented so that a baseline can be set from which the impact of changes is measured.

There are also changes which will occur as an organisation and its staff increase their understanding of a TBM Cost Model and how to use it. These will include the identification of efficiencies through cost saving and better use of existing resources, but can also include increased activity to realign costs from one Service to another. The management of this type of change needs to be governed by the TBM Office, as a Cost Model will not be open for everyone to change.

With mature use of TBM, requests for a change to the Model will come to include the business justification for the change. This tends to happen at different times for different Services, largely according to the level of engagement of the Service Owner with TBM. Some requests will be seen which are of marginal value to the organisation, but of more individual value to the Service Owner.

It can be a good practice for this type of request to ensure that movement of costs needs to be agreed at both ends before implementation. An example is where a Software License has been purchased to cover an entire organisation and the cost included in a Service, such as a Database Support License. This would be modelled at the IT Tower layer and aligned to Application Services based on usage. In this instance, a portion of the cost goes to a new Database Service at the Platform Services layer, since that cost and Service provision is never part of the same cost flow. A request from the Database Product Owner might come through asking that this cost should be split prior to their receiving it.

The justification may be correct and the change appropriate to make, but the process could still be wrong if the receiving Service Owner does not agree to it. There could be alternative licensing agreements for the Database Service or other factors to account for, so the change should have the agreement of the Service Owner receiving the cost alignment as well as the requester.

Although TBM is new to many people, some managers will fully understand its concepts as they are in many ways generic to business. This can sometimes be seen in a TBM Cost Model as it is created or reviewed, where costs appear in unexpected places due to a manager having already found a home for them outside their own span of control.

Standardisation and Patterns

One of the choices and sets of behaviour which appears to be strengthened by TBM Cost Modelling is that of standardisation. This is partly shown in the previous Chapters with respect to the definition of Services, and also in terms of the level of complexity that can be understood and managed.

Both of these can be seen as potentially limiting factors in the amount of variation that can be managed within TBM. This should not be entirely true as the limitations can be ignored and worked around, as long as Cost Model tools are capable of delivering any necessary level of complexity that is required.

One of the reasons for limiting complexity and exceptions is the difficulty they cause in measuring and managing efficiency which are core to the value seen through TBM. With too many variations, it becomes increasingly difficult to see whether changes have increased or decreased the efficiency of technology spend.

The reverse of this is that the less work a Technology department is doing to deliver individual exceptions, such as bespoke builds for its customers, and the more time on standardised patterns, the more efficient it should get.

Creation and pricing of standardised patterns of use, for example grouping Components, Products and Services in a standard way, can help drive efficient use of Technology Services. This can also be a precursor to extending the range of Technology Services in a Catalogue, where a particular pattern has widespread business use.

Chapter 15. Delivering Capability and Succeeding

As an organisation matures its implementation of Technology Business Management, the way that people interact with it gains similarity to a type of restricted capitalism. Although there is likely to be limited competition, central control of pricing and other areas of governance, the environment that is created can be described as an 'internal market for technology.'

This metaphor of a market for technology encompasses many ways in which businesses are run commercially, differing particularly in that efficiency of the organisation is the overarching goal rather than profit.

Measuring improvement against this direction and achieving specific goals within it needs particular approaches, and this chapter will review how it is possible to manage and communicate this.

The baseline implementation of TBM which this is founded on needs to be relatively mature in that:

- All relevant technology and related costs are actively managed in a generally stable TBM Cost Model.

- Product and Service Catalogues are in place for all technology Products and Services at the respective TBM Taxonomy Layer.

- A differentiation between Cost and Price is managed, with customers of Products and Services able to affect their costs by changing the volume that they use.

- Governance of the 'market' is managed by a central function such as the TBM Office, including managing changes within any of the three previous processes.

With these implementation requirements, the first two of which have been discussed in detail Chapters 8 and 10, additional TBM governance processes are needed for the extended capabilities. These include deciding how to manage the difference between costing and pricing of Services, how to manage the market itself, and new challenges such as how to handle the additional complexities of integrating pricing into financial budget processes.

Moving from costing to pricing

From a relatively early stage in the maturity of a TBM Cost Model, the alignment of some cost against Products and Services will be visible. The first step towards implementing a 'charge' for Products and Services, rather than an allocation of cost, is that the model is complete to the point where all costs are aligned to a Product or Service, and broadly validated with stakeholders.

There is always likely to be some movement or improvement required after that, and costs will vary from one period to the next, so there is not a single point at which to say that prices should be set from the TBM Cost Model. The timing for that will be based more on organisational imperatives such as financial timelines, and the capability to manage cost and charge relationships within financial systems.

Phasing in a charging or billing capability to financial systems takes time and careful thought, particularly by the Finance organisation, and can be viewed by them as an unnecessary complication with little value if introduced too early in a TBM implementation.

Business allocation as cost or charge

Once a TBM Cost Model is capable of calculating how cost is aligned to Services, there is a choice to be made about how to make that information visible to the ultimate business customer.

The simplest approach for a TBM Cost Model implementation team, based on their experience gained from building the earlier stages of the Model, is to continue to build a Model of cost alignments through to the Business User.

If the Business Users have previously been shown some form of cost allocation for Technology, the choice is largely about whether to first show them a TBM-based cost allocation, or whether to switch more directly to a charge-based allocation.

Moving from one approach to another is almost certain to cause changes to Business costs, so will generate significant amounts of discussion and questioning. These questions will be answerable with the information available through the TBM Cost Model, so this should readily be defended as being an improvement in the quality of the underlying allocation logic and accuracy of allocations.

Although allocating costs to Business customers is useful, it does not usually bring the full benefits of TBM to them. One factor limiting this is that allocation weightings at this level are more likely to be fixed for a financial year than able to be changed monthly, since the Service to Business allocation drivers are not as readily defined as those for Technology Components and Products.

Where information is available to make it possible to change the weightings monthly, business users may expect to be able to affect their Technology cost allocation in a similar timeframe, as they would with a charge-based allocation. This is generally not practical, since Financial flows will lag behind cost, so this style of implementation needs to be identified to Business users as benefitting them over a longer term, rather than immediately.

Unless this implementation approach is also the final goal for the TBM implementation, questions about the way that allocations are calculated will be repeated when a price-based allocation is introduced.

The choice of whether to show a TBM cost allocation at all may then depend on timing and the capability of the organisation, both the Financial team and Business. Bypassing this activity and moving directly to price-based billing and allocation causes no specific additional steps, so this intermediate stage may add no value to the implementation process.

Showback and Chargeback.

'Showback' is a term you can hear quite often within a TBM environment, but rarely otherwise. It is used as a term to capture the process and period when a Service Catalogue has been created along with relevant information to align cost or charges to customers, but without actually aligning financial allocations to those calculations. In similar situations, the phrase 'parallel' or 'shadow' running of the process is also used.

By contrast, 'Chargeback' is used to identify where a Price times Quantity mechanism has been implemented to allocate costs, and those charges are part of the customers recognised cost base.

The reason for identifying Showback by name with TBM is that it is sometimes seen as a final target state for an organisation's TBM implementation. A limitation of Showback is that Business users will only see a theoretical benefit of their actions rather than an actual benefit, so it is not fully effective as an incentive for them to take action.

A slightly different approach which drives towards the better behaviours, is clarity that Showback will be in place for a fixed period and will be deliberately followed by Chargeback. With this incentive, Businesses users can plan for and make changes to their behaviour to use Technology more efficiently, knowing that they will benefit from those changes when the switch occurs. An extended period running Showback processes, before fully migrating to a Chargeback capability, is a realistic option. This can even run for well over a year to tie in with Business and Financial processes, although this may generate pressure from Business users for faster implementation.

Using project charging as a model for Service charging

For a variety of Financial management purposes, including some tax efficiencies, the costs of project activity are often managed separately from business as usual activity. This can include specific price-based calculations such as setting a 'day rate' for people working on projects, with their hours spent on project activities multiplied by the day rate to calculate project cost.

The calculation of project costs is very similar to the calculation of non-project costs with TBM, in that both are based on a price and a quantity to calculate the total to be charged. The main difference is that with TBM, rather than managing a small number of day rates (possibly by skill level or location), a longer list of Services will be charged for on this basis.

The alignment of project costs to the Business is run on a regular basis by the Finance organisation. They also have processes in place to help them manage any difference between these calculated project costs and the actual costs which they manage in the ledger.

This capability for Finance, to balance in the Financial system any difference between a calculated Price times Quantity based charge and the underlying costs, is also required for Service charging. The reuse of the processes already in place for project charging can make the implementation of TBM Chargeback more straightforward than implementing something wholly new.

Pricing of Products and Services

The basis of most organisations' internal measures of success are that their Financial systems show overall financial health and profitability of Business Units, rather than at a lower level such as that of individual managers. While this does not scale perfectly and some enterprises need to manage and report finances and profitability at a lower level, this rarely extends down to the level of the internal Technology organisation or its individual Products and Services. This means that the expectation for pricing within TBM is not to make a profit for the Technology organisation, but more likely achieving a break-even position or small over-recovery.

Put in this context the target may be obvious, but when it comes to pricing Services and Products based on a TBM Cost Model the idea needs to be restated; that the Technology organisation is not there to make a profit at the expense of its own Business customers. This understanding needs to be communicated, both at the level of the Technology organisation and for its Products and Services, for several reasons.

A price-based charging system which generates a small but manageable over-recovery is usually preferable to under-recovering and needing to request balancing payments from the Business. As an example, in an organisation where Technology is one of a number of shared services that Businesses receive cost from (such as Personnel, Finance and Real Estate), an over-recovery by Technology may be useful to balance other areas with an under-recovery.

At the level of an individual Service Owner, there is a possibility that they will look at the finances for their Service and believe that it is in their best interest to increase the price, either to 'make a profit' or to fund additional investment. These approaches, if they are made by the Service Owner, can be compared to those of a monopoly supplier. In a closed, internal market where the business customers do not have the ability to buy elsewhere, this is not a useful behaviour.

Managing the price of Products and Services then comes down to working out the Unit Cost of each item to be charged for, identifying both the current state of efficiency and likely direction of those Unit Costs for the next period, and using those inputs as a basis for setting the prices.

Communicating changes to Services, and changes to their prices, becomes a sensitive issue for organisations and must be managed with significant attention to detail. An organisation's choice on how to use Technology can be materially affected by its perception of the price of Services.

Pricing based on Unit Cost

A simple rule of thumb for setting prices is to take the Unit Cost of an item and round it up to two significant figures. This takes a Unit Cost such as

$127.56 per unit and turns it into a price of $130 per unit. If there is a simple distribution of Unit Costs this gives an average of 1% over-recovery, but the actual value will be heavily affected by the pricing of the highest cost Services.

If a higher margin is desired, one simple alternative is to set the price as Cost plus a percentage. While this delivers on a target, the pricing of the same $127.56 plus 3%, at $131.39, suggests to customers that there is a level of accuracy and consistency from the Cost Model which is not truly achievable.

Combining the target margin calculation with either the rule of thumb or a similar rounding rule is a useful starting point for setting prices.

As with any rule of thumb there will be situations when it is best ignored, and these include when a price is either particularly low or high, as in the examples below.

The standard Unit for Storage, both for online and offline (backup) is per Gigabyte or Terabyte, where a Terabyte is 1000 Gigabytes. Looking at Cloud Storage, and generally at On-premises Storage, the requirements and provision are usually measured in Gigabytes (GB), as the majority of instances are still going to require fractions of a Terabyte (TB). Although they are mathematically identical, it is perceived as being easier to understand the charge for 120 GB of Storage priced at $0.023 per GB than the same charge being described as 0.12TB of Storage at $23.00 per TB.

The cost of Storage is often a material part of the total calculation of price-based allocations for a Technology organisation, so the margin can impact Business users more than for many other Services.

Breaking the rule of thumb to add an extra significant figure to the price is one option to manage this, or allowing a mid-point price such as $125 between $120 and $130. This approach has limits when working with fractions of a penny. With the Storage example, it is quite likely for people to query why the price is $0.023 rather than a simple two cents, so adding granularity to change the price to $0.0225 would not increase plausibility. Rounding the price up to the nearest whole cent, $0.03, would deliver a margin of 30% so may be unsustainable, whilst taking an 11% loss by pricing at $0.02 may cause an under recovery that is unable to be balanced elsewhere. At this stage, setting prices is about finding the balance between accuracy and achieving acceptance of the prices by your customers.

The impact of efficiency within the technology market

When setting prices for Technology Services, another factor which changes the actual margin delivered on the Service compared to its price is how the cost varies over time.

Although it may appear that technology costs are quite stable, for example a laptop computer seems to be at the same price point from year to year, the changes in the underlying technology mean that more capability is being delivered for the same price. This also applies to large scale and high cost technologies, where increased capability or capacity will be effectively shown as Unit Cost reduction, as the costs flow through a Cost Model. These become a relatively reliable driver in reducing the Unit Cost of many Technology Services, and a driver for reducing the price.

This impact is difficult to distinguish from other drivers of cost variance within a TBM Cost Model, but the net impact can be seen. The impact of Moore's Law i.e. that (historically) computer processing capability has doubled every two years, is reflected somewhat in the way that computer prices have reduced over time, although this is clearly just one component of a computer's cost.

The impact of market prices is a downward pressure on the Unit Cost of technology which can be expected but not easily measured. This effectively becomes a long term driver for price reduction, without requiring significant intervention.

Pricing for items without measurable units

Although the focus so far has been on Unit Cost as the basis for setting prices, there are several types of cost that are not easily measured or priced in this way. These can include costs which are treated as Overheads, as described in Chapter 14, or those for Products and Services which have a very low volume and need individual or bespoke pricing.

The flexibility to charge for these on a different basis to per-Unit pricing should be built into any pricing and billing system, but its use should be limited to the true exceptions.

A practical implementation is to set these items with a Unit of $1 (or the relevant currency), so that the number of Units to be charged to the customer is the amount they pay. An example might be for the provision of a new 'black-hole storage system' by a business, for which they pay $123,450 per month. This would be charged as 123,450 units at $1.00.

The calculation behind this is not transparent in the same way as an inventory-based charge, so needs to be communicated alongside the charge.

An alternative to this would be to charge for one unit at a price of $123,450. One reason to avoid this is that the purchase of a second or subsequent units each with a different price, would require each item to be managed in a Catalogue as its own separate Product with an individual price.

Even though the amount charged would be different for each device, treating this as a quantity provides flexibility until the actual number of Units reaches a level where a proper Unit Cost and price can be calculated.

A further level of flexibility can also be introduced with the concept of negative volumes. This is effectively a way to give a credit to a customer for whatever necessary reason. Most often the use of negative volumes will be in cases where an error in an inventory has been identified and the customer has been overcharged. Running a reversal of those volumes is a useful balancing transaction.

In almost all cases where negative volumes are used, the process to enter them into the billing system will be manual rather than through a standard automated source. There need to be governance processes in place to ensure that this cannot be abused, but in combination with the variable Unit of Measure, using negative volumes allows both quantity-based and arbitrary amounts to be credited.

Pricing for new and retiring services

New technologies are created regularly, sometimes at the component level of a TBM Cost Model and sometimes, particularly with Cloud technologies, more directly measured and used at the Products and Services levels within the TBM Taxonomy.

Although the impact is not as great when adding a new item to a Catalogue based on Cloud technology, the introduction of almost any new Product or Service will have some level of startup cost as well as its ongoing cost. The investment cycle, where equipment needs to be purchased to create the first instance of a Service, is still applicable to some types of technologies, so the approach to setting the initial price for these must be identified.

With the introduction of a new Service, all of the startup cost will be in the Cost Model but the actual volume used will start at zero and only grow gradually. Using this volume to calculate the Unit Cost, and setting the price based on it, will result in a very high initial price and cause users to avoid the Service, which is not the intended behaviour.

The choice of what volume to use to create a realistic Unit Cost and price will be informed by the expected usage defined in the Business Case for the new Service, the cost of equivalent services in the market, and other factors.

In the same way as not setting too high a price as a disincentive, setting too low a price so that the investment cost is never recovered from the customers is unlikely to be an acceptable approach. The balance is in finding a way to fund some investment but leaving enough room to be able to bring the price down after the Service is well established. It is a bad practice to price below the expected long term cost, as price rises are not well accepted.

The challenge for pricing of Services that are being retired is largely a reverse of the challenge for pricing a new Service. The costs of the Service will generally be reducing over time, as the original investment has often been in place beyond its planned lifetime, so ongoing running costs do not include any of the original investment or depreciation.

Although there is likely to be a planned reduction in the number of Units provided, the Unit Cost calculation is likely to be highly variable and pricing is probably best realised through a manual rather than automated process.

This is one of the instances where the price of the Service is unlikely to be as significant to the final users as other forms of management. Although an increase in the price might be noticed, a Service which is being retired is often already of both low cost and low value to the Business users, so they do not see the need to finish moving away from it.

The combination of TBM and other management disciplines, along with project management for the retirement of the Service, become a more practical approach. Setting a combination of timelines and deadlines for the Service to be switched off, with punitive charges for any users causing delays, are a more valid combination than increasing the price of the Service. Backing this up with publicising the process and naming those who are the last to leave the Service, can be more effective than a technical approach.

Price (and other) sensitivity

Setting and changing prices in a Service Catalogue become part of the standard annual financial cycles and processes once a Chargeback capability is implemented, although some flexibility in this can be retained while Showback is in use.

The primary driver for this is the need for Business units to create Budgets and Forecasts at specific times, which will include planning for their cost of Technology. These will include their projection of how much Technology they will use, and the prices set for the Products and Services.

The setting of prices must then happen at least annually, within the Budget process, although it may be possible to run it more frequently. Unlike the calculation of cost, which is best run on a monthly basis to help Technology management see patterns and movement within the technology cost base, changing prices regularly does not help Business users. Their ability to plan their cost of Technology will usually be only part of their longer term cost management, so changes to Service prices more frequently than annually can be seen by them as an unnecessary distraction.

The way in which users react to changes in Service prices is affected by their goals and perceptions, as noted above in relation to the retirement of a Service. Any change which negatively impacts a user will be more likely to be queried than one which aids them.

The most immediately noticeable change to customers is the increase in price of any Service, so any such change must be well planned, understood and justified, prior to being communicated.

This means that a price increase must not be communicated as being due to an increase in the Unit Cost of a Service. The implication of that message in isolation is that Technology costs are not being controlled or understood. A communication that describes an increase in license costs from a vendor, an investment in new technology, or an increase in the cost of managing risk and security, would all be more readily understood and more acceptable.

This can cause challenges to changing a TBM Cost Model if moving costs from one Service to another will cause the price to increase. This type of change is quite typical in a Cost Model so needs to be reviewed carefully for any impact on Service price. If a change to the Cost Model is justified, it should be made independently of the pricing so that the true business cost is not hidden, but it might be necessary to introduce the price change to the affected customers with more notice.

Apart from price increases, the other ways in which business users can see their costs increase are through their own volumes increasing and through changes to the Units associated with Services. The first of these is within the businesses' control, as they can choose not to increase their use of technology and its relevant cost, but the second is centrally managed.

The measurement and management of volumes for Chargeback are a core part of ongoing TBM processes. The best practice for this is that inventories are taken at least once per month, checked and validated, and then used as input both to the TBM Cost Model and to the Chargeback process. This output is expected to be reliable and accurate and any errors, exceptions and manual adjustments become part of the standard processing, understood by both the Service Owner and their customers.

Even with reducing prices, increasing business demand for services can drive the net cost up. The process for setting prices within an environment where demand is growing can cause some business interactions which are based on unrealistic expectations and projections. Issues can arise if a gap opens between the amount paid by Business users and the cost of Technology.

The other situation in which Business users can find their costs changing without being within their own control is through changes in the description, provision or Unit of Measure for Products and Services.

A change in the definition of a Service can be caused by multiple factors such as inclusion or removal of specific components, consolidation or separation of Services, or changes in the underlying technology. In some of these cases, the customer impact will be visible in the description and price, so the communication of the change is straightforward.

Where the change is going to cause customers to see different volumes from their previous view of the inventory, more detailed analysis and care needs to be taken with setting their expectations and checking for negative impacts.

An example of this can be seen in the case of automation of a Service, where the Unit charged used to be the number of requests managed. This might be a Service such as a resetting passwords, where modern systems automate what used to be a process requiring manual validation of the request and manual effort to reset the password.

While this might seem a simple and innocuous change, departments which were previously infrequent users of the Service can easily see an increase these costs, and will query why they are paying more for a function which they did not use.

Changes in underlying technology can also be visible as Unit Cost in a TBM Cost Model and appear wrong or counterintuitive. These are most likely to have an impact at the point of setting prices, and then need to be checked with relevant technology experts as they can drive behaviours which are not wanted. A recent example is that, at one point, disk storage appeared to be as cheap per GB as tape backup, though definitely not the best technical answer for long term archival. Pricing decisions around this needed to be taken based on the strategic technology choices as well as cost; another situation where TBM needs to mix with other management disciplines to deliver the best business result.

For price changes, with both the introduction of new Services and making changes to Services, the key to successfully delivering these is in regular and repeated communication. As reviewed in Chapter 10, the governance of changes to Catalogues and ensuring that Business users can adjust to the changes can run through much of the year.

Setting prices with changing costs and volumes

The level of detail used in a TBM Cost Model for inventory is unsustainable when it comes to future projections, such as budgets and forecasts. It is not realistic to know which inventory items, relationships and components will increase or decrease at a specific future point, particularly with a twelve to eighteen month projection, so more general and consolidated sets of data must be used.

As an example, where specific Compute Services are being projected, the best projection likely is that the volume of these will change by either a specific percentage or volume. The projected growth of Compute Services associated individually with each Application Service is unlikely to be usefully accurate. Using a broad multiplier for how all Compute Services are expected to grow can help deliver a view of how cost and price need to change.

With a Public Cloud based Service, as the price is set externally, the customer can only realistically be shown the external price plus a small increase for internal management costs. They will know that an increase in their use of the Service will cause an increase in their costs unless the external supplier reduces the underlying price, and that information on future price changes will not be available.

For internally provided Services the expectation may be different. Where an investment has been made in technology and its usage is not seen as perfectly efficient, customers might expect the price to be reduced over time and as demand and efficiency grow. This can lead to some interesting interactions between Businesses and Technology organisations when Service Demand and pricing decisions are taking place.

In a Budget cycle where Businesses are including the cost of Technology in their planning, any price changes for Technology Services can make a material difference to their total cost. In a situation where Chargeback is well established, Businesses will tend to see and assume that Technology prices will be reduced each year. This will not occur for all Services every time, but will be a regular occurrence and expected.

To meet their budget and business targets, Business users will want to understand how Technology prices will change, and they may also look at how prices are set and whether they can affect that process. If they are not told the price changes in advance, but asked for their projected demand, they may try to affect pricing through this.

With the approach to setting prices based on Unit Cost that was previously recommended, Business users projecting higher volumes than they currently have could reduce the projected Unit Cost, and see that built into the pricing. If they fail to meet their projected demand levels, they will still benefit from the reduced price, but Technology may find that not all their costs are recovered. For this reason, the use of Business projections of Technology volume need to be looked at alongside other factors such as actual volume trends and technology strategy.

In an environment where customers are told the new prices at the start of their Budget process, depending on the price changes they may have no additional work to do in order to meet cost reduction targets.

In the reverse situation to the example above, where businesses are told to reach a particular Budget target without being told what the price changes are, their only lever on their technology costs is to reduce their volumes. Calculating the projected Unit Costs based on those reduced volumes will cause increases, and potentially increased prices. As for increased Business demand, these types of decreases again need to be managed with broader understanding of the context.

The balance between these situations can be hard to find, and both may occur simultaneously for different Services. Arbitrating this is a governance function of the TBM Office; ensuring that the best information is used to set prices, since a mechanical or automated process will not suffice.

Value delivered

As Technology Business Management delivers multiple benefits to a business, the range of opportunities is sometimes a challenge in justifying the cost associated with implementing the relevant changes. Some specific and direct benefits can often be found in advance to cause TBM to be used. An ongoing understanding of the opportunities identified, actions taken, and value delivered through TBM are useful to maintain its evolution.

The reports generated through a TBM Cost Model, both for status and to track actions, are a key part of this capability, but additional activities can demonstrate specific areas of value.

How much would this have cost last year?

The delivery of increased efficiency in the use of technology spend is at the core of what TBM delivers. Measuring and showing those improvements must be a part of the ongoing engagement of a TBM governance team with all of its stakeholders.

The simplest way to communicate an improvement in the efficiency of technology is by showing a Cost reduction over time. The delivery of Unit Costs, and the parallel management of inventory throughout the technology cost base, enables net cost savings to be shown even if total costs rise.

Where prices and Chargeback are in place, the reduction can be demonstrated on the basis of a simple comparison of how much would have been charged for the current volumes but with the previous year's prices. In a Showback environment, the same can be achieved with the previous year's Unit Costs.

This can be calculated across a large part of technology spend, but there are some costs which should be excluded. This particularly applies to some forms of investment cost, such as Application Development, where business decisions on the amount of work will be strategic and not measurable on a per Unit basis. When looking at the total technology spend, investment in technology capacity should be included, as that becomes part of the Services' Unit Cost. Overhead and Orphaned costs should also be included or they risk becoming unmanaged.

Improvements in cost efficiency can be measured and reported in this way for a single technology or group of technologies, although this requires a level of integration effort when technologies are grouped. Mechanisms to create an 'Index' of overall technology efficiency can be implemented to achieve this for groups of Services and even to cover the majority of technology infrastructure.

What impact have changes made?

Within the overall improvements to efficiency that are expected to be seen and delivered through TBM, some will have been treated as general good management practice, some as inherent or automatic, some as targeted improvements, and some as improvements in accuracy and understanding.

The first two of these, good management practice and inherent or automatic improvements such as Technology price cuts, can be tracked and their impacts will be included in Unit Cost reductions. These become visible by their impact on Business cost, through standard TBM reporting.

Keeping track of the other two categories requires specific additional action, although their impacts will also be included in Unit Cost and efficiency reporting.

As reviewed in Chapter 13, Reporting can be implemented within TBM for targeted actions, strategic vendor management, application rationalisation programmes and technology changes driven by Enterprise Architecture decisions. Data already being consolidated and managed for those purposes can support ensuring that relevant reporting capabilities are in place, setting baselines and targets, and enhancing regular reviews.

TBM reporting poses a particular challenge when used to measure the impact of Cost Reduction programmes. The differentiation of costs removed and their replacement, such as consolidation of multiple vendor contracts to a single vendor, is only seen within TBM as the difference in value between the two. Some more aggressive reporting in Cost Reduction programmes might count the full value of all of the removed contracts as savings, without recognising the increased cost of the remaining vendor, which TBM could not readily differentiate and report.

The tracking of targeted actions requires additional discipline within the TBM Office as it will include not only the actions which are identified strategically by management, but also the changes and opportunities identified iteratively through the year as TBM reports are being reviewed.

With monthly reviews of TBM reports, particularly those showing overall status, trends and exceptions, specific items can highlight potential actions to improve the organisation's efficiency or the accuracy of the Cost Model.

As actions are taken to follow these opportunities, the TBM Office should be ensuring that a relevant measure is reported, setting a baseline, and tracking progress.

The additional factor of these actions being identified through TBM reports and processes does not give TBM the ability to claim credit for the actions, but tracking their identification and progress is part of the overall TBM value.

The implementation of changes to the TBM Cost Model is another part of the TBM value which needs to be tracked, even where it moves cost between Services rather than delivering a direct business benefit or overall efficiency improvement. These types of improvements in accuracy can have a long term impact on the business efficiency.

An example of this might be a decision to move the cost of a firewalled network from being charged as part of everyone's network cost to being associated with the specific applications on it. The increase in costs to the specific applications might highlight several types of inconsistency, such as some applications not needing to be in the firewall at all with others actively needing the capability but unaware of its existence. The financial benefit of this is not directly calculable, but knowledge of its origin is a useful example of TBM's wider impact.

Identifying opportunities

Where many businesses rely on managers' knowledge, experience and expertise to identify where the organisation can improve, a TBM Cost Model can be used to show technical data with a financial impact to be used as the basis for taking action.

Identifying specific opportunities within that data can still benefit from managers' and experts' knowledge and experience as many of the opportunities will already be known but their value unmeasured. Additional opportunities will be identified through ongoing and regular reviews of TBM outputs.

Capturing value and opportunities

Within many TBM reports, the integration of multiple sources of data is inherent, so the analysis of trends and exceptions is all that is required to initially identify opportunities.

These can range from simple items such as mismatches between inventories highlighting unnecessary expenditure, through to strategic opportunities such as earlier than expected over-capacity in Data Centres due to virtualisation or migration to Cloud environments.

As these items are identified they must be recorded and investigated. The process of qualifying the opportunity will include a calculation of its potential value, impacts to stakeholders, and required actions and ownership. The last of these becomes important as only a limited set of actions will be immediately able to be taken by the group identifying them. Many of the opportunities will be visible in the relationships between multiple data sets and involve multiple teams.

A governance process to consolidate opportunities as they are identified, qualify them, agree ownership and prioritisation, can be part of the role of a TBM Office, or devolved and distributed.

While there is a regular process to identify opportunities through TBM report review, the same processes to track opportunities can yield significant input from unofficial sources too. The more widespread the use of information from a TBM system, the more opportunities can be identified by specialists outside of the core reviews.

The opportunities in errors

Most errors you find in a TBM Cost Model will enable additional accuracy to be delivered in cost alignment, while a few will actively deliver cost savings. Errors which are found in Cost Model inputs can be challenging to incorporate but can sometimes be significant.

There can be a tendency in large organisations for responsibility to be specific in scope, with historic and organisational reasons given for why elements of a Component, Product or Service are excluded from an individual's remit. This can result in issues being identified where the creation of a TBM model aligns costs to a partial inventory, rather than leaving those costs unaligned.

If a Service Owner identifies that a cost should be not just for their own inventory, but also for an additional group, the customers of both will be affected. One set of customers will have been paying a higher price than necessary, while the other may have been paying nothing for their Service. In this situation, the second group might be unlikely to complain about being undercharged, while the former may have been struggling to justify business propositions.

Within a TBM Cost Model this type of error, of which there are multiple varieties, can occur throughout many stages of maturity and should not be expected to be irrelevant even after multiple years of TBM management.

These types of opportunity may not be turned into an immediate action, as the business impact may be material. Although the evaluation and qualification of the opportunity should be calculated in the same way, it is sometimes correct to defer impactful activity until the next budgetary or pricing cycle.

Errors in inventories can sometimes be significantly simpler to manage, such as by correcting the inventory when there has been a relatively immaterial gap. For slightly larger errors, it can be necessary to adjust volumes within a Chargeback model to ensure that a Business sees a correction for the error, for example charging for several months or historic inventory providing a credit for an overcharge.

Where there is a large enough error identified in an inventory, it is worthwhile deferring changes to your Model or billing until you have reviewed the impact.

Major corrections in Service consumption inventories do not just affect the customers of the Service but may require you to make an out-of-cycle change to the price of the Service as part of the adjustment. As this can change in either direction, the choice between action and deferral should be actively decided.

An example is for a Database Service, charged per instance, where it is discovered that there is an additional inventory to be added which will cause a 50% increase in volume. Assuming that the price had been set to fully charge for the costs, this will mean that there is a sudden increase in the allocation from technology and a 'profit.' Alongside this, it is likely that the Business users of this additional inventory did not know that they were not being charged for it, so will need to accept charges that they have not budgeted for.

The decision on what change to make related to this, and when, will depend on the readiness of all users of the Database Service to act for the common good, and their ability to manage change. The TBM Office may be able to offer to reduce the price of the Database Service and start charging the additional inventory. In those Business groups which are being charged for the Database Service already, this reduction in the price per instance will generally be acceptable, while the Businesses impacted by the new inventory may be more challenged but should still accept that this is correct.

The general alternative to this is to defer the same change in billing until the next pricing cycle. This will generally be unchallenged by those Businesses which have already budgeted for their use of the Service, although this type of goodwill cannot always be relied on.

A harder situation to manage is the reverse, where an inventory is found to be significantly overstated and customers charged for phantom items. This will potentially have caused the price of the Service to be set too low. This type of situation is one of the risks to a technology department budget, and to business plans, which is less likely to be acceptable to customers to adjust for. Deferring action to fix this until the next full budget or pricing cycle, which will generally require increasing prices, is generally going to be the only acceptable approach.

Strategic business decisions

If a business is planning strategic actions with a significant impact on the IT expense base, TBM can provide significant information to advise on it. This can range through the impact of mergers and acquisitions, the cost of divestments on technology, and the relevant financial position for technology outsourcing.

In any such situation, the standard TBM capabilities will be a starting point to provide data, but may need significant change to meet specific requirements.

With a stable TBM Cost Model, the challenge of integrating a strategic change is understanding which variables are required to deliver a relevant "what if" analysis. Additional concerns about this, such as the sensitivity of this type of analysis compared to the normal transparency of TBM, also need immediate focus. These issues are likely to be more sensitive than any Business as Usual functionality.

The potential complexity and security of this activity requires an early definition of the analysis process; preferably prior to its first engagement. This will include proper phases and timelines for definition and qualification of the request, sponsorship and approval, specification of scenarios, and delivery.

Requests for "what if" analysis will come in all sizes once it is known that the capability exists. The effort involved will generally only be of value at a sufficient scale to make business decisions, rather than IT decisions.

One type of strategic business decision which needs relatively little additional analysis is the value of technology outsourcing. A by-product of a full TBM Cost Model implementation is that a well-structured view of both the Unit Cost and Volume of much of the technology cost base will be immediately available. This is a directly relevant set of measures when considering technology outsourcing, and a potential key to understanding a Vendor's plans and margins in such a discussion.

Some strategic choices and actions can be reflected within a TBM system with forward planning. An example which might not be included unless the opportunity was foreseen, is on decisions around single-vendor, dual-vendor or multiple-vendor policy. This capability can be built in or added to a model, enable this to be investigated and reported, but is not relevant to every organisation.

Measuring impact

Beyond the financial impacts that can be measured with TBM, there are a number of ways in which the benefits to the Business can be recognised in the actions and behaviours of people and the organisation. These range from broad organisational maturity measures to individual recognition.

TBM maturity

Although Technology Business Management as a discipline has only been in existence since the early 2010s there have been a number of assessments and measures of maturity developed to cover aspects of it. Using these external assessment schemas can provide useful guide to potential areas for development, as well as a potential metric for comparison with other organisations.

There is also a mechanism to generate your own maturity assessment, based on standard approaches such as Capability Maturity Models. This can be a heavyweight way to measure the development of your internal systems, but the concepts and individual metrics can be very useful. A challenge in this is that one organisation's goals and scope for TBM may not be complete, although the assessment can be more specific.

Measuring the maturity of your TBM environment can be done across multiple aspects including data, model, outputs, internal and external consumers. This type of analysis may be extracted directly from a TBM system at times, enabling ready measurement of progress, although at a more functional level than for true maturity assessment.

Measuring engagement and usage

There are different approaches to the rollout of TBM systems; from maintaining them as a centralised capability to aiming for their widespread use throughout an organisation. In either design, there is an opportunity to look at whether the target users are engaging with the system as expected or if there are gaps.

A number of measures of engagement can be put in place, such as training, vendor or TBM Council qualifications, and the level of use of TBM systems and reports.

As well as individual engagement, usage of systems and reports is a useful measure by which the TBM Office can check whether specific Use Cases are being followed, as discussed in Chapter 13.

On a broad scale, the use of regular surveys to gauge stakeholder engagement with TBM is an option; measuring this every six months can show you where you're making real progress and where you need to focus.

Backing up this type of engagement metric with actions to directly solicit feedback and success stories is also a regular TBM Office function. Activities that raise internal 'brand' awareness, running roadshows, delivering regular communication, and giving awards to people for identifying and delivering efficiency improvements, can all help ensure that Technology Business Management is embedded in an organisation and its value realised.

Governance

The ongoing success of a TBM implementation and its acceptance, development and achievement, require a core TBM governance and management team to develop and promote the function and capabilities. This is often called the TBM Office, but the responsibilities must be recognised even when it is not identified by name.

This is role which usually starts during the implementation phase of a TBM deployment and whose staff are the first in the organisation to gain skills and understanding of the general principles of TBM. They also have been involved in the detailed discussions about how and why specific decisions have been taken on aspects of the implementation, which are often not fully documented.

This set of skills and knowledge base are hard to replace if there is wholesale change in the team, so spreading skills and knowledge throughout an organisation is a useful aim. Within an organisation that is regularly moving staff and managers between jobs or hiring new staff, the ongoing training of both the TBM Office staff and other stakeholders is a TBM Office responsibility.

As identified in Chapter 5, about where TBM should sit in an organisation, the range of TBM disciplines covers Finance, Technology and Management.

It is generally the case that people do not have all the skills at the required level to understand the whole of TBM when they first engage with it. The two aspects of this which need to be integrated are firstly ensuring that people reach the minimum level of knowledge required in their non-specialist areas, and then ensuring that they do not become too specialised.

An example of this is seen when working with Technology users and managers with limited Finance knowledge. Unless the person is already aware of Financial processes and timelines, there will regularly be a question of why they are looking at information that is a month or two old. The necessity to finish a month before the Finance data can be loaded to a TBM Cost Model, and how long that takes, is a straightforward concept once it has been described, but not one that is obvious unless you have been involved with it.

Monthly TBM governance

The question of when TBM output will be available is a regular feature of TBM governance. With a financial-calendar based process underlying most TBM activities, both monthly and annual, it should be possible to plan many activities in advance.

The monthly cycle of loading data to a TBM Cost Model, processing, validating, correcting it (if needed) and publishing it, can be managed in multiple ways to help formalise the timeline and set expectations. This can include multiple stakeholders in different ways. The processes affecting Finance may be sped up, such as by taking a pre-close ledger input to check for variances and understand their impact on TBM before the final data is available. If it is not fully automated, it is useful to manage and check the engagement of Component, Product and Service owners to ensure that their monthly inputs are received in good time and with correct quality, querying material variances in advance.

Reducing the amount of time taken for month-end processing is a useful goal for a TBM Office. That period of time is usually required to be significantly dedicated to the activity and cannot easily overlap with other workloads.

Semi-annual and annual cycles

Quarterly cycles are often a chance to consolidate trend and progress data from TBM and other sources to report on them. These are largely an extension of the standard monthly TBM cycles, focused on specific actions or concerns. Longer cycles, such as semi-annual and annual, can be more involved for a TBM Office, calling for varying degrees of change management and planning.

If the TBM Office has responsibility for governance of Product and Service Catalogues, a significant proportion of the year can be taken up with aspects of managing change to it. The timeline needs to be tied in with the Budget cycle, as the changes must be complete and communicated prior to the start of budgeting. This may also include the TBM Office being involved in some element of pricing for the changes.

The length of time needed for planning Product and Service changes can vary but needs to be conservatively managed, as there is very little flexibility on the end-date. It must also tie in with any other organisational dependencies, such as inter-related Catalogues (both in Finance and elsewhere) which may have their own lead-times.

An example of this is where Services are linked between TBM and financial systems for Chargeback, so that the introduction of a new Service in the TBM Catalogue must be matched by the same change being made in the Finance system Service Catalogue. Such a change, for use in next year's budgeting by business users, will have an internal Finance-team timeline which may not be published but needs to be anticipated and understood by the TBM Office.

This is a practical challenge, since a six-month process for documenting, modelling and pricing a change to a Service, plus a three month budget cycle, means that planning for the next year appears to start almost as soon as a new year has begun.

Managing breadth

As noted throughout this book, a significant combination of Technology, Finance and Management skills can be required in all TBM roles. These are more specialised and detailed within a TBM Office, but apply to many stakeholders and users too.

Mixing these requirements with both people, organisational and technical change, the need to prioritise and focus on specific action items and issues is also coordinated from the TBM Office, with decisions delegated or escalated as needed. Ensuring that decisions and changes are both understood and approved helps to limit the concentration of knowledge in too small a group, and with it the risk of knowledge being lost when individuals move jobs.

Flexibility and consistency

In Chapter 3, the purpose of Technology Business Management was described as being "To manage IT efficiently and equitably align the cost to its consumers." Although not explicitly identified in the phrase, the equity of aligning the costs is linked to Budget and Forecast processes by some TBM users, in the sense that changes to costs which are beyond their control are inequitable.

In an organisation which has historically used an annual process for setting the IT budget and charges, from a Business user's perspective their budget may be set at the start of the year and cannot be changed. From this perspective, the monthly cycle which a TBM Cost Model brings can appear out of control. This can particularly lead to a slow rate of change before implementation of a Chargeback model, while Business users adjust to being given the opportunity to manage their Technology costs. Moving from their old expectation of a single and consistent charge each month for Technology, to one where they are responsible and can cause those costs to change, is an organisational change that needs preparation.

This challenge also applies when there is a Chargeback capability, if there is a change in price or other charges which are beyond the Business users' control. If the Business users understand that they can control their costs by controlling their demand for IT Services, a change to the price of a Service affects their financial forecasts and profitability, so they will object. The most constructive response to this from a TBM governance perspective is to clearly identify when in the Financial cycle the prices and charges will change.

The requirement for consistency is not limited to Business users and is equally impacting on the Finance department, particularly at the start of data flowing through a TBM Cost Model. Except in situations where the Finance department are running a regular update to their forecasts, there are specific times at which a Finance manager will clearly benefit from having a TBM Cost Model which is locked down with no further changes allowed. The most frequent example of this is the creation of a formal, agreed budget.

It difficult for a TBM Office to balance this with the need to provide regular Model updates. The TBM Office needs to ensure that they can manage and report on both 'static' scenarios, usually historic, while at the same time continuing with regular 'dynamic' capabilities.

Documentation

A Cost Model usually will not be able to tell you a narrative of what costs reach a certain point and why. 'What' is traceable through a TBM Cost Model, but 'why' needs to be documented separately.

Documentation of a TBM implementation is a bit like documentation of Application Development; it is important to ensure that you do it while the work is in progress, or it is likely to never happen. The documentation also needs to be very flexible, due to the usual high rate of change and rework during implementation and even afterwards.

As with Application Development, it is useful to put comments into the coding of a TBM Cost Model at multiple levels. At various points it will be necessary to have information about where the model is conforming to the TBM Taxonomy or varying, about the specific logic that is following a standard or has been built to a unique business requirement, and about the individual logic of a formula.

With this in place, it is possible to work out how to extract the information to turn into relevant documentation.

Different roles will need different paths through the documentation of a TBM implementation. Some of these paths will show generic information relevant to a role. This type of documentation is most likely to be the basis of education and training on TBM for a role, and broad rather than deep.

Building more specific documentation based on Use Cases can provide a high level of confidence and specificity, allowing users to reach relevant information quickly but still with context. This can apply to specific documentation of reports, but also needs to refer to how the information in those reports is derived.

Although requiring effort to achieve, users will find it easier to understand a 'narrative' of cost flows in a TBM Cost Model than a technical description. As such, documenting a Cost Model usually needs to be about "what" a cost is and "why", followed by "how" it relates to its source or consumer. It should rarely, if ever, be about "how many" or "how much", which is the job of reporting.

Chapter 16.   The Bloopers reel

If, like me, you can look at the index of a book and then choose to jump to a particular Chapter based on the headings, welcome! This Chapter is designed less as a summary or set of stories to be read in sequence (although you're welcome to do so), but more as a set of illustrations of how some of the ideas covered in the book can fail to work as expected when they meet real world situations.

However hard you have tried to reach perfection in a Technology Business Management context, there are circumstances (and sometimes people) that make this impossible to maintain. A large majority of the issues which arise are straightforward to deal with and become part of the regular processes that are needed in a company using TBM disciplines. However, some are unusual in the scale of their impact or in the root cause once they are traced.

This Chapter brings together a few anonymised examples of the more unusual situations that can occur, from huge errors, through deliberate manipulation of data, to easily overlooked issues of internationalisation.

$100 trillion gap in the budget

In an organisation running a Price x Quantity allocation mechanism to charge Application Owners for their use of IT Infrastructure, the first run of a budget cycle showed that the Technology department had made a $100 trillion over-recovery ... and the receiving businesses were about to make the equivalent loss!

In Chapter 9 there is a section reviewing why it is difficult to manage low volume Products and Services in a TBM environment. When this is combined with those same Products being of significantly high value, there is a need to look at how to pass those costs to their consumers most effectively.

In this case, the Product was a new form of technology which was effectively a 'black box' that a Business could buy as a single unit, rather than having to purchase components from different sources and integrate them. The cost of each device was millions of dollars, each was a custom configuration and price, and this was paid for by the Technology department and then charged to the Business customer as depreciation over a five year period.

As these boxes were each individual and custom, there was no way to set a standard price, so a price of $1.00 was set in the Service Catalogue and the amount to be charged to the customer was set as the volume e.g. a box costing $1.2m would be charged back at $20,000 per month or technically as 20,000 units at $1.00.

After a few years, there was enough volume for a standard configuration to be created for these devices and it was decided that they would be charged at the price of $22,000 per month for each unit, to include the costs of maintenance and operations on top of the purchase price. This was communicated to the Business users in advance of the Budget cycle, so that they would know to change their demand volumes appropriately.

Wherever the gap occurred, the first Budget cycle included the new price of $22,000 per month, but one of the Businesses had kept their old customised volumes of around 20,000 per device.

The result was that this individual Technology Service charge to customers was reported to be over $100,000,000,000 and caused much of the Budget to be considered unusable.

The situation was easily remedied, as the correct quantities for each customer had been calculated in advance and just needed re-entering into the finance calculations. A quick calculation shows that this was still a relatively low volume product, with only around 20 units, so this might not have been the best timing to change the approach to billing.

Individual pay affecting behaviour

In some businesses, and particularly in the financial sector in around the turn of the millennium, there was a significant amount of individual pay that was calculated based on the profit generated at a business group or individual level. This type of situation, where incentives are directly linked to a particular type of achievement, led to issues in the markets but also affected how some groups managed their Technology cost.

An example of this occurred in an environment where the Business were charged on a Price x Quantity basis for their use of Servers.

In one instance, the mechanism for charging the cost of Servers was to look up the cost and price of a Server based on the data held in the TBM system, and to combine that with ownership information for Servers provided by the Compute Service Owner, to create a bill.

A Business user discovered that they could change their Server name in the Service Owner's database to include a trailing 'space' character. This would be invisible to anyone manually comparing the lists, but the system creating the bill for Servers would not find a matching name so the owner would not be charged.

What might have started as the identification of a small error in the coding could have become a factor in the Business users pay and bonus. This issue was found early due to costs being out of line between the TBM and billing systems. A correction was made to the overall quantity for the year to make up for the 'lost' charges, along with additional checks on the accuracy of the billing process.

Measuring at a point in time or for average usage

It is useful to look at how different the approaches of vendors have become for billing technology usage. One of the ranges is between the way that IBM charge for mainframes, based on regular measurement of the usage and charging based around the peak value. In comparison, the charging for Cloud Services is also based on regular or continuous measurement but often charged per minute of actual compute usage.

Both of these rely to some extent on continuously tracking the use of resources, but for many technologies this is neither realistic nor necessary. In most TBM implementations the inventory that is used will be a monthly snapshot, often taken at a specific date in the calendar.

This can lead to inaccuracy when a customer's processes cause monthly peaks and troughs in their usage that are not captured in the inventory used for TBM and billing.

An example of this was seen in terms of one business group who were working with a high-performance trading system using large amounts of data. They reasoned that additional performance could be gained by 'defragmenting' their data each month, which could be achieved by temporarily moving all of the data off its high performance (and high price) disk storage to a lower performance, lower price location, and then moving it back.

Your acceptance of this description might depend on your understanding of the technologies involved, but this also just happened to be scheduled to take place at the same time as the monthly inventory extracts were taken for TBM and billing calculations.

The impacts of this situation were limited to the single application involved, as the data was not of sufficient size to materially affect the overall volume of either the high or low performance Storage. The longer term fix was to review the volatility of Technology Service inventories over time i.e. how much they changed and how often, to identify and change any areas that might be affected in this way.

Thousands and Thousandths

Unless you work in a multinational workplace, you may never have questioned the way that you were taught to write numbers at school. The British are slightly aware of how the meaning of numbers change, since the word "billion" used to mean a million million to them until the financial markets became more global and 'everyone' started using the American usage of a billion being a thousand million.

Even then, both America and Britain both write numbers with a "point" as the separator between whole numbers and mantissa (... the fractional part). Both may also choose to use a comma to separate thousands, millions and other groups, for example $12,345,000.67

The last sentence did not finish with a full-stop as the context would have made it potentially dangerous!

If you work with other countries it is important to note that this way of writing numbers is not close to being universal, and the level of issue that this can cause is as bad (or worse) than the difference between decimal and imperial units.

A simple example is that the same number as above, when written in Italy, would be €123.456.000,67

The use of the comma as a separator between units and tenths is more common globally than the use of a point, as can be seen in several online references. The use of a point separator between thousands and millions, as shown in the Italian example, is also somewhat limited and many countries instead use a space.

Any individual data set that is used in a TBM system, or elsewhere, would normally be expected to use a single format, but it becomes important to ensure that all numbers that are used for calculation are treated correctly.

The worst case in this context is where multiple data sources are consolidated, or manually edited, without the common numeric format being followed. If you are given the following table to convert to a single numeric format, the job is impossible without further information.

Location	Value ($ thousand)	Interpretation
USA	12,000.00	Definitely $12 million
France	12,000	Either $12 thousand or $12 million
Germany	12.000	Probably $12 thousand but possibly $12 million
Italy	12.000,00	Definitely $12 million

Unrealistic expectations

Although it is generally been covered in Chapter 11 on how to respond to queries starting with "But ...", it is very important to recognise that some expectations and questions can't be simply answered just with data, but need to be more fully explained.

This can be a matter of understanding the context that the people asking and answering the question are working from.

In one of my fist roles as a Business Manager in Technology, I was trying to understand a $10 million gap between the financial plans of my department and what I'd been sent as the Budget from the central finance organisation. My role sat within Technology at the time, and this was around 20% of my department's Budget for the year.

I spoke to the local Finance team who said that the numbers didn't come from them but were globally administered and gave me a person to call, which I did.

The call was brief. I described who I was and what the gap was that I was querying, and the call was immediately terminated with the answer that my question was "neither material nor strategic."

At the time, $10 million and 20% of my Budget felt very material and strategic to me, and both those numbers still do, but I had never looked at the context managed by the person I was calling. I do try to make enough time to explain this when put in a similar situation now, but also understand how my call, in the middle of a Budget cycle, could bring the response it did.

Changing the Unit of Measure

In Chapter 10, the description of various Product and Service Catalogues, their governance and change management, included processes and timelines for collecting changes, testing and validating them before rollout.

One change that had an unexpected effect, which made it through all the testing, validation and approval processes, was to the Unit being charged for a Service. Both the reason for the change and its impact are useful to note in this situation.

In a Mainframe processing system, a Technology Operations team existed whose job was to run and manage batch jobs; a series of tasks that were run regularly, with clearly defined documentation showing the processes for how they were started, along with how errors should be handled and escalated. Much of this was already automated, and the role was not a separate Service from the rest of Mainframe processing.

Alongside this a team were responsible for Change Management of the batch jobs. Their role was a separate Service and charged to Application Owners based on the number of changes that they requested and implemented.

Automation reached this function, and a self-service capability (including testing) was put in place so that Application Owners could make changes to the batch jobs themselves. This meant that instead of the cost driver being how many technology staff were needed to administer changes, the cost of the Service was that of the automation software.

This cost still needed to be charged out, so an alternative billing measure was chosen; the number of batch jobs in the system. How wrong could this go, when all systems needing batch jobs must have a broadly comparable requirement for change?

The answer to the last question turned out to be material to at least one Application. It turned out that one Application had separate test requirements for each of its customers' countries, so had around 20 separate test environments, each with a full copy of all the batch jobs. Although a batch change request might only apply to one country at a time, so in the past this cost very little, the new billing unit meant they were continually charged for 20 copies of every batch job they managed.

In an environment with hundreds of Applications, this change to the Catalogue entry did not show up in testing as causing a material impact, but to the specific Application and the department using it the change could have been the difference between profitability and closing down.

A pragmatic answer needs to be reached in these situations, which in this case was for the Application to be treated as a special case and only charged for one copy of its test environments, although the overall Application design and test processes were also reviewed.

The difference between succeeding and going viral

The final example in this book is one which, in many ways, you may hope to achieve. Once you have understood the potential value that can be delivered by creating a Technology Business Management system, there is usually some level of frustration that you will feel that it is not going as far or as fast as it could.

The opportunity, and risk, of this becoming a huge success and going viral in a business, can be the result of active marketing of TBM or through more organic growth. Both of these can be positive once the TBM capability is sufficiently robust, but need to be treated with the utmost care if the core TBM Cost Model and reporting is not complete.

The positive situation is most likely to arrive at around the point when a TBM Cost Model has been built and validated, with reports starting to be made available to people outside the groups involved in the implementation process.

Once a wider range of business users start to see the information and take advantage of something that is clearly understandable to them in their own context, they will talk to each other about how to do this.

This can start with a single point, such as a manager seeing for the first time how much their department is paying for desktop computers and asking why. If they see in their TBM reports that they have more computers than people, they kick off an effort to clean this up, tell their colleagues how much they expect to save as a result, and everyone starts looking at this question.

If all the managers are looking at TBM output to identify the value of this problem's resolution to them, some will also find other opportunities and start to take the same approach.

It is possible to plan for a gradual and controlled rollout of TBM access across an organisation, which would limit the likelihood of this type of unexpected success. However, if the opportunity arises to increase the rate of adoption and value rapidly, most people will take it.

The question at this point, for both Technology Business Management and for the Technology organisation, is whether they are ready and able to deal with the volume of requests and queries that are suddenly and unexpectedly being generated.

For the TBM team, this will not stop with people using the information in positive ways, and the number of queries about data will grow hugely. All of the challenges covered in Chapter 11, starting with the word "But ..." should be expected, but instead of being spread out will appear in a short time.

Coordinating with the Technology team so that they know how to structure their own responses to this type of situation is also hugely important. They should know what their customers are looking at, how it is delivered within the TBM Cost Model, and be able to explain how they manage their Service for the customer's benefit. This approach, where a Technology Service Owner look at their own Service from their customer's perspective, is one that does not always happen. When it does, it becomes a key mechanism for showing how Technology Business Management can bring value by being properly integrated throughout a business.

Chapter 17.   Glossary

This glossary is not formal or based on standard definitions for accuracy, but specific to the way that terms are likely to be used within the context of Technology Business Management implementations. Common understanding of terms is important for communication between Technology, Finance and Business functions and the use of these terms may vary from situation to situation.

Many terms used in the book are defined within the TBM Taxonomy and can be found in the Appendix. Where such terms are also listed in this Glossary, it is because of their repeated use in the book.

Activity Based Costing, ABC

A method for aligning costs to activities, and aligning those activities to Products and Services to work out their total cost. This is fundamentally what a TBM Cost Model does, with IT Towers, Products and Services as sets of common activities. The term Activity Based Costing is not usually used within a TBM context as it is more often part of a formal Finance process.

Business Case

A Business Case is the justification used to analyse and approve project or investment spend, usually as a document with supporting material. TBM systems can help provide structured information about technology cost, so that this is more complete and accurate than manual processes.

Business View

The Business View refers to TBM information provided to Business Users when following the TBM Taxonomy. This is generally related to the cost of Services and how those costs align to Business Units and Capabilities.

Capability Maturity Model

Originally defined as a hierarchy describing the way that software development can be classified and its quality improved, this has been extended to provide similar measurement in many other environments.

Catalogue

A structured list of items available for use. Catalogues exist in multiple places within organisations, many of which need to be integrated as part of a TBM implementation. (See Chapter 10)

Chargeback

The process of creating prices for Products and Services, and multiplying this by inventory-based quantities to allocate cost to customers based on this. This implies that customers can change the quantity they consume to affect their cost for the Products and Services.

Chart of Accounts

A catalogue of the Finance accounts categorising how costs and revenues will be listed in the ledgers. The Chart of Accounts is usually used within TBM as the basis to align costs to Cost Pools.

Cloud

See Private Cloud/ Public Cloud

CMDB, Configuration Management Database

A database identified in ITIL, intended to contain information about technology components (ITIL 'Configuration Items') and their relationships to each other.

CoBIT, Control of Business IT

A structured set of tools and processes to help manage and govern technology in an organisation. CoBIT extends beyond technology management to include risk and controls, but does not extend particularly into Business & Financial management.

Component

A unit that could have a price, which is only provided to other Products and Services and only consumed by other items in the Cost Model e.g. Storage for Applications. (See Chapter 10)

Converged Infrastructure

A type of technology where multiple types of hardware and software are combined by a vendor into a single consolidated offering.

Cost Centre

This term has multiple meanings. The most general is the point in a financial hierarchy at which costs are grouped and managed in a financial system. The terms is also used to describe an overall view of the value of an organisational function which does not generate revenue. (see Profit Centre)

Logical groupings of accounts in the General Ledger. These are defined in the TBM Taxonomy and used in TBM as part of the first stage of Cost Modelling to align those costs to their relevant first-stage inventory.

Cost Source

Another term for the General Ledger layer in a TBM Taxonomy, in which the full set of costs to be managed through a TBM Cost Model are captured. This can cover regularly updated costs, and budget or forecast costs covering longer periods.

Enterprise Architecture

A business discipline where a set of processes and tools enable an organisation to document its current business and technology estate and processes, describe a future state, and drive change to reach that future state. (See Chapter 4)

Finance View

This refers to TBM information provided to Finance Users when following the TBM Taxonomy. This is generally related to the costs which are initially loaded into a Cost Model and their transformation up to IT Towers.

IT Financial Management, ITFM

A related discipline to TBM, developed from a financial background and is more directly focused on ensuring correct accounting and alignment of IT costs for financial management and reporting. (See Chapter 6)

ITIL, IT Infrastructure Library

A library of processes and tools which are designed to provide a structure for IT Service Management. ITIL is more focused on managing service delivery and service quality, with limited requirements for financial management.

IT Towers, IT Sub-Towers

This is a catalogue of functions defined in the TBM Taxonomy. Within a TBM Cost Model they are the point at which technology costs are grouped according by what they do (their function) rather than what they are (their cost).

'Orphaned' costs

Costs which are identified as relating to a technology function or component which cannot be aligned consistently to inventories. These are potential points for improving data quality or technology efficiency. (See Chapter 14)

Private Cloud / Public Cloud

Technology Services provided via a network, which can replace the need for similar Services to be owned by an organisation. Public Cloud describes where these are provided over the Internet, while Private Cloud is where equipment is owned within a single company.

Product

A unit that could have a price, which can be consumed by both within the Cost Model and by business units e.g. Virtual Servers used for Application Development and for Application Delivery. (See Chapter 10)

Product and Service Catalogues

One or more Catalogues showing what is provided by a Technology organisation to its customers, including lists or the items and their descriptions. Within TBM this relates most frequently to the TBM Taxonomy Products & Services layer.

Profit Centre

Within the context of internal business finance, this describes whether the organisational entity is treated as balancing its costs with revenues as a Profit Centre, or just causing cost. (See Chapter 6)

Reference Data

Data which is unlikely to change, or to change very infrequently. This is differentiated from data which is required to be updated regularly, such as financial data and technology inventories.

Service

A unit that could have a price, which is mostly consumed by Business Units e.g. a desktop workstation. (See Chapter 10)

Service Catalogue

See Product and Service Catalogue

Service Owner

The role of Service Owner is distinct from that of a Technology Manager in that they are responsible for all the components of their Service, rather than just a single technology. Within TBM they may also be responsible for the Service definition, cost and sometimes pricing, as well as non-TBM disciplines such as Service delivery, quality and risk management.

Showback

The process of setting prices for Products and Services, and showing customers how much cost they would be allocated based on this and inventory-based quantities that they consume. This is not connected to financial allocations (see Chargeback) but can be a precursor to it.

TBM Council

The Technology Business Management (TBM) Council is a nonprofit business entity focused on developing a definitive framework for managing the business of IT. (See Appendix)

TBM Taxonomy

A set of organised and interlinked hierarchies, used for aligning financial, technology and business functions into a TBM Cost Model. (See Appendix)

TBM Office, TBMO

An organisational entity which is responsible for governance and management of TBM and a TBM Cost Model.

Total Cost of Ownership, TCO

This describes the consolidated cost of a Product or Service, bringing together all available cost components to give a complete view, rather than requiring additional data sources or calculation.

Technology View

This refers to TBM information provided to Technology Users when following the TBM Taxonomy. This is generally related to the cost of Technology between the IT Towers and Business Units, requiring these users to be aware of both Finance and Business Views as well.

Unit Cost

The average cost per unit of a Service (or Product or Component). This is a calculated output from a TBM Cost Model, being the total cost of the Service divided by the total number of units (defined by the Unit of Measure).

Unit of Measure

The metric describing how a Service (or Product or Component) is counted. This may physical or logical, such as a computer or a transaction, but must be countable and kept as an inventory if it is to be used in a TBM Cost Model.

Transfer Pricing

Where costs within an organisation are expended in one unit and then charged to another, this can cause a requirement for Transfer Pricing to be calculated for tax and accounting purposes. This particularly occurs when charging is between countries, but can also be between units within a business. This is a specialist area of Financial management and outside of core TBM disciplines.

Work Breakdown Structure

In a set of Financial accounts, the Work Breakdown Structure may be used as a description of the purpose for which an expense has been incurred. This is additional to the Account, which describes the type of expense. This originates from Project Management, where it may be used within a Project to define activities and their cost.

Appendix : TBM Taxonomy

Much of this book refers to the TBM Taxonomy developed by the Technology Business Management Council. The entire TBM Taxonomy is included in this Appendix. Any more recent updates will be available on the TBM Council website.

The TBM Taxonomy is ©2020 Technology Business Management Council, All rights reserved. Used with permission.

TBM COUNCIL

TBM Taxonomy
Version 3.0
November 2, 2018

This paper provides a detailed description of the Technology Business Management (TBM) taxonomy. It is designed to be shared with the TBM Council Standards Committee for the purpose of gathering feedback and communicating changes and updates. The document is also made available via the TBM Council's community web site, TBM Connect (www.TBMConnect.org), for all members to read and use the information. For more information on the Standards Committee, see last page of this document or refer to the TBM Council Standards Committee Charter, also available on TBM Connect.

Revision History

Editor/Author	Date	Reason For Changes	Version
TBMC Standards Committee	10/31/2016	Final revision for TBMC endorsement	V2.0
TBMC Standards Committee	03/18/2018	Final revision for TBMC endorsement	V2.1
TBMC Standards Committee	11/02/2018	Final revision for TBMC endorsement	V3.0
TBMC Standards Committee	04/19/2019	Added missing High Performance Computing	V3.0.1
TBMC Standards Committee	07/18/2019	Added missing "Foundation Platform," "Order Management" and "Facility & Equipment Maintenance & Repair" definitions.	V3.0.2

Note: A complete document history is maintained in the Standards Committee on TBM Connect.

TBM Taxonomy: Version 3.0 (November 2018)
©2016-2018 Technology Business Management Council. All Rights Reserved.

Table of Contents

Introduction to the TBM Taxonomy 1

Layers of the TBM Taxonomy Explained 2

Finance Layer: Cost Pool and Sub-Pool Definitions 4

IT Layer: IT Tower and Sub-Tower Definitions 8

Business Layer: Products & Services Definitions 15

End User Services 18

Delivery Services 21

Infrastructure Services 27

Platform Services 30

Business Services 32

Shared Services 34

About the Technology Business Management Council 43

About the TBM Council Standards Committee 43

TBM Taxonomy: Version 3.0 (November 2018)
©2016-2018 Technology Business Management Council. All Rights Reserved.

Introduction to the TBM Taxonomy

Technology Business Management (TBM) is a value-management framework instituted by CIOs, CTOs, and other technology leaders. Founded on transparency of costs, consumption, and performance, TBM gives technology leaders and their business partners the facts they need to collaborate on business aligned decisions. Those decisions span supply and demand to enable the financial and performance tradeoffs that are necessary to optimize run-the-business spending and accelerate business change. The framework is backed by a community of CIOs, CTOs, and other business leaders on the Technology Business Management Council.

To gain alignment between IT, Finance, and Business Unit leaders, TBM provides a standard taxonomy to describe cost sources, technologies, IT resources (IT towers), applications, and services. The TBM taxonomy provides the ability to compare technologies, towers, and services to peers and third-party options (e.g., public cloud). Just as businesses rely on generally accepted accounting principles (or GAAP) to drive standard practices for financial reporting — and thus comparability between financial statements — the TBM taxonomy provides a generally accepted way of reporting IT costs and other metrics. A simple view of the TBM taxonomy is shown below.

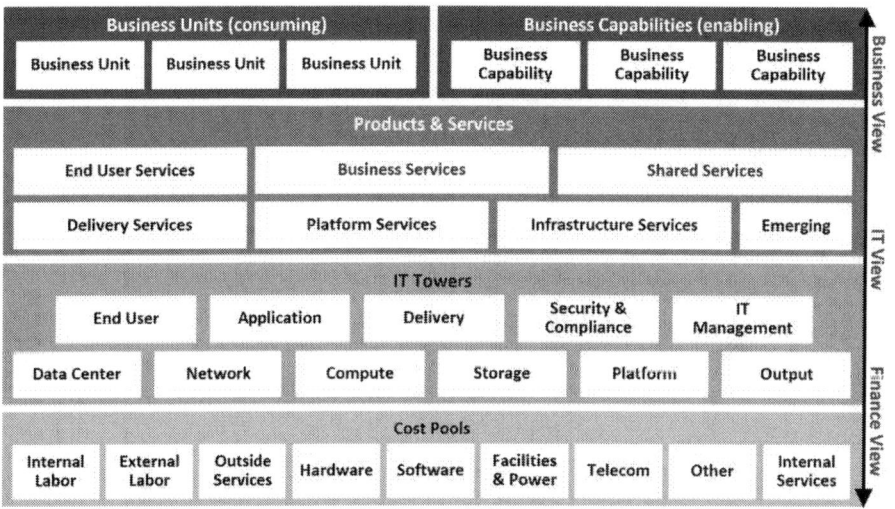

Figure 1: The TBM taxonomy provides a standard set of categories for costs and other metrics

The TBM taxonomy is needed in order to support the modeling of costs and other metrics. A TBM model maps and allocates costs and resource consumption from their sources to their uses, from the hardware, software, labor, services, and facilities IT leaders procure to the applications and services they develop, deliver, and support. In essence, the model is what translates between the layers of the taxonomy (e.g., IT Towers to Products & Services). The TBM model includes the taxonomy objects and layers plus the data requirements, allocation rules, and metrics needed to create transparency and enable the reporting that is needed for the value conversations of TBM.

TBM Taxonomy: Version 3.0 (November 2018)
©2016-2018 Technology Business Management Council. All Rights Reserved.

The TBM model relies on the TBM taxonomy to bring into agreement often disparate and contentious definitions of IT cost components and object classes. This creates a common language so that the terms *server* and *compute* for example are understood by everyone (IT and non-IT stakeholders alike) to mean the same thing and to include the same types of underlying costs calculated using the same methods.

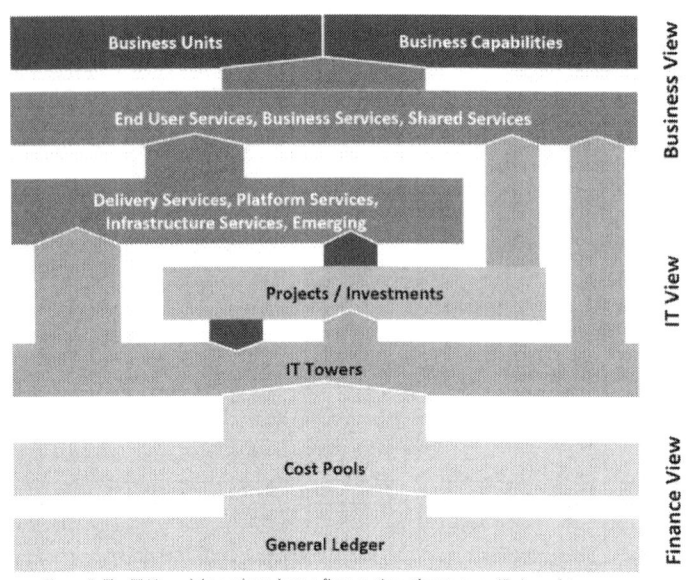

Figure 2: The TBM model translates from a finance view of costs to an IT view of towers, projects, and services and then into a business view of costs

By using the TBM taxonomy and model, CIOs can illustrate, for example, how user demand shapes the cost of applications, services, and technology architectures they maintain. And non-IT leaders can use the same data and insights to guide their consumption (demand).

Perhaps more importantly, these TBM tools allow for benchmarking and trend analysis of IT costs. This includes comparing the unit costs of technologies, such as a virtual Windows server or a terabyte of tier 1 storage, from one business unit, vendor, or data center to another. It also includes comparing unit costs over time, or even looking at ratios such as the IT cost per employee or the storage cost as a percentage of total IT spending.

These are powerful tools used more extensively in the private and public sectors including a diverse array of over 300 organizations: ExxonMobil, Microsoft, First American, Telstra, Zurich Insurance Company, U.S. General Services Administration (GSA), Fannie Mae, Federal Home Loan Bank of San Francisco, and the State of Washington.

Layers of the TBM Taxonomy Explained

The three layers of the taxonomy represent different views into the same costs and other metrics. The model starts with the Finance layer as the foundation of the taxonomy:

- **Finance:** The lowest layer begins with the general ledger, but may include other cost sources unique to the organization. This provides for a standard set of **cost pools**: hardware, software, internal labor, external labor, outside services, facilities and power, telecom, internal services and other. Cost pools not only make cost allocations easier, they enhance reporting because they can be traced through the model to reveal the composition of costs and allow comparability of composition (e.g., how much internal labor is in this service versus that one?).

- **IT:** The middle layer includes a standard set of **IT towers and sub-towers**, such as servers, storage, voice and data networks, application development and support. These are common amongst nearly all companies and can be viewed as the resources or basic building blocks of specific applications, services, and so on. While the tower definitions are standard, in practice they come in many forms. They may be sourced internally (i.e., via hardware, software, internal labor, and facilities & power), largely sourced externally (e.g., outside service, external labor), or as a hybrid of the two. Regardless, this view enables IT leaders to assess the cost-effectiveness of IT technology and service delivery.

- **Business:** At the highest layer the taxonomy provides a standard but generic set of **product** and **service** categories along with higher-layer **business units** and **business capabilities**. It is at this layer of the model we anticipate the creation of industry-specific elements extending this standard organizing taxonomy and following the same general principles present in the model. This will allow for more meaningful reporting and comparisons within each industry, without losing the cross industry comparisons that are possible at the other layers via common apps, services, and capabilities. This layer also includes the business unit consumers.

Because the taxonomy enables IT and financial leaders to bucket infrastructure, applications, and services into standard categories, it enables discussion of these buckets in terms that make sense — and *matter* — to business leaders.

Extensibility is one of the design principles to the TBM Taxonomy. Extensibility will enable companies to use the standard TBM Taxonomy while enabling industry or organization specific extensions to the taxonomy while still supporting compatibility with the standard. Extensions that are supported include the addition of new categories or sub-categories that do not conflict with the definition and meaning of any existing, standard categories. This enables an organization to isolate costs for any unique technology (e.g., medical devices, SCADA equipment) that are not part of an existing standard category. This allows costs to be tracked independently and does not corrupt the definition of an existing standard category.

Types of changes to the TBM Taxonomy that are not supported and are not considered extensions include: 1) splitting an existing category into two or more categories thereby changing the definition of the original category; 2) consolidating two categories into one category; and 3) changing the definition and composition of a published standard category. One of the main reasons for not allowing these types of extension is the impact on benchmarks. If changes are made to the definition and expected composition of costs, then the benchmark values will no longer be relevant. Examples of changes that are not supported as an extension include: 1) splitting the *Enterprise Data Center* IT Tower into Company Owned Data Centers and Co-Location Data Center Facilities. A better solution is to use the optional level 3, IT Sub-Tower Element to distinguish these costs. 2) Consolidating Database and

TBM Taxonomy: Version 3.0 (November 2018)
©2016-2018 Technology Business Management Council. All Rights Reserved.

Middleware into a single Tower. If one of the towers is not material in an organization's environment, don't use it or allocate any costs to it. 3) Changing the definition of the Voice IT Sub-Tower to include both voice equipment and voice telecommunication costs which changes the standard definition of the Voice sub-tower.

The following sections describe and define the finance, IT and business layers of the TBM taxonomy.

Finance Layer: Cost Pool and Sub-Pool Definitions

Cost pools are low-level categories that are often aligned easily to general ledger accounts. Not only do cost pools make cost allocations easier, they enhance reporting because they can be traced through the model to reveal the composition of costs. For example, application total cost of ownership (TCO) can be broken down into hardware, software, internal and external labor, outside services, facilities, and telecom costs.

The following graphic defines the cost pools and sub-pools in the TBM taxonomy.

	INTERNAL LABOR	EXTERNAL LABOR	OUTSIDE SERVICES	HARDWARE	SOFTWARE	FACILITIES & POWER	TELECOM	OTHER	INTERNAL SERVICES
Operating Expenditures	Expense	Expense	Consulting	Expense	Expense	Expense	Expense	Other	by Shared Service*
			Managed Service Provider	Lease	Licensing	Lease	Lease		
			Cloud Service Provider	Maintenance & Support	Maintenance & Support	Maintenance & Support	Maintenance & Support		
				Depreciation & Amortization	Depreciation & Amortization	Depreciation & Amortization	Depreciation & Amortization		
CapEx	Capital	Capital	Capital	Capital	Capital	Capital	Capital		

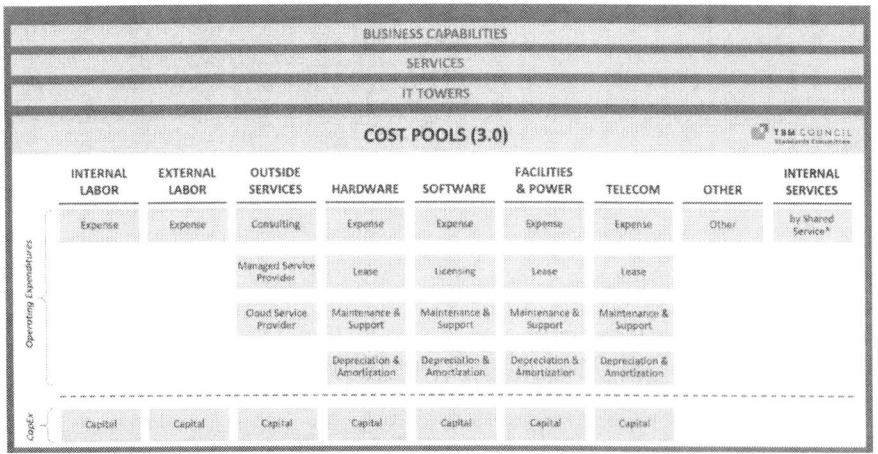

Figure 3: Finance Layer: Cost Pool and Sub-Pool Summary View

TBM Taxonomy: Version 3.0 (November 2018)
©2016-2018 Technology Business Management Council. All Rights Reserved.

Cost Pool	Cost Sub-Pool	Description
	Operating Expenditures (OpEx)	
Internal Labor		Internal Labor includes the full range of personnel costs and activities required for delivering or supporting the IT services – including direct operational activities, support and management and administration activities.
	Expense	Employee wages, benefits, expenses & occupancy.
External Labor		External Labor includes the costs of external personnel required for delivering or supporting the IT services – including direct operational activities, support, management and administration activities.
	Expense	External contractor fees, travel, and expenses.
Outside Services		Outside Services include IT services purchased from external service providers including consulting services, managed services and public cloud services. Specific examples of outside services include managed network services, cloud storage for end user backup, and externally provided email services.
	Consulting	External consulting project-based services.
	Managed Service Providers	External managed service providers.
	Cloud Service Providers	External public cloud service providers including IaaS, PaaS, and SaaS.
Hardware		Hardware includes all physical technology assets excluding property, office space or raised floor facilities. The range of assets varies by IT Resource Tower; examples include servers, PCs, storage arrays, network appliances, printers and so on. Where a device contains embedded software (firmware), for example in a network firewall, the cost should be reported as hardware even if the software can be upgraded for a separate fee.
	Expense	Hardware expense of non-capitalized purchases (e.g., spare parts, consumables or equipment below capitalization threshold).
	Lease	Hardware lease expenditures (e.g., hardware purchased through a supplier or financial services leasing arrangement).
	Maintenance & Support	Hardware maintenance and support expenditures.
	Depreciation & Amortization	Hardware depreciation of capitalized purchases.

TBM Taxonomy: Version 3.0 (November 2018)
©2016-2018 Technology Business Management Council. All Rights Reserved.

Cost Pool	Cost Sub-Pool	Description
Software		Software includes the licensing, maintenance and support costs for all software including operating system, middleware, databases, system management and administration tools, desktop applications and utilities and business applications. Software costs include enterprise or per instance licenses, client-access licenses, maintenance/update costs, customization fees.
	Expense	Software expense of non-capitalized software purchases.
	Licensing	Software license expenditures for the use of non-SaaS provided software. SaaS subscriptions belong under Outside Services > Cloud Service Providers.
	Maintenance & Support	Software maintenance and support expenditures.
	Depreciation & Amortization	Software depreciation of capitalized software license purchases & software development efforts.
Facilities and Power		Facilities & Power costs include the floor space as well as the power, cooling, and other utilities costs, environmental control (fire suppression), power distribution, rack infrastructure, outside services and personnel costs related to managing the data center environment.
	Expense	Data center space, power, security and other operating expenses (e.g., co-location facility services, electricity, water, etc.).
	Lease	Data center lease expenditures.
	Maintenance & Support	Data center maintenance & support expenditures.
	Depreciation & Amortization	Data center depreciation of facility build and leasehold improvements (e.g., raised floor investments, power/PDU infrastructure, and rack build-out).

Cost Pool	Cost Sub-Pool	Description
Telecom		Telecom is for all telecommunications charges, including leased line, domestic and international voice (including mobile), MPLS, ISP and other charges. Telecom costs include the circuits and any associated usage fees for providing voice and/or data telecommunication services between data centers, office locations, the internet and any customer, supplier or partner. This is typically transmission across the wide area network (WAN).
	Expense	Voice and data network connectivity expenses including circuit and usage expenditures.
	Lease	Telecom lease expenditures.
	Maintenance & Support	Telecom maintenance & support expenditures.
	Depreciation & Amortization	Depreciation/amortization of any capitalized telecom expenditures; typically, this will show up under Hardware or Facilities depreciation/amortization.
Other	Other	Miscellaneous or non-standard expenses.
Internal Services	Shared Service	Miscellaneous charges received from other internal shared services groups (e.g., HR service fees from the HR department). Real estate management fees for space and power should be included in the *Facilities and Power* cost pool.
Capital Expenditures (CapEx)		
Internal Labor	Capital	Capitalized labor (internal employees)
External Labor	Capital	Capitalized labor (external contractors)
Hardware	Capital	Capitalized hardware expenditures
Software	Capital	Capitalized software expenditures
Outside Services	Capital	Capitalized services
Facilities & Power	Capital	Capitalized leasehold improvements
Telecom	Capital	Capitalized telecom expenditures

TBM Taxonomy: Version 3.0 (November 2018)
©2016-2018 Technology Business Management Council. All Rights Reserved.

IT Layer: IT Tower and Sub-Tower Definitions

IT towers and sub-towers are the basic building blocks of services and applications. Examples include compute (e.g., servers, Unix, mainframe), network, application (e.g., application development, application support and operations) and IT management. They are sometimes called domains or functions. Many IT shops have dedicated departments or cost centers for towers that are then delivered as shared resources for product and service owners.

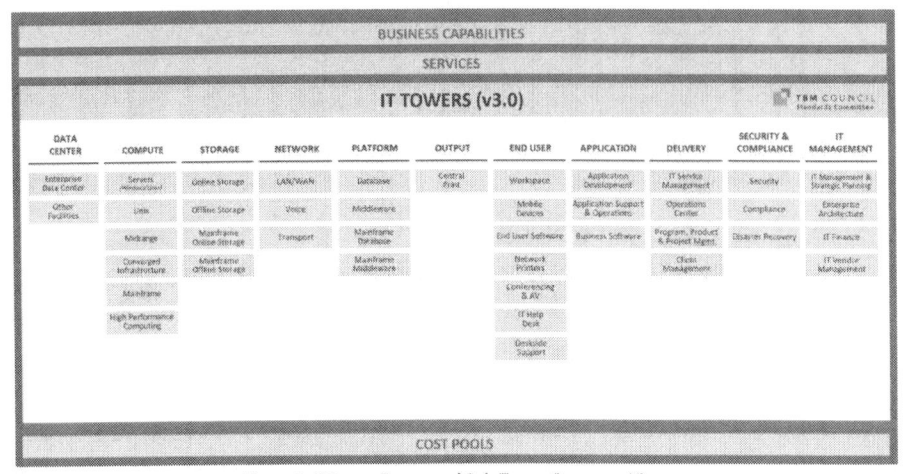

BUSINESS CAPABILITIES									
SERVICES									
IT TOWERS (v3.0)									TBM COUNCIL
DATA CENTER	COMPUTE	STORAGE	NETWORK	PLATFORM	OUTPUT	END USER	APPLICATION	DELIVERY	SECURITY & COMPLIANCE	IT MANAGEMENT
Enterprise Data Center	Servers (Non-Unix)	Online Storage	LAN/WAN	Database	Central Print	Workspace	Application Development	IT Service Management	Security	IT Management & Strategic Planning
Other Facilities	Unix	Offline Storage	Voice	Middleware		Mobile Devices	Application Support & Operations	Operations Center	Compliance	Enterprise Architecture
	Midrange	Mainframe Online Storage	Transport	Mainframe Database		End User Software	Business Software	Program, Product & Project Mgmt	Disaster Recovery	IT Finance
	Converged Infrastructure	Mainframe Offline Storage		Mainframe Middleware		Network Printers		Client Management		IT Vendor Management
	Mainframe					Conferencing & AV				
	High Performance Computing					IT Help Desk				
						Deskside Support				
COST POOLS										

Figure 4: IT Layer: Tower and Sub-Tower Summary View

The following table defines the IT towers and sub-towers in the TBM taxonomy.

Tower	Sub-Tower	Description
Data Center		Data Centers are purpose-built facilities to securely house computer equipment. Data Centers provide racks/cabinets & cabling, clean & redundant power, data connectivity, environmental controls including temperature, humidity and fire suppression, physical security and the people to run and operate the facility and its infrastructure.
	Enterprise Data Center	Purpose-built data center facilities that house and protect critical IT equipment including the space, power, environment controls, racks, cabling and "smart hand" support.
	Other Facilities	Computer rooms and MDF/IDF/telco closets that house IT equipment in corporate headquarters, call centers or other general purpose office buildings.

Tower	Sub-Tower	Description

Appendix : Page 8

Tower	Sub-Tower	Description
Compute		Compute refers to both general and special-purpose devices and software that are programmed to carry out a set of arithmetic or logical operations. In essence, it provides the "brains" to process application and user requests. Compute includes a wide range of physical and virtual servers differentiated by platform and operating system. The Compute tower should include all direct hardware, software, labor and outside service costs.
	Servers	Physical and virtual servers running a version of Microsoft's Windows Server or the Linux operating system; includes hardware, software, labor and support services. Optional Level 3 categories include: Windows, Linux and Public Cloud Compute.
	Unix	Servers running vendor-specific, proprietary Unix operating systems (e.g., IBM AIX, Sun Solaris, HP UX); includes hardware, software, labor and support services.
	Midrange	Servers running IBM AS/400 platform including hardware, software, labor and support services.
	Converged Infrastructure	Purpose-built appliances that provide compute, storage and network capabilities in one box.
	Mainframe	Traditional mainframe computers and operations running legacy operating systems.
	High Performance Compute	High-Performance Computing (HPC) is used for solving complex computational problems through massive concurrent use of computing resources and parallel processing techniques. HPC technology is applied in areas such as scientific and industrial research, product engineering and development, and complex business modeling, simulation and analysis. HPC hardware and software technologies are specialized and optimized for massively parallel computing and processing vast amounts of data.

TBM Taxonomy: Version 3.0 (November 2018)
©2016-2018 Technology Business Management Council. All Rights Reserved.

Storage	Storage provides centralized data storage and securely holds information and data to be retrieved later. Storage may hold data for application programs and code, databases, files, media, email and many other forms of information. The storage tower includes distributed and mainframe storage that provides on-line storage for real-time access and archival storage solutions that may enable near-term retrieval or long-term archival. The storage tower excludes the internal storage included with a typical server configuration or end-user device such as a laptop, desktop or mobile phone, or tablet.	
	Online Storage	Central storage such as SAN, NAS and similar technologies for the distributed compute infrastructure; includes the equipment, software and labor to run and operate. Optional Level 3 categories include: On-Premise, Public Cloud Storage.
	Offline Storage	Offline storage resources used for archive, backup & recovery to support data loss, data corruption, disaster recovery and compliance requirements of the distributed storage.
	Mainframe Online Storage	Mainframe attached storage arrays and the associated equipment, software and labor to run and operate.
	Mainframe Offline Storage	Any storage resources used for archive, backup & recovery to support data loss, data corruption, disaster recovery and compliance requirements of the mainframe storage.
Network	Network includes the data and voice equipment along with the transport methods to connect systems and people and to enable people to converse. Networks provide core connectivity within the enterprise data centers as well as connectivity to and access within office building and remote locations.	
	LAN/WAN	Physical and wireless local area network connecting equipment within the core data centers and connecting end users in office working areas to the organization's broader networks. Wide area network equipment, labor and support services directly connecting data centers, offices and third parties (excludes telecom and communication services). Optional Level 3 categories include: LAN, WAN.
	Voice	Voice resources which enable or distribute voice services through on premise equipment including PBX, VoIP, voicemail and handsets (excludes telecom and communication services).

TBM Taxonomy: Version 3.0 (November 2018)
©2016-2018 Technology Business Management Council. All Rights Reserved.

Tower	Sub-Tower	Description
	Transport	Data network circuits and associated access facilities and services; includes dedicated and virtual data networks and internet access. Also includes usage associated with mobility and other data transit based on usage billing. Voice network circuits and associated access facilities and services. Also includes usage associated with standard telephone calls and 800 number service. Both voice and data transport may include terrestrial and non-terrestrial (e.g., satellite) technologies. Optional Level 3 categories include: Data, Voice.
Platform		Platform includes all costs associated with distributed and mainframe databases and middleware systems. Costs include DBMS software and tools, labor and outside services.
	Database	Distributed database services focused on the physical database (versus the logical design) including DBAs, DBMS, tools and operational support.
	Middleware	Distributed platform, application and system integration resources enabling cross application development, communications and information sharing.
	Mainframe Database	Mainframe database services focused on the physical database (versus the logical design) including the DBAs, DBMS, tools and operational support.
	Mainframe Middleware	Mainframe platform, application and system integration resources enabling cross application development, communications and information sharing.
Output		Output includes the central print services to provide high-volume printing of customer bills, checks, product documentation or other customer support materials. Output also includes additional post print processing support (e.g. fold, stuff, apply postage, bundle).
	Central Print	Central print services; often provided to support customer billing or customer documentation support processes. Unit of measure: page.

TBM Taxonomy: Version 3.0 (November 2018)
©2016-2018 Technology Business Management Council. All Rights Reserved.

Tower	Sub-Tower	Description
End User		End User includes end user computing devices and support for end users. The scope includes costs to build, manage and run end user computing devices for the enterprise and deliver centralized support to end users.
	Workspace	Client compute physical desktops, portable laptops, thin client machines, peripherals (including monitors, pointer devices and attached personal printers) used by individuals to perform work.
	Mobile Devices	Client compute tablets, smart phones (iOS, Android, Windows Mobile) and apps used by individuals to perform work.
	End User Software	Client related software used to author, create, collaborate and share documents and other content. Examples include email, communications, messaging, word processing, spreadsheets, presentations, desktop publishing, graphics and others. Optional Level 3 categories include Productivity; Communications; Collaboration.
	Network Printers	Printers located on or near users' desktops. Examples include network connected personal printers, ink-jet printers, laser printers, departmental or copy-room printers. Only include network connected printers. Do not include printers connected to an end user computer.
	Conferencing & AV	Audio and video conferencing equipment typically used in conference rooms and dedicated telepresence rooms to enable workforce communications.
	IT Help Desk	Centralized Tier 1 help desk resources that handle user requests, answer questions and resolve issues.
	Deskside Support	Local support resources that provide on-site support for moves, adds, changes and hands on issue resolution.

TBM Taxonomy: Version 3.0 (November 2018)
©2016-2018 Technology Business Management Council. All Rights Reserved.

Tower	Sub-Tower	Description
Application		The Application tower includes costs related to applications in the enterprise. The scope includes the cost of business software and the costs to develop, manage and run applications for the enterprise.
	Application Development	Resources involved with the analysis, design, development, code, test and release packaging services associated with application development projects. Optional Level 3 categories include: Development, QA
	Application Support & Operations	The operations, support, fix and minor enhancements associated with existing applications.
	Business Software	Software expenditures including licensing, maintenance and support related to off-the-shelf software purchases.
Delivery		The delivery tower includes the costs to monitor, support, manage, and run IT operations for the enterprise and includes the IT Service Management (ITSM) functions.
	IT Service Management	Resources involved with the incident, problem and change management activities as part of the IT Service Management process (excludes the Tier 1 help desk).
	Program, Product & Project Management	Resources involved with managing and supporting IT related projects and/or continuous product development (e.g. Agile) across business and IT-driven initiatives.
	Client Management	Resources or "account managers" aligned with the lines of business to understand business needs, communicate IT products, services and status of IT projects.
	Operations Center	Centralized IT Operations Center resources including monitoring and intervention e.g., NOC (network operations center), GOC (global operations center).

Tower	Sub-Tower	Description
Security & Compliance		The Security & Compliance tower includes service costs related to IT security compliance and disaster recovery. The scope includes costs to define, establish, enforce, and measure security, compliance, and disaster recovery readiness for the enterprise.
	Security	IT Security resources setting policy, establishing process & means, measuring compliance and responding to security breaches and providing real-time operational security such as vulnerability scanning, managing firewalls, intrusion prevention systems, and security information and event management (SIEM). Optional Level 3 categories include: Cyber Security. The implementation actions defined by security policies (e.g. mitigating security breaches by applying patches) are not included in the Security sub-tower and are part of the respective towers where the actions take place (e.g. Compute, Storage, Network).
	Compliance	IT Compliance resources setting policy, establishing controls and measuring compliance to relevant legal and compliance requirements. Optional Level 3 categories include: Data Privacy. The implementation actions defined by Compliance policy (e.g. implementing controls like multi-factor authentication) are not included in the Compliance subtower and are part of the respective towers where the actions take place (e.g. Compute, Storage, Network, Application, End User).
	Disaster Recovery	IT Disaster Recovery resources setting DR policy, establishing process & means, dedicated failover facilities, performing DR testing. NOTE: DR designated equipment is included directly in its own sub-tower (e.g., extra servers for DR are included in Compute tower, etc.). The implementation actions defined by Disaster Recovery policy (e.g. building DR servers) are not included in the Disaster & Recovery sub-tower and are part of the respective towers where the actions take place (e.g. Compute, Storage, Network).

TBM Taxonomy: Version 3.0 (November 2018)
©2016-2018 Technology Business Management Council. All Rights Reserved.

Tower	Sub-Tower	Description
IT Management		The IT Management tower includes the costs to manage, administer & plan IT for the enterprise. It includes executive management, strategic management, enterprise architecture, IT finance, and vendor management.
	IT Management & Strategic Planning	IT management and administration resources; typically CIO, senior IT leaders and administrative support including centralized IT strategy and planning.
	Enterprise Architecture	Enterprise architecture services including business, information, application and technical architecture to drive standardization, integration and efficiency among business technology solutions.
	IT Finance	Resources involved in the planning, budgeting, spend management and chargeback of IT expenditures and the costing of IT products and services.
	IT Vendor Management	Resources involved in the selection, contract management, oversight, performance management and general delivery of services by 3rd party vendors and external service providers.

Business Layer: Products & Services Definitions

Products & Services are what IT delivers to end consumers: business leaders, end users and often external parties such as partners and customers. In more mature, service-oriented organizations, services are well defined, advertised in a service catalog, priced or costed, and measured for consumption, among other practices. Service definitions should convey business value to business leaders, users or other stakeholders. In IT organizations that have adopted the latest in Lean-Agile thinking which incorporates continuous delivery, the concept of Products, rather than Services, may be assumed. The categories and classifications defined by the TBM Taxonomy are appropriate across these different IT operating models. Throughout this document, the term Services is used rather than calling out a distinction between Products or Services terminology.

The following graphic represents the service hierarchy including service types, services categories and services defined in the TBM taxonomy.

TBM Taxonomy: Version 3.0 (November 2018)
©2016-2018 Technology Business Management Council. All Rights Reserved.

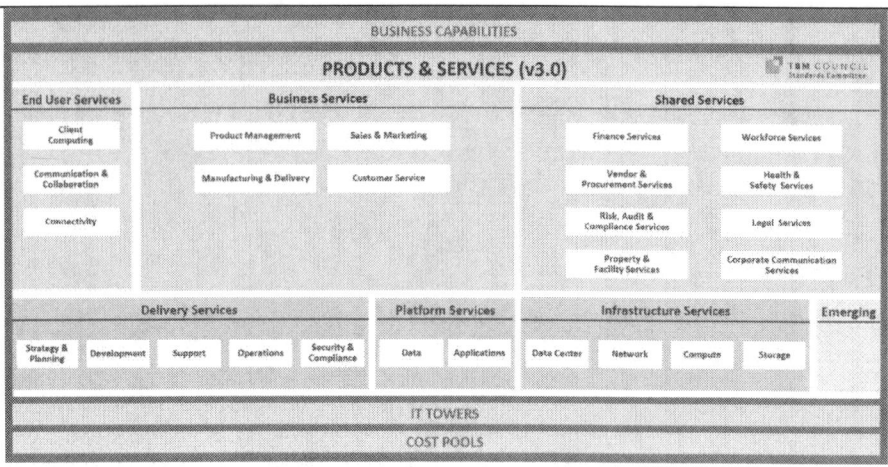

Figure 5: Business Layer: Services Summary View

The service hierarchy is grouped by service type (e.g., end user services, platform services), service category (e.g., client computing, communication & collaboration) and service name. Service offerings, as shown below, would be specific to the organization and are included in the TBM taxonomy as representative examples.

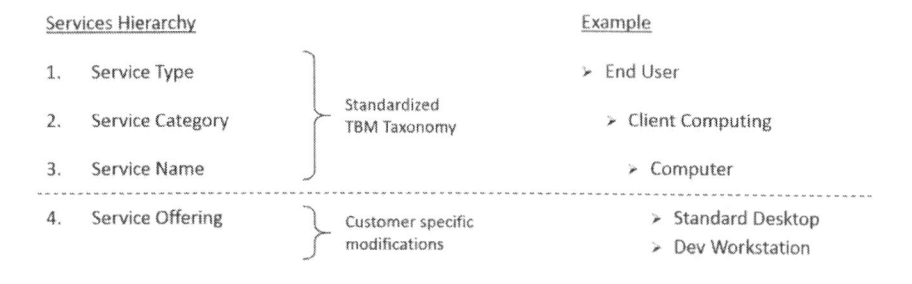

Services Hierarchy		Example
1. Service Type	⎫ Standardized TBM Taxonomy	➤ End User
2. Service Category		➤ Client Computing
3. Service Name	⎭	➤ Computer
4. Service Offering	Customer specific modifications	➤ Standard Desktop ➤ Dev Workstation

Figure 6: Services Hierarchy

The six Service Types defined in the standard TBM taxonomy include:

- **End User Services** include the client computing devices, software and connectivity to enable the workforce to access business applications; to communicate with other employees, partners and customers; and to create content using productivity software. These are always "user-facing" services.

- **Business Services** are delivered by IT to enable product and external customer focused business capabilities that enable the business to win, serve, and retain customers.. The TBM Taxonomy includes a generic set of capabilities that most enterprises perform including Product Management, Sales & Marketing, Manufacturing & Delivery and Customer Service. Additional technology extensions may be developed which provide specific business application services unique to an industry. Industry-specific extensions that have been endorsed are published in a separate addendum.

- **Shared Services** are delivered by IT to enable internally focused corporate services which automate and support the organization's internal operations. These are often referred to as business support or shared services which enable the core operating capabilities of an enterprise or organization (e.g. Finance, Human Resources, Legal, etc.).

- **Delivery Services** are those to build, deploy, support and operate the End User Services (above), Business Application Services (below) and Shared Application Services (below). Development services create and change business-facing services, typically through projects. Additional support and operations services assist users, and maintain and ensure the availability of the business-facing services.

- **Platform Services** include the application infrastructure (database, middleware, etc.) that enables business-facing applications and services. Typically, these are not directly consumed by users. They are components required by the end user, business application and shared application services (see below for the latter two types). However, for some IT operating models, the shared "infrastructure and operations group" may directly provide these Platform Services to their customers.

- **Infrastructure Services** include the core infrastructure — facilities, compute, storage and network services — that are required to deliver any technology automation. Typically, these are not directly consumed by users. However, for some IT operating models, a shared "infrastructure and operations group" may directly provide these Infrastructure Services to their customers.

- **Emerging Services** are new trending services in the market with limited adoption across the enterprise. These services or offerings are early in enterprise adoption. The TBM council places services/offerings in the emerging services to provide visibility into possible future designation within the overall TBM taxonomy. The emerging services or offerings will be reviewed annually and organized into existing or new types, categories or services; or removed depending on the maturity and adoption of the service.

Note that many services can be delivered using traditional delivery models (e.g., on premise data centers) or via different cloud delivery models (i.e., public cloud, private cloud, hybrid cloud). These are not specifically reflected in the taxonomy categories below as they can apply to many types of services. Furthermore, the standard cloud service models (i.e., Infrastructure as a Service, Platform as a Service, and Software as a Service) are not included specifically. However, TBM models should incorporate those as classifications (e.g., labels or metadata) of the service offerings where needed for reporting and decision making.

The following tables defines the services in the standard TBM taxonomy.

End User Services

End User Services

Client Computing
* Computer
* Mobile
* Bring Your Own Device
* Virtual Client

Communication & Collaboration
* Collaboration
* Communication
* Productivity
* Print

Connectivity
* Network Access
* Remote Access

Figure 7: End User Services

Category	Name	Description
Type: End User Services		
Client Computing		Client Computing includes all the physical and virtual devices and associated services that enable a user to interact with the enterprise's technology systems. This includes desktops, laptops, mobile devices and virtual desktop environments.
	Bring Your Own Device	A set of services that enable users to bring in their own personal computing devices (laptop, tablet, smartphone) and connect to the organization's corporate network in accordance with the organization's security and other standards. Standard support may include connectivity to access business applications, information and other technology resources; as well as other security, back-up, updates and patches, remote access and centralized service desk.
	Computer	A selection of IT-provided computers, workstations, laptop or tablet configurations. Each type may be ordered with additional memory and storage. Standard corporate image will be loaded on each device. Requestor may order optional software through the Productivity services. Includes network and remote network access. Standard support package including security, back-up, antivirus, updates and patches, remote access, centralized service desk.
	Mobile	A selection of IT-provided smartphone configurations. Includes network access. Standard support package including security, encryption, back-up, updates and patches, remote access and centralized service desk.

TBM Taxonomy: Version 3.0 (November 2018)
©2016-2018 Technology Business Management Council. All Rights Reserved.

Category	Name	Description
	Virtual Client	The virtualization of desktop and application software enables PC and tablet functionality to be separate from the physical device used to access those functions – whether a fixed or mobile workspace environment. Virtual Workspaces may have different, pre-configured packages of software application and enable access from multiple devices. Advanced desktop management provides higher levels of flexibility, security, backup and disaster recover capabilities.
Communication & Collaboration		Communication and Collaboration includes the services that allow an end-user to communicate with other people via email or chat, to collaborate through shared workspaces, and to create and print content such as documents, presentations, videos and other forms.
	Collaboration	A selection of collaborative software offerings that enable people to work together to achieve common goals across locations and time zones. Enables the sharing of documents and deliverables across distributed users.
	Communication	Communication represents a broad set of integrated or individual services that enable users to communicate with other users, partners or customers. This communication may occur via electronic mail, calendaring, messaging, social communities, audio conferencing, video conferencing and voice calls. More robust, unified messaging service offerings provide file transfer, file sync and share, embedded images, clickable hyperlinks, Voice over IP (VoIP) and video chat.
	Print	A variety of peripheral devices that enable the distribution of information. Specialized devices may offer one or all of these services - print, copy, and fax. Printing output creates a "hard copy" of digital documents, presentations, spreadsheets, etc. Scan inputs a hardcopy document into a digital format for a computer to use.
	Productivity	End user application software enabling the creation and distribution of information in a variety of formats including: documents, presentations, spreadsheet, modeling tools, project management, databases, desktop publishing, web design, graphics and image editing, audio/video editing and CD/DVD recording.

Appendix : Page 19

TBM Taxonomy: Version 3.0 (November 2018)
©2016-2018 Technology Business Management Council. All Rights Reserved.

Category	Name	Description
Connectivity		Connectivity includes the network services that provides a user access to the enterprise's technology systems. This includes wired and wireless access while on premise and remote access while away from the enterprise.
	Network Access	A set of connection services which enable users to access a private or public network from their client computing device. Once connected, as part of the network they can access business applications and information; and can communicate and collaborate with other users on the network. Often times, this may be bundled with a Client Computing service.
	Remote Access	A set of connection services which enable users to access the organization's internal private network from their client computing device when away from the corporate facilities. Once connected, the user can access the organization's business applications and information. Often times, this may be bundled with a Client Computing service.

TBM Taxonomy: Version 3.0 (November 2018)
©2016-2018 Technology Business Management Council. All Rights Reserved.

Delivery Services

BUSINESS CAPABILITIES

Delivery Services

Strategy & Planning	Development	Support	Operations	Security & Compliance
* Technology Business Mgmt * Innovation & Ideation * Enterprise Architecture * Program, Product & Project Mgmt * Business Solution Consulting * IT Vendor Mgmt	* Design & Development * System Integration * Testing	* Service Desk * Application Support * IT Training * Central Print	* IT Service Management * Event Management * Scheduling * Capacity Management * Deployment & Administration	* Identity & Access Management * Security Awareness * Cyber Security & Incident Response * Threat & Vulnerability Management * Data Privacy & Security * Governance, Risk & Compliance * Business Continuity & Disaster Recovery

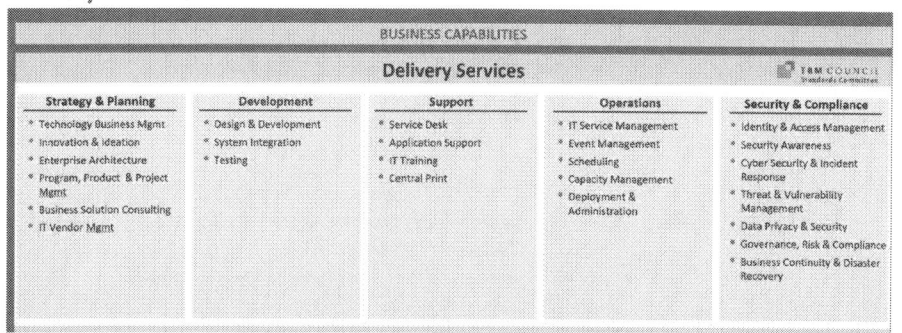

Figure 8: Delivery Services

Category	Name	Description
	Type: Delivery Services	
Strategy & Planning	Strategy and Planning includes all the services that the CIO and IT leadership team leverage to efficiently plan and manage the enterprise technology environment. This includes planning, architecture, consulting, innovation and R&D, project and agile management, and vendor management. Many of the ITSM strategy services are included in this service category.	
	Enterprise Architecture	Enterprise architecture guides organizations through the business, information, process, and technology changes necessary to execute their business and IT strategies.
	Business Solution Consulting	Business solution consulting services help the enterprise improve their performance, primarily through the analysis of existing business problems and development of plans for improvement. This includes business relationship management, demand management, business process analysis as well as technology selection.
	Technology Business Management	The disciplines and value conversations for improving the business outcomes enabled by the technology portfolio. Enables technology leaders and their business partners to collaborate on business-aligned decisions. Includes IT management, IT finance and costing, IT billing, business value, metrics, benchmarking, service portfolio management, service catalog management, service level management and availability management.

Category	Name	Description
	Innovation & Ideation	The investment, development and incubation of new technologies to create new or better solutions which meet unarticulated or existing market needs. Includes new technology solutions and new product incubation services.
	IT Vendor Management	The management of technology suppliers who provide, deliver and support technology products and services. Includes services across the life cycle of a vendor including selection, negotiation, contracting, procurement, maintenance and subscription renewals, and performance management.
	Program, Product & Project Management	Program Management is the process of managing several related projects, often with the intention of improving an organization's performance. Product Management refers to a more collaborative and continuous planning, prioritization and delivery process (e.g., Agile methodologies) to provide frequent releases of small packages of new functionality in an iterative approach. Project Management is a traditional method of discrete planning, budgeting and execution of projects to deliver new capabilities, enhance existing capabilities or retire applications or services. Project Management services initiate, plan, execute, control, and close the work of a team to achieve specific goals and meet specific success criteria. Representative service offerings for this service include: Portfolio Investment Planning, Project Planning & Delivery, and Continuous Planning & Delivery.
Development	\multicolumn{2}{l	}{Development includes all the services to plan, design, build, test and release new application software and services.}
	Design & Development	Design and Development services provide the planning, design, programming, documenting, testing, and fixing involved in creating and maintaining a software product.
	System Integration	Development services that link together different computing systems and software applications physically or functionally, to act as a coordinated whole. This can be accomplished across systems that reside within the enterprise's data centers as well as with SaaS services that reside in the provider's facilities.

TBM Taxonomy: Version 3.0 (November 2018)
©2016-2018 Technology Business Management Council. All Rights Reserved.

Category	Name	Description
	Testing	Testing services execute a program or application with the intent of finding errors or other defects. The investigations are conducted to provide stakeholders with information about the quality of the product or service and allow the business to understand the risks of software implementation. Testing may take multiple forms including functional, system, integration, performance and usability.
Operations		Operations includes the costs to monitor, support, manage, and run the enterprise technology systems for the enterprise. It includes IT Service Management, capacity management, event management, capacity planning, and scheduling. These are typically services provided behind the scenes and not directly user-facing.
	Deployment & Administration	Includes the release management and software distribution services to deploy new and/or the most recent software version to the host servers or client computing devices. Also includes ongoing operating system (OS) support and patch management.
	IT Service Management	IT Service Management refers to the incident, problem and change management services necessary for IT to plan, deliver, operate and control the IT services offered to its customers. Software tools and services for assessing, recording and managing asset configurations, such as server settings or network router tables.
	Capacity Management	Services which ensure that IT resources are right-sized to meet current and future business requirements in a cost-effective manner. Takes into account the expected demand from the business or consumer along with the availability and performance of existing capacity and projects future requirements. Capacity management occurs across data center, compute, storage, network and other IT resources.
	Event Management	Services to monitor resources and applications. Services that records API calls and delivers logs and insights. Services that provide log data consolidation, reporting and analysis to enable IT administrators and security personnel to understand asset utilization, user logins, and information access.
	Scheduling	Services involved in the execution of tasks required to operate an IT Service and are often automated using software tools that run batch or online tasks at specific times of the day, week, month or year.

Appendix : Page 23

TBM Taxonomy: Version 3.0 (November 2018)
©2016-2018 Technology Business Management Council. All Rights Reserved.

Category	Name	Description
Support		Support includes the centralized services which directly support the end user community and includes training, application support, service desk and central print services.
	Application Support	Application Support services provide the ongoing operational activities required to keep the application or service up and running, provide Tier 2 and Tier 3 technical support to more complex or difficulty user questions and requests. Application Support may also include minor development and validation of smaller application enhancements (e.g., minor changes, new reports).
	Central Print	Central Print services provide high-volume and advanced printing for invoices, product literature or other complex documents for mass distribution. Additional post-print services may include folding, envelope stuffing, postage and bundling to expedite distribution.
	IT Training	IT Training provides educational services to the organization's users on how the access and effectively use the organization's business application services, as well as common productivity software and tools.
	Service Desk	Service Desk provides a single point of contact to meet the support needs of users and the IT organization. Service Desk services provide end users with information and support related to IT products and services, usually to troubleshoot problems or provide guidance about products such as computers, electronic equipment, or software. Help desk support may be delivered through various channels such as phone, website, instant messaging, or email. Additional service delivery offerings include IT knowledge management, request fulfillment, desk-side and "tech bar" service offerings.

TBM Taxonomy: Version 3.0 (November 2018)

©2016-2018 Technology Business Management Council. All Rights Reserved.

Category	Name	Description
Security & Compliance		Security & Compliance includes all the services to ensure the integrity, protection and proper use of the enterprises technology systems and data. It includes identity & access management, security awareness, cyber security & incident response, threat & vulnerability management, data privacy & security; governance, risk & compliance, business continuity & disaster recovery.
	Identity & Access Management	Identity and access management (IAM) services set policy, business processes, establishes controls and provide technologies to facilitate the management of digital identities by ensuring individuals have the appropriate access to necessary systems at the right times. Specific areas include authentication, identity management and identity governance & administration. Specific areas included: Authentication/Authorization, Identity Management, Identity Governance & Administration, Privileged Access Management, and Certificate Management.
	Security Awareness	Security awareness sets policy, procedures and provides corporate knowledge training to members of an organization to promote an understanding for all individuals regarding the protection of an organizations physical and digital assets. Specific areas included: Security Training, Security Advisory, and Security Policies and procedures.
	Cyber Security & Incident Response	Cybersecurity services provide policies, procedures and technologies to recognize existing and emerging threats as well as determine associated risk to ensure the organization has the appropriate defense and responses to each incident. Specific areas included: Cyber Security Monitoring and Security Incident Response.
	Threat & Vulnerability Management	Threat and vulnerability management services ensures an organizations applications and infrastructure vulnerabilities are proactively identified, classified and corrected to ensure they are not exploited by unauthorized individuals or parties. Specific areas included: Application Vulnerability Management, Infrastructure Vulnerability Management, and Network / Endpoint Security.
	Data Privacy & Security	Data privacy and security ensures corporate and user data is not used or accessed by unauthorized individuals or entities by ensuring data and identities are classified appropriately, the correct controls are in place to prevent data loss and data is appropriately secured. Specific areas included: Data Classification & Identification, Data Loss Prevention, Data Encryption, Data Access, and Database Security.

TBM Taxonomy: Version 3.0 (November 2018)
©2016-2018 Technology Business Management Council. All Rights Reserved.

Category	Name	Description
	Governance, Risk & Compliance	IT Compliance services set policy, establish controls and measuring compliance to relevant legal and compliance requirements. Ensure risks are met, alignment with regulatory needs (SSAE16, HIPAA, PCI DSS, SOX, TRICARE etc.), Documented and communicated to business owners. Ensure third parties meet risk and security requirements.
	Business Continuity & Disaster Recovery	Business Continuity ensures the continuous operation of the enterprise. Services include business impact assessments, business resiliency plans, disaster recovery capabilities and the associated exercise, testing, training and awareness to support people, process and technology recoveries in case of an incident.

TBM Taxonomy: Version 3.0 (November 2018)
©2016-2018 Technology Business Management Council. All Rights Reserved.

Infrastructure Services

Infrastructure Services

Data Center	Network	Compute	Storage
* Enterprise Data Center * Other Data Center	* Data Network * Voice Network * Internet Connectivity * Virtual Private Network * Domain Services * Load Balancing	* Physical Compute * Virtual Compute & Containers * Compute on Demand * Mainframe	* Networked Storage * File & Object Storage * Backup & Archive * Distributed Storage (CDN)

Figure 9: Infrastructure Services

Category	Name	Description
Type: Infrastructure Services		
Compute Services		Compute Services includes all the physical and virtual computing services that run business applications, software tools and system services. These compute services can be dedicated or on-demand and may be provided on-premises or through external managed services or public cloud offerings.
	Compute on Demand	Offer transient compute services that are executed automatically, either on a schedule or triggered by a predefined event or set of events.
	Mainframe	Offer transactional and batch oriented compute services supported by a mainframe infrastructure.
	Physical Compute	Offer a variety of compute configurations comprised of physical servers. These are typically distributed compute services based on the Windows, Linux or UNIX operating systems for predefined configurations of memory, CPU and storage. Standard operational support includes security hardening, backup, updates, patches, and centralized monitoring.
	Virtual Compute & Containers	Offer a variety of compute configurations delivered through the virtualization of physical compute resources. May include on-demand provisioning and de-provisioning based on user interaction or the performance of the application itself. These virtual instances are typically running Windows or Linux operating systems and have pre-defined configurations of virtually allocated memory, CPU and storage. Standard operational support includes security hardening, back-up, updates and patches and centralized monitoring.

TBM Taxonomy: Version 3.0 (November 2018)
©2016-2018 Technology Business Management Council. All Rights Reserved.

Category	Name	Description
Data Center Services		Data Center Services include the various facility services that provide a secure and controlled environment for housing compute, storage, network and other technology equipment. These may include large, dedicated data centers owned by the enterprise or leased through co-location services. Smaller computer rooms and distribution rooms within the enterprises office buildings provide space for on-premises equipment.
	Enterprise Data Center	Purpose-built facilities to securely house computer equipment providing physical security, clean & redundant power, data connectivity and environmental controls – temperature, humidity, fire suppression. Includes data centers owned and operated by the enterprise, as well as co-location or point-ofpresence services operated by other service providers. Additional services may include shipping and receiving, assembly, rack and stack and maintenance.
	Other Data Center	Other data center services that may be delivered through dedicated secure rooms or telecom closets with a facility.
Network		Network Services includes the voice and data network and supporting services such as load balancing, domain services, virtual private network and the internet to enable communications within and outside the enterprise.
	Domain Services	Domain services provide lookup capabilities to convert domain names (e.g., www.acme.com) into the associated IP address to enable communication between hosts.
	Internet	Telecommunication services using the public internet to enable communications across the organization including its data centers, office buildings, remote locations, partners and service providers. Virtual Private Networks may be created to limit access and provide security.
	Load Balancing	Offer ability to optimize incoming application/workload requests through load balancing and traffic management to deliver high availability and network performance to applications.
	Virtual Private Network	Virtual Private Network (VPN) services offer a secure method to authenticate users and enable access to corporate systems and information. VPN can also isolate and secure environments in the data center across physical and virtual machines and applications.
	Data Network	A selection of network connection offerings that enable direct data communications across the organization including its data centers, office buildings, remote locations as well as partners and service providers (including public cloud service providers) without traversing the public internet. Typically provides a greater level of performance, security and control. The available service offerings may include terrestrial and non-

Category	Name	Description
		terrestrial (e.g., satellite) technologies as well as field networks or special-use networks.
	Voice Network	Telecommunication offerings for voice circuits to deliver "plain old telephone service" and other advanced features including 800-services, automatic call distribution, etc. The available service offerings may include terrestrial and non-terrestrial (e.g., satellite) technologies.
Storage Services	Storage Services includes various offerings for persisting information, data, files and other object types. The services offerings range from supporting real-time, high-performance data retrieval to slower retrieval to long-term archive storage. Different storage offerings also provide recovery point objectives to meet the business needs of an application based on a business impact assessment.	
	File & Object Storage	Secure and durable object storage where an object can be unstructured data such as documents and media files or structured data like tables.
	Backup & Archive	Secure, durable and lower-cost storage service offerings for data backup and archiving. May include disk backup, tape backup, optical backup and off-site storage services.
	Networked Storage	Storage services that provide a pool of storage to a server for the purposes of hosting data and applications, or to a virtualization environment for the purposes of hosting servers. Networked Storage services enable redundancy, ease of management, rapid move/add/change/delete capabilities, and economies of scale. Storage array network (SAN), network attached storage (NAS) and solid state drives (SSD) storage are example technologies.
	Distributed Storage (CDN)	A content delivery service for storing high-bandwidth content at the edge network to reduce latency and improve application performance.

Platform Services

Platform Services

Data Services
- Database
- Distributed Cache
- Data Management
- Data Warehouse
- Data Analytics & Visualizations

Application Services
- Application Hosting
- Foundation Platform
- Message Bus & Integration
- Content Management
- Search
- Streaming
- Decision Intelligence & Automation

Figure 10: Platform Services

Category	Name	Description
	Type: Platform Services	
Application Services		Application Services include a wide-range of application-based services that run on top of the compute platform and enable other business applications. Application Services include application hosting, message bus and system integration, audio/video streaming, content management, search and a variety of artificial intelligence and machine learning services.
	Application Hosting	Fully managed application and web hosting services including the general computing server, database server, web and application server services. Includes standalone Web Service and App Service platform services.
	Foundation Platform	Foundation Platform includes the core foundation capabilities provided by large ERP systems, as well as the "platform as a service" provided by many SaaS applications. ERP foundation platforms (like SAP R/3 Basis or SAP S/4 HANA) are the technical underpinning that enables the ERP application to function. It typically consists of programs and tools that support the interoperability and portability of ERP applications across systems and databases. Many SaaS applications also provide a platform capability to enable integration and development of additional applications or modules that complement the primary application suite. Examples include Salesforce's Force.com product, ServiceNow's Now Platform and Appian.
	Message Bus & Integration	A messaging infrastructure to allow different systems to communicate through a shared set of interfaces. Includes event streaming to multiple applications, subscribe and publish notification service for enterprise and mobile messaging, task completion alerts and threshold alerts.

TBM Taxonomy: Version 3.0 (November 2018)
©2016-2018 Technology Business Management Council. All Rights Reserved.

Category	Name	Description
	Content Management	A set of services that support the creation and modification of digital content using a simple interface supporting multiple users in a collaborative environment. Includes records management and digital asset management.
	Search	A keyword search service for web and mobile applications.
	Streaming	Services that deliver live and on-demand media streams including audio and video.
	Decision Intelligence & Automation	Decision Intelligence & Automation services allow software and devices to utilizing large datasets to become more accurate in predicting outcomes without being explicitly programmed. Natural language processing, facial recognition, object recognition, intelligent personal assistants and robotic process automation are offerings that utilize these technologies to augment the human thought process.
Data Services		Data Services include a variety of data-related services that capture and retrieve transactional activities in a database, store the data in a centralized data warehouse, provide analytical and visualization tools to explore the data and caching technology to distribute information to the edge to improve performance and response times.
	Database	A relational database service for applications to access transactional data. A No-SQL database service for applications that need consistent, low-latency scaled out document/key-value store models.
	Distributed Cache	An in-memory cache service that helps improve web application performance.
	Data Management	A set of data analytic services that automate the movement and transformation of data including extract, transform and load (ETL) processes, data quality management and master data management.
	Data Warehouse	Services supporting a central repository or set of repositories of integrated data from one or more disparate sources. Stores current and historical data and are used for creating analytical reports for knowledge workers throughout the enterprise.
	Data Analytics & Visualizations	Software services and BI tools to analyze and communicate information clearly and efficiently to users via graphs, charts and other visual representations including geospatial analytics. Also includes real-time streaming analysis of data by providing low latency, highly available, scalable complex event processing over streaming data in the cloud.

TBM Taxonomy: Version 3.0 (November 2018)
©2016-2018 Technology Business Management Council. All Rights Reserved.

Business Services

Business Services *(for generic company)*

Product Management	Sales & Marketing	Manufacturing & Delivery	Customer Service
* Product Development * Product Planning	* Customer Analytics * Marketing & Advertising * Sales Force & Channel Mgmt * Customer Sales	* Resource Planning * Manufacturing * Inventory & Warehousing * Product Delivery * Service Delivery	* Order Management * Customer Care

Figure 11: Business Services

Category	Name	Description
	Type: Business Services (Generic)	
Product Management	Product Development	Applications and services that enable product design and development including innovation management, computer aided design, simulation visualization, enterprise feedback and social product feedback/crowdsourcing.
	Product Planning	Applications and services that enable product life-cycle management including requirements management, product data management, change and configuration management, manufacturing process management, quality management, product analytics, and risk and compliance management.
Sales & Marketing	Customer Analytics	Applications and services that enable customer and product analytics and voice of the customer input.
	Customer Sales	Applications and services that enable B2C commerce platforms, B2B commerce platforms, product configurations, POS platforms and payments.
	Marketing & Advertising	Applications and services that enable marketing automation, online marketing, mobile marketing, and ad technologies.
	Sales Force & Channel Management	Applications and services that enable sales force automation, sales enablement and training, partner relationship management and pricing management.
Manufacturing & Delivery	Inventory & Warehousing	Applications and services that enable inventory management, supply chain scheduling, warehouse management and returns management.
	Manufacturing	Applications and services that enable prototyping, production scheduling, fabrication/manufacturing of tangible products,

Appendix : Page 32

TBM Taxonomy: Version 3.0 (November 2018)
©2016-2018 Technology Business Management Council. All Rights Reserved.

Category	Name	Description
		equipment maintenance, software development of digital products and quality testing.
	Product Delivery	Applications and services that enable the logistics and delivery of physical products including supply-demand matching, fleet/transportation management, tracking systems and GIS/routing optimization.
	Service Delivery	Applications and services that enable the delivery of nontangible services including resource scheduling, engagement management, professional services, education, and service quality.
	Resource Planning	Applications and services that enable demand forecasting, demand planning, and partner sourcing.
Customer Service	Order Management	Applications and services that enable order management, contract management, pricing optimization, billing and payment processing.
	Customer Care	Applications and services that enable multi-channel customer communication (ACD, CTI, IVR, speech recognition, predictive dialing, email response, change, co-browse), knowledge management, customer service workforce automation, and field service.

TBM Taxonomy: Version 3.0 (November 2018)
©2016-2018 Technology Business Management Council. All Rights Reserved.

Shared Services

Shared Services

Finance Services
- Planning & Management Accounting
- Revenue Accounting
- Accounts Receivable
- General Accounting and Reporting
- Project Accounting
- Payroll & Time Reporting
- Accounts Payable & Expense Reimbursement
- Treasury
- Tax

Workforce Services
- Recruitment
- Employee Transitions & Separation
- Workforce Management
- Performance, Retention & Rewards Management
- Benefits Management
- Policy Management
- Employee Development
- Employee Communications & Relations

Vendor & Procurement Services
- Sourcing & Procurement
- Supplier Management
- Contract Management

Health, Safety, Security & Environment Services
- Policy & Governance
- Oversight & Enforcement
- Healthcare Services
- Occupational Safety

Risk, Audit & Compliance Services
- Risk Management
- Breach Management & Remediation
- Business Continuity Planning & Management
- Auditing
- Investigations
- Records Management

Legal Services
- Legal Counsel
- Case Management
- Contract Review

Property & Facility Services
- Development & Space Planning
- Workspace Services
- Physical Security
- Operations, Maintenance, Repair & Improvements
- Fleet Management (non-logistics)
- Food & Beverage

Corporate Communication Services
- Stakeholder Relations
- Government Relations
- External Communications
- Community Outreach

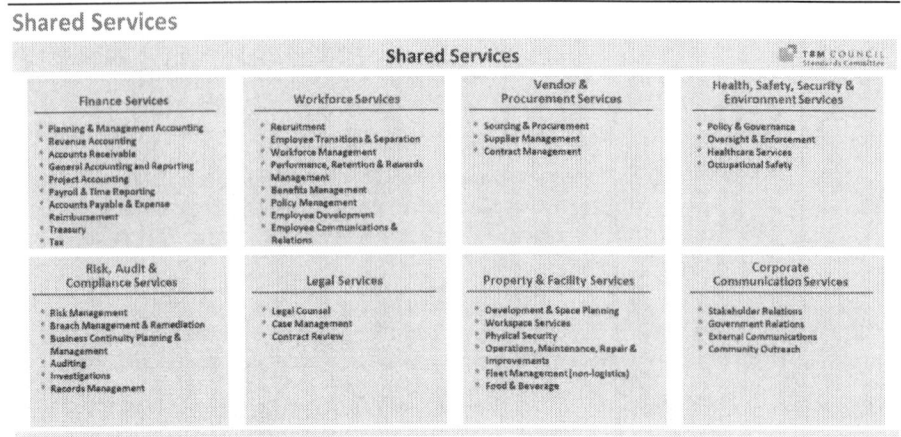

Figure 12: Shared Services

Category	Name	Description
Type: Shared Services		
Finance Services		Applications and services that enable the ability to manage the financial aspects of running the business or organization. In the broadest terms, it includes the activities to manage financial & general accounting and reporting, revenue accounting, accounts payables, payroll, treasury operations, tax management and internal controls.
	Planning & Management Accounting	Applications and services that enable the strategic allocation of funds in support of established future and current business goals, including planning, budgeting and forecasting, ad-hoc analysis and reporting to inform and guide leadership in the ongoing determination and understanding of business strategy related financial goals, incentives, progress and impact. Specific service offerings may include: planning/budgeting/forecasting, cost accounting & control, cost management and financial performance.
	Revenue Accounting	Applications and services that enable the comparison of revenue targets to actual achievement. Supervisory responsibility over all transactions and entries (receivables, payables, intercompany movements) that pass into the final periodic accounts of an entity, and support int./ext. analysis and communication of profit on a monthly, quarterly or annual basis. (Determination of whether this includes the actual lifecycle processing of payments due from customers, is based on entity type, sector and scale - see Accounts Receivable). Specific service offerings may include: customer credit, invoicing, accounts receivable, and collections.

Category	Name	Description
	Accounts Receivable	Applications and services that enable the complete lifecycle of invoicing and receipts processing to ensure the business is paid by its customers, including Invoicing, payment receipt, processing, error handling, PO setup (as a supplier) reconciliation, reporting and collections.
	General Accounting & Reporting	Applications and services that enable financial statement preparation (balance sheet, statements of income, cash flows, shareholders' equity etc.) in accordance with accepted accounting principles. Also includes responsibilities to classify, determine, analyze, interpret, consolidate and communicate financial information to support up-to-date business decisions for better management & control, and regulatory/legislative compliance (in conjunction with Management Accounting) of costs, assets & equipment. In certain contexts can include grant activities related to the funding and reporting of nonrepayable funds provided to corporate, academic or agency entities. Specific service offerings may include: general accounting, fixed asset accounting, grant management, and financial reporting including regulatory and compliance reporting.
	Project Accounting	Applications and services that enable managing accounts for large investment projects, often requiring significant capital outlays over multiple years. Managing investment against major milestone, product or activity expenditures during the course of a project, supporting project, portfolio and program leadership with insight to understand their progress & efficiency toward target. Specific service offerings may include: capital planning, capital project accounting & analysis.
	Payroll & Time Reporting	Applications and services that enable the handling of reported time, and the ongoing processing and payment of wages, salaries and benefits, including quality assurance and error handling (but excl. benefits management). Also inclusive of time keeping, and the capture, aggregation, measurement, validation and transmission of staff time. Specific service offerings may include: time reporting payroll, and payroll taxes.
	Accounts Payables & Expense Reimbursement	Applications and services that enable the processing of payments due to suppliers, lenders and other operating expenses, including those related to employees. Supports the development of policies and procedures around processing of accounts payable & employee expense reimbursement across the entity. This process often includes the receipt & review of invoices and reimbursement requests, payment processing, PO & payment issuance via check, wire transfer or other forms of payment transfer. Specific service offerings may include:

Category	Name	Description
		accounts payable, expense reimbursement, corporate credit cards.
	Treasury	Applications and services that enable the management and optimization of daily liquidity, excess cash, and financial risk via investment activities (e.g. hedging, debt instrument purchase/sale, overnight and short term institutional investments, and funds transfers) focused on supporting ongoing business operations across the entire company, or regionally. Also includes the governance, control, assessment and risk management activities required to ensure effectiveness. Specific service offerings may include: Treasury policies & procedures, cash management, in-house bank accounts, debt & investment, hedge transactions.
	Tax	Applications and services that enable managing the organization's financial accounts specific to the world-wide management, optimization and payment of tax, and related evidence & documentation. This includes, planning, estimations & analysis of the tax position and impact, related transfer pricing strategies, tax return preparation, timely payment, and required authorizations. It also encompasses the orchestration of record retention in support of regulatory requirements and internal policy. Specific service offerings may include: tax strategy, tax planning & analysis, transfer pricing, and tax processing.
Workforce Services		Applications and services that enable the ability to manage the employee workforce of the business or organization. In the broadest terms, it includes the activities to select, recruit, develop, reward, retain, counsel and retire employees. Includes the management of employee information including workforce analytics.
	Recruitment	Applications and services that enable determining and handling employee recruiting, sourcing and selection, including requirements gathering; advertising; order creation; agency placement; application receipt, review, filtering; candidate & agency contact; applicant screening & investigations; offering & negotiations; records management. Can also include prior employees.
	Employee Transitions & Separation	Applications and services that enable managing employee (and less commonly vendor staff) transitions of a vertical, horizontal, geographic, mission, or structural nature, including management & administration of programs for: foreign assignment, reassignment, re-deployment, promotion/demotion, separation, outplacement, leave of absence, repatriation, and retirement.

Category	Name	Description
	Workforce Management	Applications and services that enable managing employee focused processes and information for workforce analysis & reporting; inquiry & resolution; employment verification; HR data / information; refreshing / updating indicators of employee retention and motivation, working with time & attendance systems (excluding items like actual survey or assessment delivery).
	Performance, Retention & Rewards Management	Applications and services that enable creating frameworks for, and performing the management & administration of, programs for rewarding, motivating and recognizing employees with the objective of retaining them and enabling career path growth (incl. distributions).
	Benefits Management	Applications and services that enable the management, administration & processing of employee benefits, benefit plans, staff enrollment, claims, funding & entitlements; and includes analysis and planning, provider selection, employee communications & education, and regulatory compliance.
	Policy Management	Applications and services that enable creating strategies, standards, and supporting policy, for purposes of setting and managing standards of conduct, corporate and legal HR compliance and breaches, skills and competencies, and resource Performance, Rewards & Transitions. Includes planning, supervising and implementation of workforce policy inclusive of modeling, analysis and reporting.
	Employee Development	Applications and services that enable employees (and less commonly contractors/providers), with skills, knowledge, and/or capability development, and education. This extends to new hire onboarding / orientation; technical or business skills training; safety, security, conduct, ethics & compliance training; procedural and other legal or organizational aspects. (Excludes education as part of employee Transitions). Also includes program & course creation, delivery, management and reporting.
	Employee Communications & Relations	Applications and services that enable crafting and execution of employee communications plans, its supporting messages, distribution channels and formats, to initiate interaction for: promoting horizontal or vertical employee engagement across the organization; creating awareness (e.g. of new policy, practices, or other internal / external events or actions of relevance); assessing satisfaction and engagement levels and drivers.

TBM Taxonomy: Version 3.0 (November 2018)
©2016-2018 Technology Business Management Council. All Rights Reserved.

Category	Name	Description
Vendor & Procurement Services		Applications and services that enable the ability to manage the indirect procurement of goods and services required for a business to enable its activity including development of sourcing strategies, vendor selection, contract negotiations, ordering of materials & services and ongoing vendor and contract management.
	Sourcing and Procurement	Applications and services that enable creating strategies, standards and processes for procuring goods and services from approved sources. Establish a procurement process that describes the approach, policy and guidelines for purchasing activities including evaluation & sourcing of suppliers. Create sourcing relationships in order to continuously improve price performance. Re-evaluation and assessment of purchasing activities, standards, pricing and impact across the value chain and supplier landscape.
	Supplier Management	Applications and services that enable evaluating supplier options to select the most effective, efficient and low risk suppliers. Validate selected suppliers. Use internal/external data, analysis and feedback to rank and manage strategic and non-strategic suppliers to optimize vendor spend and output, including the ongoing management and reporting of supplier performance (e.g. output quality, delivery cycle times). Can also include survey & research activities.
	Contract Management	Applications and services that enable the intake and management of vendor contracts. Keeping contracts current with routine evaluation. Ensure proactive dissemination of knowledge to key stakeholders regarding renewals, expirations, price changes, volume thresholds or other contract aspects, to provide adequate lead times and avoid lapses in service, or surprise / unplanned expenditures.
Health, Safety, Security & Environmental Services		Applications and services that enable the ability to provide a safe environment for the organization, environment and local residents including policy, oversight, healthcare, occupational safety and threat assessment.
	Policy & Governance	Applications and services that enable determining the desired outcomes, obligations, conduct and impacts related to personal and environmental health and safety. Creating and implementing the HSSE program. Train and educate employees of the on the HSSE program. Oversee and manage the HSSE program.
	Oversight & Enforcement	Applications and services that enable monitoring and oversight of policy adherence and enforcement activities (including investigations) related to environmental, health and safety

Appendix : Page 38

TBM Taxonomy: Version 3.0 (November 2018)
©2016-2018 Technology Business Management Council. All Rights Reserved.

Category	Name	Description
		standards, should activity fall outside of defined processes, regulations or legislation.
	Healthcare Services	Applications and services that enable the definition and structuring of health services provided to/by the workforce, to promote preventative health and basic treatment, including the provision of on-site health services.
	Occupational Safety	Applications and services that enable the programmatic evaluation and management of risks & opportunities that may affect industry-specific or role-related personal health and safety of employees, contractors or other 3rd parties. Provide required compliance and reporting as required by local and national governing bodies.
Risk, Audit & Compliance Services	**Applications and services that enable the ability to proactively manage the risk of the business and ensure adherence to regulatory requirements.**	
	Risk Management	Applications and services that enable establishing umbrella frameworks, management activities, policy and related procedures and requirements for the entire organization, to defend against risks that may negatively impact the viability, growth, performance, health, stability, competitiveness, preparedness, or reputation of an ongoing concern, state, product or service. Ensures the identification, detection, assessment, monitoring and communication of risk and the execution of risk management activities across all levels of the organization, including all risk facets, including but not limited to sector, organization, operations, compliance, data, personal privacy, cyber, espionage, geo-political, etc.
	Breach Management & Remediation	Applications and services that enable administering the efforts and activities for breach assessment / estimation of impact and causality, as well as containment and remediation efforts. This may require the creation of plans for corrective action, even in collaboration with government agencies and pertinent professional services firms specialized in remediation efforts relevant to the organization's operations. Includes generation of new recommendations for implementation by Risk Management to be embedded as part of the ongoing capability/process.
	Business Continuity Planning & Management	Applications and services that enable the plans, processes and resources required to rapidly adapt and respond to any internal or external disruption, threat or event that may present an opportunity or result in degradation or catastrophic failure of business operations.

Category	Name	Description
	Auditing	Applications and services that enable the internal or external planning, preparation, execution and review of internal control mechanisms, policies and procedures in order to manage internal controls. Includes observation, reviews, interviews, fact-finding and the generation of recommendations and designs of control activities to be implemented. Monitor and review control effectiveness, remediate control deficiencies, and enable compliance functions. Can also include the implementation and maintenance of technologies and tools to enable internal controls-related activities.
	Investigations	Applications and services that enable following up on a breach of standard operating procedures to identify, locate and understand the impact of the breach. An investigation can include searching, research, interviews, evidence collection, data preservation and various methods of investigation, as well as the gathering and documentation of findings & observations, and reporting of them.
	Records Management	Applications and services that enable managing codified information in an organization throughout its life cycle and state/form, from the time of creation or inscription to its access and eventual disposition. This includes identifying, classifying, storing, securing, retrieving, tracking and destroying or permanently preserving records, including digital and physical.
Legal Services		Applications and services that enable the ability to provide legal counsel and support to the organizations governance and operations including discovery, litigation, contract reviews and intellectual property protection.
	Legal Counsel	Applications and services that enable providing guidance and legal practices to abide by the law involving the practical application of legal theories, laws, regulations and knowledge to govern the organization's messaging, product, and business operations. This includes the safeguarding (incl. litigation) and defense of intellectual property, brand value, confidential information, corporate and personal exposure to liability (physical or environment injury, cyber etc.) and many other forms and applications of law.
	Case Management	Applications and services that enable managing the (mostly) administrative lifecycle of legal cases, including matter management, time and billing, document completion and submittal, monitoring case status, scheduling hearings and meetings, time and billing, orchestration of litigation support, collaboration and communications, record storage and search.

TBM Taxonomy: Version 3.0 (November 2018)
©2016-2018 Technology Business Management Council. All Rights Reserved.

Category	Name	Description
	Contract Review	Applications and services that enable reviewing and negotiating terms to reach a final draft of a contract that is acceptable to all parties. Contracts may include non-disclosure agreements, master service agreements, statements of work and other types of contracts.
Property & Facility Services		**Applications and services that enable the ability to provide for the non-productive facilities for the organization including development & space planning, physical security, workplace services, fleet management (non-logistics), food services and the maintenance of facilities and equipment.**
	Development & Space Planning	Applications and services that enable planning the use, services, acquisition and construction or build out, of nonperforming or performing real property (whether owned or leased) for the organization. Execution of the planning, approvals, and acquisition of a site, for the build out or installation of real property or assets that may or may not yield direct income or house staff, equipment, or inventory. Creation of long-term vision, strategies and standards for acquiring, developing and managing purchased / leased / retained property and improvements.
	Workspace Services	Applications and services that enable provisioning workspaces and related assets, and management of that provisioning effort. The orchestration and/or installation of office, shared community or light industrial spaces according to requirements (e.g. tables, chairs, couches, monitors, AV equipment, privacy screens, cubicles, doors, appliances, lighting, cabling, shelving, racks etc.). *Not intended for large scale industrial/plant construction.* Excludes Physical Security.
	Physical Security	Applications and services that enable managing the physical safety of property, facilities, equipment and people through the presence of physical barriers, workforce authentication and authorization, and visible or unseen manned or unmanned security services.
	Operations, Maintenance, Repair & Improvements	Applications and services that enable preserving and improving productive assets through the planning, managing, and performance of preventative, routine, and critical maintenance work, and occasional improvements to those existing facilities or equipment.
	Fleet Management (non-logistics)	Applications and services that enable managing vehicles used to support the transportation of the workforce and may include vehicle financing, maintenance, telematics, and scheduling. Vehicles may include cars, vans, trucks, motorized carts, bicycles and other forms of transportation. Does not include

Category	Name	Description
		transportation associated with the shipment of the organization's products or service delivery.
	Food & Beverage	Applications and services that enable providing and managing on-site food and beverage services for consumption by the organization's workforce.
Corporate Communication Services		Applications and services that enable the ability to manage and orchestrate all internal and external communications aimed at creating a favorable view among stakeholders including public relations, stakeholder relations, government relations, external relations and community outreach.
	Stakeholder Relations	Applications and services that enable fostering external relationships with stakeholders of the entity, including investors, government and industry, the board of directors, and the general public. This is not related to customer management.
	Government Relations	Applications and services that enable creating and maintaining relationships with government and industry representatives. Persuading public and government policy at the local, regional, national, and global level (subject to government regulations).
	External Communications	Applications and services that enable developing and managing relations with media. Develop connections with journalists to solicit critical, third-party endorsements for a product, issue, service, or organization.
	Community Outreach	Applications and services that enable developing and administering community relations. Establish business connections with the people constituting the environment the organization operates in and draws resources from in order to foster mutual understanding, trust, and support. Create programs that promote the organization's image in a positive and community-oriented way.

About the Technology Business Management Council

The Technology Business Management (TBM) Council is a nonprofit business entity focused on developing a definitive framework for managing the business of IT. It is governed by an independent board of business technology leaders from a diverse group of the world's most innovative companies. The TBM Council established a set of tools and best practices including organizational traits, management disciplines, a common taxonomy, and metrics. Members are encouraged to develop and contribute to their understanding of TBM through the Council's research, standards, education offerings, and community engagements. Members collaborate with their peers through an annual global conference, regional meetings, and an online community.

About the TBM Council Standards Committee

The Standards Committee, working together with TBM Council Staff, oversees, reviews and manages the development and maintenance of TBM standards, including but not limited to the TBM taxonomy and TBM KPIs/metrics. The Committee reports and is accountable to the TBM Council Board of Directors. The Committee has the responsibility to keep the Board informed regarding standards development and is also responsible for documenting and publishing the standards for all TBM Council members to see, use and comment upon.

The Committee is comprised of a chairman (James LaPlaine, CIO, Red Ventures), 15 voting members from industry, a Federal government liaison (non-voting), and TBM Council Alliance Partner representatives (from ISG and KPMG). Service Provider representatives from firms such as IBM, HCL, Atos, Hexaware and others also participate in the Council as non-voting members.

Printed in Great Britain
by Amazon